Where Are the Children?

Where Are the Children?

A Class Analysis of Foster Care and Adoption

Betty Reid Mandell

Lexington Books
D.C. Heath and Company
Lexington, Massachusetts
Toronto   London

Library of Congress Cataloging in Publication Data

Mandell, Betty Reid.
    Where are the children?

    1. Foster home care—United States. 2. Adoption—United States.
3. Social classes—United States. I. Title.
HV875.M357   362.7'33'0973   73–6832
ISBN 0-669-88963-6

Published simultaneously in Canada.

Printed in the United States of America.

International Standard Book Number: 0–669–88963–6

Library of Congress Catalog Card Number: 73–6832

DEDICATED

TO ALL THE CHILDREN WHO ARE BEYOND THE SOUND OF THEIR
PARENTS' VOICES

CONTENTS

ACKNOWLEDGMENTS

Thanks

to Marvin, my husband, for helping me to clarify and simplify;

to my daughter Christine, who spent many hours caring for her young sister while I wrote;

to friends who made helpful suggestions: Larry Beeferman, James Black, Robert Bourne, Nathaniel Raymond, Mary Low Schenck, the Boston State College Social Welfare class of Fall 1972;

to John Quinn, who transcribed the research tapes while a work-study student at Northeastern University;

to all the parents, foster children, foster parents, and agency staff members who helped me to formulate my ideas in practice;

to Child and Family Services, Inc., of Hartford, Conn., who gave me the time and the freedom to do research on foster care. The agency is not responsible for the ideas I put forth here, and some staff members will probably disagree with many of them, but it is to the agency's credit that it encourages free inquiry wherever it may lead!

Staff members besides myself who were involved in the Foster Care Research Project at Child and Family Services in 1968–1969 were Delores Taylor, research director; Lynette Anderson, Rosemarie Carbino, Charlotte Craig, Ronald Long, and Kathleen Olmstead, all social workers; Salvatore Alessi and George Rogers, psychologists; and James Black, psychiatrist. The foster parents were assured of confidentiality when they participated in the project, and I regret not being able to credit them by name for doing the most important part of the project.

Where Are the Children?

CHAPTER ONE
WHERE ARE THE CHILDREN?

*"Children! Where are the children?" Where indeed? Nowhere.
My mother's cry would ring through the garden, striking the great
wall of the barn and returning to her as a faint exhausted echo.
"Where . . . ? Children . . . ?"*

Colette, *My Mother's House* [1]

Colette and her siblings delighted to hide from their mother. It was a game sweet with the sureness that their mother wanted to find them and, remembering her mother's anxious search, Colette the grown woman says, "That lovely voice; how I should weep for joy if I could hear it now!" [2]

But there are thousands of children who are beyond the sound of their parents' voices, and thousands of parents who have given up calling for their children. Thousands of children are being cared for by people other than their biological parents in foster homes, adoptive homes, and institutions. This book studies two systems of child care which substitute non-biological parents for biological parents—foster care and adoption. Society grants adoptive parents a legal right to their adoptive children, while foster parents are responsible for the care of children without having any legal jurisdiction over the children. Sometimes natural parents retain full legal jurisdiction over their children in foster care; sometimes the court and/or a social agency has legal jurisdiction. When a court assumes jurisdiction over children, it usually charges the parents with neglect and declares children dependent upon the state, or it may adjudge the children delinquent.

Many children in the United States are living apart from their parents in foster homes and they are being joined on the average by about 9,000 more every year: in 1969 there were 249,000 of them in public and private voluntary foster homes, and it is estimated that by 1975 they will number 302,100. [3] In 1970 alone, there were about 175,000 adoptions: 51 percent by nonrelatives, and the rest by stepparents or other relatives. [4] In 1969 there were 74,000 children in institutions for the dependent, neglected, and emotionally disturbed. [5]

The children of the poor are a political issue. A disproportionate number of the poor belong to minority groups. Poverty is often equated in the public mind with minority status, so the impoverished children of minority groups are the hottest political issue. Elimination of poverty requires large-scale redistribution of income and changes in property relations between the haves and the have-nots and have-littles. The affluent resist such changes, and substitute programs for the children of the poor, as safe alternatives to radical changes in existing economic arrangements. Thus the most politically popular program of the "War on Poverty" was the Head Start program to educate preschoolers. Larzerson [6] points out that early childhood education as a substitute for housing and jobs is cheaper and less controversial than active enforcement of civil rights and antidiscrimination legislation. The Republican Ripon Society has proposed day care for the poor as a politically acceptable "antipoverty" program.[7] A host of policy makers and academicians are centering their attention on the children of the poor, and on the reproductive habits of the poor. Some of their recommendations are spine-chilling.

The accusation by some black leaders that some policy makers have genocidal intentions does not seem farfetched when Roger Freeman, a former special assistant to President Nixon, proposes a cash bonus for welfare parents who volunteer for sterilization in a "birth prevention" program.[8] Freeman also proposed that Congress consider taking children away from some welfare mothers and raising them in "well-run" government institutions. An electrical engineer at Stanford University, William Shockley, taking his lead from the Stanford psychologist Arthur Jensen, purports to prove that black Americans are innately less intelligent than white Americans. He also proposed "as a thinking exercise" that the government offer bonuses to those citizens who, paying no income tax, submit to voluntary sterilization. The sociologist Edward Banfield, formerly of Harvard University, considered the advisability of sterilizing members of the "lower class," as have some state legislators. Bruno Bettelheim, the director of a treatment institution for disturbed children, believes that group care similar to that in Israeli kibbutzim should be instituted for disadvantaged children.[9] Child welfare specialist Martin Wolins, dismayed by the failure of the foster care system and impressed by Israeli and European forms of group care, also recommends group care for the children of the poor.[10] The child development specialist H. Skeels, encouraged by the positive results of the effects of adoption on children from institutions, proposes a large-scale adoption program to counteract poverty and both sociocultural and maternal deprivation.[11]

Nevertheless, for the past several decades, the children of the poor who have been removed voluntarily or involuntarily from their parents have been placed in institutions, foster homes, or adoption homes. More recently, however, child welfare agencies have preferred foster homes to institutions, under the assumption that a nuclear family (a husband, wife, and young children, living by themselves in their own house) is the best environment for child-rearing, for it has a better chance of duplicating the biological family. Healthy, white babies who have been relinquished by their unmarried mothers have generally been placed in middle-class and upper-class adoptive homes. Relinquished black children have been more likely to grow up in institutions or foster homes.

Foster care is, in the words of the director of the Child Welfare League of American, "a mess."[12] Adoptive care is not a mess, but it has serious problems. The problems in both the foster care and adoption systems flow out of the problems of the larger society. Chief among these problems is the gap between social classes, resulting in gross inequalities of wealth and status. Related to this is industry's single-minded concentration on profit-maximizing, with its inordinate emphasis on material possessions and status achievement. Corporations' requirements for maximum geographical mobility of their workers destroy bonds of family and community, so that primary bonds of solidarity can not provide for dependents as they once did. The American value of individualism hinders the development of social supports to supplant family and community supports. Continued Puritanical proscriptions on extramarital sexual behavior perpetuate stigmatization of those who engage in more permissive sexual behavior. Women and children continue to be devalued, despite an official rhetoric of egalitarianism and concern for children.

I believe that a class analysis of adoption and foster care will pinpoint the problems of the systems more precisely than does a purely psychological analysis of individual motivation and personality dynamics, or an analysis of role relationships divorced from a view of the larger social system. Most child welfare research has been based on individualistic psychological theoretical assumptions, viewing the middle-class two-parent nuclear family as the "ideal type." When sociological research has focused on role functioning, the roles have often not been viewed as flowing out of a specific political and economic system which shapes these roles. Nevertheless, much of the research that has been done contains information which points to a class analysis even when the theoretical formulations have not centered on class as a crucial factor.

A materialist view, on the other hand, views social institutions and individual psychology as flowing out of the objective material conditions of a society. The culture and psychology created by material conditions take on a reality of their own, which in turn influences the material conditions, but the material conditions remain the most potent forces. The theoretical assumptions guiding my analysis of substitute child care are drawn partially from Frederick Engels [13] and Wilhelm Reich.[14]

Engels' theory of the development of the family has long been held in disrepute by most sociologists and anthropologists. Nevertheless it contains rewarding leads for understanding substitute child care. In 1884, Engels described how he believed the patriarchal monogamous family had served the function of stratifying society by assuring inheritance of surplus goods through the male lineage. Basing his reasoning on data compiled by Lewis H. Morgan on the Iroquois Indians, Engels postulated that when societies could hunt and gather only enough food for subsistence, accumulation of property did not occur, nor were there exploiting and exploited classes, since each man's labor was necessary to feed himself. When societies developed agriculture and herding of animals, it was possible to accumulate a surplus of food and property, and it was then that inheritance of property became an issue and exploitation of a person's labor became a possibility.

For the inheritance system to work, said Engels, a man had to be sure who his heirs were. In a society where sexual promiscuity was condoned and a woman could have children by many men, a man could not be sure he was the genitor of a child. Therefore, according to Engels, monogamous marriage was instituted, along with patrilineage. From this came the requirement of premarital chastity for women, prohibition of extramarital affairs for women, and the double standard of sexuality. Since men were allowed free sexual expression, prostitution arose to serve the mens' sexual needs and adultery was condoned for men but not for women.

Engels traced the historical development of societies through savagery, barbarism, and civilization. The patriarchal societies are at their apex in the beginning stage of civilization; the exploitation of wage-labor and masculine domination of women through monogamous marriage mark this stage of civilization. However, Engels envisioned a time when through struggles workers would end their exploitation by the propertied class; the state as the instrument of oppression by the propertied class would wither away; since property would be social rather than private, inheritance would be abolished; women would end their oppression by leaving their domestic slavery to join with men as equals in doing society's work; society would provide for the care of the children through nurseries and public schools; much of the domestic work would be done communally; marriage would proceed to a "higher form of monogamy" in which the woman and man would be equal partners; the double standard would be abolished; and marriage would be based on completely free choice rather than on economic necessity.

Anthropologists tell us that Engels' description of the evolution of societies is wrong, and for several decades evolutionary theory was not fashionable in anthropology. The unlimited promiscuity and group marriage that Engels postulated in the early stage of savagery did not, as far as anyone knows, ever exist. Societies did not progress in a near unilinear fashion through the three stages that Engels described. The theory was neat, but the facts were more complex. Yet when one studies adoption and foster care in historical and cross-cultural perspective, there is a recurring suspicion that, wrong as Engels might be about some things, he sheds light on some data which would not otherwise make sense.

The stigma of illegitimacy is clearly related to the perpetuation of property within the monogamous, patriarchal nuclear family, as is the double standard of sexual permissiveness for males and females. In many preliterate subsistence economies in Eastern Oceania, [15] for example, kinship is matrilineal; the clan is the most important socioeconomic unit of society; the sibling group is more important than the marital unit; children are regarded as communal, rather than private, property; clan property is owned communally; illegitimacy and sexual permissiveness are not stigmatized. Adoption among consanguinal kin is a common practice, and children retain ties with the natal clan and parents as well as with their adoptive parents. This is in sharp contrast to Western civilization, where the patriarchal nuclear family is the norm; illegitimacy and sexual permissiveness are strongly stigmatized; property is owned privately and the accumulation of property is highly valued; most people are engaged in wage-labor; children are regarded as private property; adoption is atypical and, until relatively recently in some countries, tied very closely to inheritance laws. Some countries, such as France, Greece, Spain, and most Latin American countries, still do not allow adoption when it would interfere with the inheritance rights of biological heirs. The rigidly patriarchal countries of ancient Rome, ancient Greece, India, Japan, and pre-revolutionary China, allowed adoption only for the securing of heirs for a propertied childless family. In those countries illegitimacy was strongly stigmatized and women were devalued—so much in pre-revolutionary China and in ancient Rome that female infanticide was practiced. After the Russian Revolution the Bolsheviks—perceiving the relationship between adoption and inheritance—not only abolished inheritance, but also abolished adoption in 1918. They legalized it again in 1926, apparently because of the need for homes for the many homeless children after the civil war.

The foster care system mirrors a polarized class society. The majority of foster children come from the most socially stigmatized families: the unmarried mothers, the impoverished, and the minority groups—especially blacks, Puerto Ricans, Mexican-Americans, and Indians.[16] Most of the families are poor, and disproportionate numbers of them live in crowded and substandard housing, have severe health problems, and are headed by one parent, usually a woman.[17]

There is no clear proof that the foster child's lot improves after the state takes charge of him. If he is removed involuntarily from his biological family, he stands a good chance of not returning home, of losing contact with his family, and of not gaining permanent ties to another family.

Although many foster homes have given good care to children, and many foster children regard their foster parents as if they were their "real" parents, the system of foster care has not given the majority of foster children the benefits that society claims to want for children: long-term physical nurturance and environmental stability; socially defined roles in which the children can feel secure; consistent and stable object relationships to aid children in developing a strong sense of identity; assurance from a family and/or society that children will have a reasonably equal opportunity with other citizens to achieve success as adults. A large number of children have been as severely neglected by the state in foster care as their parents—from whom the state removed the children—were alleged to have neglected them. A study in the 1960s found children in 43 percent of public placements and 17 percent of voluntary foster care suffering from neglect and abuse.[18]

As for developing a stable identity, Wolins sums up the situation:

> The identity of a child in (a foster home) is often unclear, his stay is uncertain. He will probably find himself a wanderer, packing his affections, if any, and his problems and transferring them to at least several foster homes before he matures. Although the outcome for some foster children has been favorable, the overall effect of the program is unknown.[19]

Foster children are given an ambiguous, marginal, and stigmatized role. They are invisible even to some social scientists. In their study of "The New Englanders of Orchard Town, U.S.A.," the Fischers said:

> A number of "state" children board with various families in the town who receive remuneration for their care. At least one of these families keeps

such children isolated from other children of the town for fear parents would be worried that state children would be a bad influence. None of these families were interviewed. Some "state" children were reported to be nice children.[20]

The term "state child" is anathema to foster children and their natural parents. An adult woman who grew up in foster homes that she remembers positively has this to say about the term:

I think that most people take you for what you are, but once they find that you're a state child, then you're no good. That's the first impression . . . the boy who was in the last foster home that I was in was going steady with a girl for 3–4 years and they were going to get married. But he was a state child and her parents kept at her to stay away because he was a state child and he was no good. . . .[21]

The biological parent of a foster child says, " . . . I always felt low. Like I was kind of an outcast. I don't know why. This is just my nature."[22] Another parent of children in foster care speaks of foster parents who

in a misguided effort to show my children how much they cared for them told them that they enjoyed and cared for the children so much that they would keep them even if they were not being paid for their care. My children, instead of being flattered and pleased, were resentful. They did not like to feel that they were receiving charity from either the county or the foster parents.[23]

A foster parent describes some community attitudes toward the parents of foster children:

But I can sympathize with taxpayers who are tired of paying high welfare for this. Now I know a family in our town who are struggling to raise their children and it's difficult, and the kids don't have much. But (my foster child) has two times as much as they have. Now they're tired of working, and why shouldn't they sit down and say, "Look, I want the state to help me for a while." Ah, but they're not. I had to take one of (my foster children) down to the dentist and [was] telling them, and they said, "We'd like to, but we can't afford it." So you really can't blame a hard-working woman or man who feel this way. . . . They imply that his natural parents are running around having a fine old time, trying everything as far as I know. . . . Ah, but I mean they have this feeling of why should they struggle for rent paying, just to be able to hold their head up.[24]

What of adopted children? Do they fare better than foster children? Since the majority are born out-of-wedlock, they become less stigmatized by becoming part of a legal family. Since the majority of adoptive children are born to poor parents, their socioeconomic status is raised through adoption. Yet their social status is problematic. Since it is an atypical status, they may be subject to "genealogical bewilderment."[25] There are endless and seemingly insoluble problems about how to deal with the fact of their adoption and how to deal with the natural parents who have relinquished their rights to the children. Reviewing the research on adoption, Kellmer Pringle concludes that adoptive children are Maybe more vulnerable than natural children because (1) a majority are conceived out-of-wedlock, and the mother is likely to be under stress during pregnancy; (2) the baby is likely to have an anxiety-laden atmosphere in the early months since both the natural mother and adoptive parents are assailed by anxiety and fear; (3) there is deep-seated social disapproval of illegitimacy; (4) adoptive families are a minority group, "in the sense that adoption is not the generally prevailing pattern of child rearing," and there is a good deal of evidence that minority groups share certain psychological characteristics.[26] Sexual anxieties of adoptive parents make it especially hard for them to discuss an out-of-wedlock child's origins. Added to this are the anxieties many adoptive parents feel about infertility, so that it is often difficult for them to deal unambiguously with the adoptive child's developing identity.

Several studies show that adopted children are curious about their origins: McWhinnie [27] reported that many of her subjects remembered feeling curious about their origins, and the difficulty in getting information; Goldman [28] stressed the existence of curiosity about natural origins in both successful and unsuccessful adoptions; Paton [29] found in her study that about half of the adoptees when grown searched for natural parents. Most who did so reported poor relationships with adoptive parents. Jaffee and Fanshel [30] also found in their study that the adoptive children who had the most problems were also the children most likely to want more information about their biological parents. Most of the adoptive parents in Jaffee and Fanshel's study had psychologically "killed off" the children's natural parents by not discussing them with the children. Some had not even told the children they were adopted, contrary to the advice of the social workers at adoption agencies. Ansfield [31], a children's psychiatrist, recommends never telling the child of his adoption, by swearing relatives to secrecy and, if necessary, telling lies to neighbors and representatives of community institutions, as well as to the child. Kirk, [32] on the other hand, speaking from a sociological perspective, believes that the socially healthier adjustment of adoptive parents is "acknowledgment of difference" rather than the denial of difference. He advises encouraging open communication between adoptive parents and natural parents before the child is placed, to help the child cope with questions about his background. I know of no agency, however, which has followed Kirk's advice.

Adoptive children in Western countries sever all ties to the biological family and become the exclusive possession of the adoptive parent. This radical severance of ties to biological parents, coupled with the stigmatized status of mothers bearing children out-of-wedlock, is what seems to constitute the most problematic aspect of adoption in the United States.

To summarize, the main problems of foster care seem to center around class stratification; stigmatization of illegitimacy; devaluation of women and children; breakdown of the social insurance functions of the family and breakdown in community solidarity; the unwillingness of the state to substitute adequate supportive structures to compensate for the breakdown of the family; and a pervasive attitude of contempt for poor people. The main problems of adoption seem to center around the stigmatization of illegitimacy; the removal of children from all contact with the biological families; the social requirement of proof of fertility in order to achieve adult status, and especially the social definition of woman's primary role as child bearer and rearer.

A society's property relationships and its system of inheritance create and perpetuate the class structure of society. To illustrate, my next chapter focuses on an historical and comparative view of the relationship of adoption to property ownership and inheritance practices.

Notes to Chapter One

1. (Garden City, N.Y.: Doubleday Anchor Books, 1955), pp. 4–5.
2. Ibid., p. 6.
3. National Center for Social Statistics, *Child Welfare Statistics*, 1968, Report CW-1, US/DHEW, Table 23, p. 29; Table 10, p. 20; *Child Welfare Statistics*, 1969, CW-1, US/DHEW, Table 22, p. 30.
4. *Statistical Abstract of the United States* 1972, Bureau of the Census, Table 497, p. 305.
5. *Child Welfare Statistics*, 1969, CW-1, US/DHEW, Table 22, p. 30.
6. M. Larzerson, "Social Reform and Early Childhood Education: Some Historical Perspectives," *Urban Education*, April 1970, pp. 84–101.
7. B. Mooney, "Day Care: A Proposal," *Ripon Forum*, April 1970, pp. 18–19.
8. Courtesy of the *Boston Globe*, 28 January 1972.
9. Bruno Bettelheim, *The Children of the Dream* (N.Y.: Macmillan, 1969).
10. Martin Wolins, "Political Orientation, Social Reality, and Child Welfare," *Social Service Review*, 38 (December 1964): 429–442; "Group Care: Friend or Foe?" *Social Work*, vol. 14, no. 1 (January 1969): 35–53. "Another View of Group Care," *Child Welfare*, vol. 44, no. 1 (January 1965): 15–16.
11. H. Skeels, "Effects of Adoption on Children From Institutions," *Children*, vol. 12, no. 1 (1965): 33–34; M. Skodak and H. Skeels "A Final Follow-up Study of One Hundred Adopted Children," *Journal of Genetic Psychology*, 75 (1949): 85–125.
12. Joseph H. Reid, "Patterns of Partnership" (mimeographed, N.Y.: Child Welfare League of America, 1969), p. 11.
13. Frederick Engels, *The Origin of the Family, Private Property, and the State* (N.Y.: International Publishers, 1942).
14. Wilhelm Reich, *The Sexual Revolution* (N.Y.: Orgone Institute Press, 1951).
15. Vern Carroll, ed., *Adoption in Eastern Oceania* (Honolulu: University of Hawaii Press, 1970).
16. David Fanshel, "The Exit of Children from Foster Care: An Interim Research Report," *Child Welfare*, vol. 50, no. 2 (February 1971): 65–81; Jenkins and Norman, "Families of Children in Foster Care," *Children*, vol. 16, no. 4 (1969): 155–159.

17. Alfred Kadushin, "Child Welfare," in *Research in the Social Services: A Five-Year Review*, ed. by Henry S. Maas (N.Y.: National Association of Social Workers, Inc., 1971), pp. 34–38.

18. Abraham S. Levine, "Substitute Child Care: Recent Research and Its Implications," *Welfare in Review*, vol. 10, no. 1 (January–February 1972): 3.

19. Martin Wolins, "Another View of Group Care," *Child Welfare*, vol. 44, no. 1 (January 1965): 15–16.

20. Beatrice Whiting, ed., *Six Cultures: Studies of Child Rearing* (N.Y.: John Wiley & Sons, 1963), p. 935.

21. Foster Parent Discussion Group, Child and Family Services, Inc., Hartford, Conn., 7 January 1969 (taped).

22. Ibid., 4 February 1969 (taped).

23. Phyllis Johnson McAdams, "The Parent in the Shadows," *Journal of Public Social Services*, vol. 1, no. 4 (December 1970).

24. Foster Parent Discussion Group, Child and Family Services, Inc., Hartford, Conn., 15 October 1968 (taped).

25. H. J. Sants, "Genealogical Bewilderment in Children with Substitute Parents," *British Journal of Medical Psychology*, 37 (1964): 133–141.

26. M. L. Kellmer Pringle, *Adoption: Facts and Fallacies* (N.Y.: Humanities Press, 1966), p. 27.

27. Alexina McWhinnie, "A Study of Adoption–the Social Circumstances and Adjustment in Adult Life of 58 Adopted Children," (Ph.D. diss., University of Edinburgh, 1959).

28. R. J. Goldman, "A Critical and Historical Survey of the Methods of Child Adoption in the United Kingdom and the United States" (M.A. diss., Birmingham, England, 1958).

29. J. M. Paton, *The Adopted Break Silence* (Acton, Calif.: Life History Study Center, 1954).

30. Benson Jaffee and David Fanshel, *How They Fared in Adoption: A Follow-up Study* (N.Y.: Columbia University Press, 1970).

31. Joseph G. Ansfield, *The Adopted Child* (Springfield, Ill.: Charles C. Thomas, 1971).

32. H. David Kirk, *Shared Fate* (N.Y.: The Free Press, 1964).

CHAPTER TWO
INHERITANCE AND ADOPTION

To whom it may concern:
If anything should happen to me I hereby leave the
following people the following things.
1. to Joe and Vito = I have some mony at home about
30 or 40 dollars, I want you two to have it. P.S. = I love youre
very much. Take what you want.
2. To Little Vinnie = I love you most of all. I have 100
dollars in the bank in Brooklyn. Take 50$ of it. I have a suede vest
I also want you to have. So take that too. Anything else you want,
take. PS = Take good care of yourself, I'll love you always.
3. To Ann = Take 30 dollars out of the $100, thats for
helping us. Look thru my stuff anything else you want take.
You've been a good friend.
4. To Sal = Dear friend you may have the remaing $20
of the hundred dollars. You can get Granny a new rolling pin. You
have been a good friend to me. I'll never forget you.
5. To Paolo = You can have my posters. Rosa told me
you liked posters. You can have my inflated pillows too. Your
Good people, I'll never forget you.
6. To Sammy = You can have my raccoon fur and two
medallions of mine. Anything you find that you really want, you
can have. Your a beautiful Person Sam, You'll go a long way.
7. To marion = You can have my peasant shirts and stuff
like that. Help yourself. Your a good friend, I'll always remember
you.
8. To = Ray, Phil, Dick, Kenny, Mike, Dave, Butch,
Ronnie, and all you other people take what you can find. I can't
think of anything specific to give. I love all of you every last one.
PS = tell Marciano I said goodbye. I don't even know him and
I'll miss him.

Dear Friends,
I hate to leave you, I really love all of you, I love being
with you. Whether I die or live and go to another place, I want
you to have these things. To Gloria = thanks for your help, I'll
always be your friend. P.S. = tell Carl how much I love him and
how much it hurts me to leave him. Tell Joe I love him, but not as
much as Carl. I'll always love Carl. Thats all I guess, take care of
yourselves, where ever I am I'll be thinking about you.

Love
Sarafina

The "will" of a 13-year-old girl placed in an institution for
dependent children. She had no contact with her parents, and had
been living with her grandmother, whom she claimed to hate.
Names have been changed.

Poor Aunt G . . . she has the wildest imagination . . . her bottom drawer is full of money—thousands of dollars—any day they will come to take her to court but Roy says not to worry—she says he's been so good to her (he really has) that she's leaving all her property to him. She's leaving me all her beautiful dishes and furniture because I've been pretty good too. . . .

Letter from the niece of a 95-year-old woman in a nursing home, propertyless, and supported by Old Age Assistance.

The 13-year-old girl and the 95-year-old woman were in institutions supported by the state. They are financially and psychologically impoverished, yet in their imaginations they reach out for love and try to establish their value to themselves and others through inheritance. Property and the passing on of property is embedded in most people's imaginations, whether they actually possess property. This key factor must be understood in order to understand social relationships fully.

Witmer points out that "inheritance runs through the history of adoption and non-adoption so much more prominently than any other factor . . . that its importance can hardly be overestimated."[1] The United Nations Analysis of Adoption Laws, studying fifteen European, North American, and Latin American countries, says that in the statutes of all the countries, "provisions concerning the rights of inheritance between the adoptee and his adopter are given prime attention and the most detailed analysis."[2]

Goody [3] relates adoption practices directly to economic factors, including the property relationships of a society, distribution of resources, and inheritance practices. In his cross-cultural study of adoption, he compares Euro-Asian systems of adoption to traditional sub-Saharan African societies, where adoption was almost an unknown practice. Goody argues that Africa did not practice adoption because agriculture was extensive rather than intensive. There has been less land to inherit; therefore property has been less problematic and may pass through brothers and nephews. Inheritance has been horizontal as well as vertical, and personal continuity has often been maintained through taking on wives rather than children.[4] The Islamic religion forbids adoption, as does the Jewish religious code. The Moslem code of *Hukum Shara* does not recognize adoption.[5] Islamic religion allowed polygyny, one way of assuring male heirs if a wife is barren. Witmer cites Biblical references as evidence that adoption was practiced by the Jews, with emphasis on heirship, [6] but Horowitz says that adoption is forbidden in the Jewish religious code, and no national adoption law was proposed in Israel until 1958.[7]

Euro-Asian Societies

In contrast to African societies, Euro-Asian societies practiced intensive agriculture. Inheritance was vertical rather than horizontal, and monogamy was the norm. I shall summarize some of these Euro-Asian adoption practices:

Classical Greece

In classical Greece, adoption served the function of securing an heir to pass on the family line and property. A man could adopt his daughter's husband or one of his sons as an heir. Men adopted their grandsons or (as in China) their agnatic nephews, and sometimes their nieces to succeed as *epikleroi*. The adopted cut off their ties with their natal family. Only if an adopted son had begotten a son could he return to his natal family, and if he did he was cut off from his own progeny. Only citizens could adopt and be adopted, for only they could own property. Only males could adopt, although girls were sometimes adopted as heiresses.

> Adoption involved a continuation of the worship of the family shrines and this too could not be properly carried out by a foreigner. An adopted son had to look after his adopted father in his old age, bury him when he died, and worship him after his death. Perhaps even more than in Rome, the practice was connected with continuity, both of property and worship, in the direct line of descent.[8]

Ancient Rome

The Roman practice of adoption was to prevent a family line from dying out by providing a son and heir who could inherit the property, continue a man's family line, and perpetuate the worship of ancestors. The adopted person broke off all contact with his natal family. In one form of adoption, adrogation, he renounced the worship of his original family gods and took over the new gods of his adopted family. He took all his property and descendants with him, and his family line was extinguished. In another form of adoption, adoption *alieni juris* from the *potestas* of his or her paterfamilias, a man or woman came by themselves, leaving their children (if any) under their original paterfamilias—and they would have no property to bring.[9]

Because inheritance was only through the paternal line, males had to adopt males. Women could not adopt, though they could be adopted (not adrogated).

> Inheritance of property and worship of the dead were intimately associated in Roman society; for this reason a man wanted to provide himself with a specific descendant to carry out both these tasks. . . . It was not the deprived but only citizens who were adopted, often the sons of other big families. For the giver there was a gain in the shape of an alliance between the two houses, while the recipient perpetuated his own line.[10]

Leslie [11] points out the relationship of adoption practices to changes in the social structure after the wars with Carthage. Prior to that time, fathers had the right to dispose of their sons' property. Caesar gave sons the right to dispose of property they had acquired during military careers. The power of fathers over children was restricted. "While infant exposure, never common, was still permitted, the power of life and death over children was taken away. . . . Only very poor parents were permitted to sell their children's labor. . . ."[12] The birth rate fell, abortion was widely practiced,

> exposure of infants reached scandalous proportions. To correct this situation, laws were passed taxing the inheritances of childless couples at 50% of the inheritance. The laws exempted children by adoption, however, and it became fashionable to adopt adult children for the purpose of receiving inheritances. Both the couples doing the adopting and the adopted entered such relationships according to calculated advantage.[13]

Hindu India

Adoption has been an important practice from ancient times to the present to continue the patriarchal line, inherit property, and perform the appropriate rituals when the father dies. The adopted son cut off ties from his natal family, but despite the severance he was still forbidden to marry anyone in his natal family. As in China and Greece, adopters preferred the adopted son to be as close a kinsman as possible, preferably a brother's son.[14] Some authors emphasize the religious significance of adoption since it was related to the ancestral cult, but Mayne argues that adoption was only practiced by propertied people: "Paupers have souls to be saved, but they are not in the habit of adopting."[15]

Present adoption practice in India gives some recognition of the child welfare function of giving an "orphan or a child of a relatively poor family . . . a good home and security,"[16] but in practice adoption still functions mainly as a device for providing a male heir. Basham argues that adopted sons were poor substitutes for true sons in performing the *strāddha* funeral ceremony, which insured a father's safe transit to the other world, and the efficacy of an adopted son was dubious.[17] Mandelbaum points out how the incidence of adoptions can be stimulated by economics:

> In one Mysore village where irrigation has made land far more remunerative than before, the orderly transmittal of an estate is of high importance. Among the landowners, 10 percent of all the males had been adopted. But in a nearby village, where the lands are not irrigated and economic opportunities are not so bound in with the land, only 2 percent of the men of the same *jati* had been adopted.[18]

Alan Fanger [19] describes adoption among the Hindu Kumaonese villagers of the Himalayas as an uncommon practice. The village is primarily agricultural, although about 20 percent of the adult population are engaged outside the village in service occupations such as servants and soldiers. Most of the villagers are relatively poor. During the period Fanger studied the village, there were two cases of adoption out of a population of about 500-600. Only males were adopted, and only for the purpose of inheritance, land cultivation, and performance of the death rites. Although the Sanskrit specifies that a Brahman priest should sanctify the adoption, there was no ceremonial recognition of adoption among the Kumaonese. The boys were adopted as infants, and simply moved from one house to another. In one case, a man adopted his brother's son, and the biological father became the child's uncle. A practice more common than adoption was the custom of *ghar jamai* (*ghar* translates as "house"; *jamai* translates as "son-in-law"). This means that if a man has no sons but has a daughter, he can get his son-in-law to move in with him. The son-in-law does not inherit land but becomes a kind of manager or regent. He can still inherit from his own parents, but usually does not. His son can inherit land. Fanger says that there is a tendency to adopt within one's own caste, and probably within one's own village. If there are no sons to inherit, the property goes to collateral relatives of the father, preferably his brother or brother's son. Child welfare functions of caring for orphans or children of poor parents are performed by the joint family system.

Pre-revolutionary China

Adoption in pre-revolutionary China "meant the acquisition of a son by an heirless male from among his close agnates,"[20] and disputes of adoption were in reality disputes of inheritance.[21] Men might take concubines as an alternative to adoption, or a son-in-law might take the place of a son by marrying his wife at her parents' house. Leslie points out that the traditional Chinese family was patriarchal, patrilineal, patrilocal, and monogamous. The *tsu* or clan included all persons of a given surname descended from a common ancestor. Sons were necessary to meet one's obligations to one's ancestor and to ensure one's own future worship as an ancestor.

> A man without sons might adopt them, but the practice was disapproved of and adopted sons were looked down upon. Occasionally peasant families permitted their sons to be adopted into gentry families, but it was more common for men to take concubines, who were generally purchased from peasant families. The concubines' children were legitimate, but had only limited rights of inheritance unless the wife bore no sons.[22]

The Chinese Communist government since 1949 has virtually eliminated female infanticide and outlawed concubinage. Communes established between 1958 and 1960 have not abolished the conjugal family, but they were intended to replace the extended family. Illegitimacy, almost a new problem in China, is on the increase. Previously concubinage had handled the extramarital affairs of the males, and the children were legitimized and cared for by the extended family. Although China never had a puritanical attitude toward sex, the government is now urging a more puritanical morality in an effort to reduce illegitimacy rates.[23] According to Leslie, the rising divorce and illegitimacy rates and the plight of the aged have "forced the communists to retreat somewhat from their ideal of completely independent womanhood and from their attacks on the doctrine of filial piety."[24] Another factor contributing to this change in policy, not mentioned by Leslie, may be the objective of the ruling class to industrialize rapidly, with the concomitant reintroduction of authoritarian family values and structures, similar to the reintroduction of the authoritarian family by the Stalinist regime in Russia.[25]

Japan

David and Vera Mace say that in Japan, as in China,

> It was a common practice to adopt into the family a boy who would count as the son of the childless man, and would be willing to perform the necessary sacrifices to the ancestors.[26]

An alternative method of obtaining sons was to adopt as a son the prospective husband of a man's daughter. He was called *yoshi*, or "foster son," and frequently he was persuaded to divorce his wife after he had produced a son for the family.

From Inheritance to "Child Welfare"

A study of the history of adoption practices in Europe, North America, and Latin America reveals a gradual shift in some of these countries from an exclusive concern with protecting the natural heirs to what is now called a "child welfare" focus. Adoption was not legal in England in the past because it interfered with the inheritance rights of biological heirs. When English law did not even provide for land to be conveyed by a will, adoption would be out of the question. Witmer indicates that this refusal to share an inheritance with anyone outside the natal family is related to keeping a kingdom intact:

> In the thirteenth century no wide gulf could be fixed between the inheritance of a kingdom and other impartible inheritances.[27]

After the Statute of Wills was passed in 1540, an outsider was not wanted in the family because adoption would involve not only the adoptive parents' estate, but might also involve the estates of all members of the adoptive parents' family and even of his collaterals.[28] In the United States this is still a problem to which states apply varying legal solutions.

The practice of adoption disappeared almost completely in the Middle Ages and was reintroduced in France in 1792. The U.N. *Analysis* gives the following French history:

> When the Civil Code was being drafted (1800–1804), the section dealing with adoption met with strong opposition, but the First Consul secured its retention, because at that time he (the future emperor) was thinking of providing himself with an heir by means of adoption. However, only adults could be adopted. The only provisions for minors were the "benevolent" guardianship (*tutelle officieuse*), an institution intended to allow adoption by will, which was authorized in the case of the guardians' death; and adoption as a reward (*adoption rémunératoire*), so called because it was allowed when the adoptee had saved the adopter's life. Both were extremely rare. The spirit and nature of adoption were profoundly modified by the Act of 19 June 1923 and by subsequent provisions which made it possible to adopt orphaned or deserted minors. Besides "regular adoption," which does not completely sever the links of the adoptee with

his natural parents and can be revoked, the Ordinance of 19 October 1945 introduced, on behalf of children under five years of age who are total orphans, abandoned, or of unknown parentage, "adoptive legitimation," which integrates the child completely into the adopter's family. According to the experience of French adoption agencies, there is amongst would-be adopters a marked preference for adoptive legitimation, in spite of its being irrevocable.[29]

A shift from the exclusive concern with inheritance to a concern with the "child welfare" functions of adoption began to be evident in the laws of the United States and England in the middle of the nineteenth century. Prior to the passage of the first state adoption statutes (Texas and Vermont, 1850)[30] the most common legal means of transferring custody was through a contract or indenture, deeding the child as a piece of property and setting out the understanding of the parties.[31] This "fictitious apprenticeship" was described by the drafter of a civil code for New York State in 1865 as "so inappropriate a form in every case that it is rarely resorted to."[32] Adoptions were made either informally or by a separate legislative act for each case. Witmer says that formal adoption laws simply legalized what was already occurring. He states that England's adoption statutes were passed to protect children and parents and because,

> by reason of the low birth rate, the war, and the influenza epidemic, the practice of *de facto* adoption had become common. Children were in need of protection against both those who profited financially from placing them in foster homes and from those who profited from taking them in their own homes. Natural parents needed protection against giving children up unwillingly and unnecessarily, while adopting parents needed protection against natural parents' later claims.[33]

The U.N. *Analysis* says that

> at the beginning of the twentieth century, and particularly since the First World War, adoption took a surprising bound forward, a movement which can be traced primarily to the desire to provide new homes for war orphans and homeless children. The same motive has influenced many people since the Second World War. . . .[34]

Legal adoption did not become possible in England and Wales until the passage of the first adoption law in 1926; in Northern Ireland in 1929; and in Scotland in 1930.[35] Scotland's adoption law differed from England's in that adoptive children were not allowed to inherit from their adoptive parents, and in this respect was the same as the "old" English law. When a will merely mentioned "my child" or "my children" or "issue," the adopted child was excluded.[36] At that time the committee which deliberated laws of succession in Scotland explained in its report that adoptive children could not inherit "because of the legal complications which might ensue under our existing law of intestate succession, more particularly because of its rules of primogeniture and preference of males over females."[37]

Differences in adoption laws and practices among countries, states, provinces, and even among different communities in the United States, can be partially understood by examining differing orientations toward inheritance and property relationships. The U.N. *Analysis* points out that

> in countries whose legal system derives more or less from Roman Law or the Code Napoleon, the adopted child's links with his own parents are not broken. He is not only entitled to inherit from them and their relatives, but may still be called upon to support them, and reciprocally they may have to support him if the adopter fails to do so. Some of these provisions can easily be explained when it is realized that the original pattern of adoption was a family one, i.e., when the few children adopted were either illegitimate children adopted by their own natural father, or orphans adopted by relatives. This is still the prevailing pattern in some instances, as in Latin America. This is why in France and Uruguay adoptive legitimation, which completely integrates the child into the adopter's family, is restricted to full orphans and children of unknown parentage. It exists side by side with so-called "regular adoption" where the natural links are not completely severed.[38]

In Greece, adoption statutes "show traces of Roman law as preserved in Byzantine law and modified by European influences. Adoption is still considered mainly as a means of satisfying the desire of childless persons and couples for children, without prejudice to the adoptee."[39]

In countries concerned with inheritance rights, the inheritance rights of "blood relatives" are protected in adoption legislation in a variety of ways, for example, by (1) setting a high age limit for adopters (Bolivia, 50 years; Spain, 45; Switzerland, Argentina, and France, 40 years—with some exceptions possible); (2) restricting adoption to people who have no other children (Guatemala, Denmark, Argentina, Bolivia, France, Greece, Switzerland, Peru); (3) voiding the adoption if a subsequent child is born to the adopters (all of the countries which make provision with respect to the existence of other children except Argentina, where such an occurrence merely makes the adoption voidable); (4) allowing the adoptee to inherit only if the adopter leaves no ascendants, descendants, or spouse (Guatemala and Uruguay); (5) limiting or extinguishing the rights of the adoptee to inherit if the adopter gives birth to children (Yugoslavia); and (6) giving biological children a larger share of the inheritance (Norway and Sweden).[40]

Adoption legislation that does not sever ties between parents and children seems more closely tied to traditional concerns about inheritance, and the fear of an adopted child interfering with inheritance rights of "blood relatives." This kind of legislation seems more typical of countries, and sections of countries, which followed Roman law or the Code Napoléon. The Code Napoléon of 1804 prevented adoption when it interfered with inheritance by biological heirs. The Louisiana Civil Code of 1808 was modeled after this. Spanish law when Mexico controlled Texas prohibited adoption by a person with a legitimate child.[41]

Adoption legislation that gives the adopted child the same inheritance rights as a natural child seems more oriented to what is generally considered a "child welfare" concept of adoption. This kind of legislation seems more typical of countries, and sections of countries, which followed the English common law. For example, Massachusetts' first adoption statute (1851) "was drawn with the avowed object of securing to adopted children a proper share in the estate of adopting parents who should die intestate."[42] The U.N. *Analysis* says that the five Latin American countries studied—Argentina, Guatemala, Uruguay, Peru, and Bolivia—were strongly influenced by Roman law.[43] People in all these five countries rarely resort to adoption and they almost never think of it as a means of providing for neglected and homeless children: adoption is still mostly of the "family" pattern.[44] Adoption was first introduced in the United States in states where the legal system was based on English common law, and reintroduced by others which had abolished it previously. In the latter states legislation was influenced by Roman law.[45] Kornitzer says that the oldest British colonial adoption law was that of Malta, whose civil code of 1870 was on the Continental European plan derived from the Code Napoléon. It was framed to protect the inheritance rights of natural heirs (only people over 50 years of age who had no legitimate descendants were allowed to adopt.)[46]

Switzerland's adoption law cautions that adoption "must serve legitimate interests and not encroach on the rights of others," and, before the adoption can become legal, requires adoptive parents to be already caring for the child or to prove that their motives are good. Kornitzer points out the anxiety expressed in this law "lest adoption be undertaken from caprice or from the desire to spite one's legitimate heirs."[47] The original reason for a probationary period before legalizing an adoption was for the protection of heirs, as in France. In Switzerland the local guardianship authority supervises children given for adoption, so that "the shift of emphasis from legal to welfare requirements has taken place without a change of legal form."[48]

Spain, as of 1952, prohibited both illegitimate children and non-Spaniards from being adopted by their own parents. A distinction was drawn between civil code adoptions made for "family pride or convenience" and social welfare adoptions, which are called "family placements" and are actually foster homes given a deed of adoption by a judge and supervised by institutions which retain legal guardianship.[49]

The distinctions between familial and child welfare functions in Switzerland and Spain illustrate the transition from concerns with inheritance to concerns with "child welfare." A shift to a "child welfare" philosophy loosens or abolishes inheritance ties to natural parents and tends to substitute the state for the natural parent. In both Switzerland and Spain, adopted children retain rights of inheritance from their natural family. A shift to a "child welfare" focus in Switzerland involves the state as supervisor of the adoptive parents, whereas a shift to a "child welfare" focus in Spain involves the state as legal guardian to foster children, in a separate status from adoptive children. In countries such as France and Uruguay where there are two kinds of adoption, the form called "adoptive legitimation" severs a child's ties to natural parents completely, Uruguay doing it in the more sweeping fashion by allowing the adoptive parents to register the child in the record of vital statistics as having been born to them in wedlock, and forbidding the very mention of adoption.[50] It seems that as countries, and sections of countries, move toward a "child welfare" orientation where the children do not inherit from their natural parents, the latter do become excluded. The history of adoption and foster care in the United States bears this out.

Eastern Oceania

Inheritance and land tenure figure prominently in adoption practices also in Eastern Oceania, yet the differences between Oceanic and Western practices are vast. Oceanic societies have been changed to varying degrees by Western colonial administrators, and the clash of primitive subsistence societies with industrialized colonialists of the major world powers highlights the effect of socioeconomic factors on child care. Adoption is very common in Oceania, even in Hawaii, which has been the most fully incorporated of all Polynesian societies into Western civilization. Howard et al. assert that the importance of adoption to Hawaiians is one distinguishing difference between Hawaiians and other American ethnic groups.[51] Traditionally, Oceanic cultures have been organized upon clan and lineage lines, and the sibling group owned most land corporately. Adoption almost always took place among close relatives; and one of its most important functions in many Oceanic societies was to distribute the land equitably among consanguinal kin. Other functions included strengthening kinship ties and providing a form of social insurance for the aged.

I shall examine some of the property relationships and inheritance practices of Oceanic socieites that are in various stages of transition from a clan-lineage polity to a polity based on private property, a centralized state, and Western inheritance practices.

Hawaii

In the past, Hawaii used adoption to retain the power in a ruling house and to "keep the blood undefiled and so to perpetuate this *mana* or psychic force in the clan."[52] Only the children of a brother or sister were adopted. People also adopted to pass on wealth to the adopted relative; to provide for themselves in old age; to help close relatives who had more children they they could care for. Also they liked children. At the present time, inheritance and kinship motives are no longer important in adoption except that people who own homestead land sometimes adopt someone of at least half-Hawaiian ancestry since homestead land can be owned only by people of at least half-Hawaiian ancestry. Hawaiians prefer informal rather than institutional relationships, and turn to an agency for adoption only as a last resort. They show a strong preference for adopting relatives or children of close friends because they believe that a child's character is inherited, and fear that one who is not a relative or friend might break the adoption contract. They encourage an adopted child to continue his contact with his natural parents after adoption. Hawaiians still emphasize kinship seniority, and grandparents frequently adopt their grandchildren. Adoptions are usually carried out between matrilineal kin. Because of the importance Hawaiians attach to "passing on the name," there is a slight preponderance of males adopted, especially among legal adoptions. There is a trend toward more legal adoptions of both related and unrelated children, but especially of unrelated children. This is sometimes motivated by a desire for legal protection of the child's inheritance, but the reason given most often is a fear that the natural parents will take back the child. Adoptive parents claim to give adopted and natural children an equal share of the inheritance, and espouse complete egalitarianism between adopted and natural children.

Society Islands[53]

These islands include Tahiti, the largest. They have probably been changed more than any of the other Polynesian islands except Hawaii by the administering colonial power (France). However, their land tenure and adoption arrangements provide an interesting contrast to Hawaii since the Roman law of France seems to lend itself more favorably to existing socioeconomic arrangements than does the English common law of the Americans. The native polity based on a tribal system, and the concept of inherited rank, has disappeared. Family and domestic economies involve the production of cash crops and the purchase of building materials and foodstuffs. However, adoption is still common, and adopted children are usually taken from among close kin. "Children, like land and personal names, are regarded as resources to which rights are held by categories of people claiming a common ancestor."[54] At the beginning of the century, the French codified land boundaries and claims of ownership, and they have since regulated land transfers according to French law. Most of the land is passed on according to French rules of succession,

> which provide for the land rights of an intestate person to be transferred, at his death, in specified proportions to various categories of legitimate and natural consanguinal kinsmen. Legitimate children succeed to the total estate in equal shares without regard to either sex or birth order.[55]

However, most rural Tahitians have not made testaments and although their land rights legally pass on to their children in equal portions, they have not actually partitioned the land but rather divide rights in the land so that now each section has a large number of co-owners. Some co-owners live in or near each section of land to work it; others live elsewhere where they or their spouses have land rights, or where they can get wage-labor. Tahitians conceive of bodies of co-owners as a descent group, traced from a common ancestor. "Thus the Tahitian, and widespread Polynesian, ideology linking land rights with membership in a descent unit is maintained within the letter, if not the spirit, of French civil laws."[56] Under this system, adopted children do not inherit intestate from their adopters, but inherit from their natural parents. Adopters rarely deed land to adoptees by testament. Often grandchildren are adopted, and since they are the grandparents' heirs anyway, they inherit from the grandparents.

In the rural community of Maupiti, a poor community, large numbers of adults leave the island to seek wage-labor elsewhere, and adoption is more frequent than in the neighboring more prosperous community of Murifenua. Much of the adoption in Maupiti is of grandchildren, so that the "economically necessary sequence of household development is maintained."[57] Another commonly advanced reason for adopting children is the same as that given by Hindus: adoption provides heirs who will bury their parents correctly and make use of their house and land. "For those who have no natural children, adopted children are the universally preferred alternatives. Unmarried persons, either male or female, may adopt children."[58] French law—but not kin—discriminate against illegitimate children. Tahitians attach no social stigma to illegitimacy. A Tahitian woman often has one or two children before beginning an approved conjugal relationship.

> It is an ethically neutral act for a woman to give such children to her parents or to other close relatives for adoption. The woman is thus freed to continue . . . "the business of adolescence" if she should wish to do so.[59]

Rangiroa Atoll[60]

Rangiroa Atoll, in the Western Tuamotus, provides an interesting example of how a shift to French inheritance laws create anxiety about inheritance rights between adoptive and natural children. Adoption has been very common since ancient times; traditionally it served the function of allocating and redistributing people among small localized descent groups called 'ati. The sibling group as a whole owns the land. Ownership is distinguished from use rights, which are good only during a person's lifetime and cannot be inherited. French law does not recognize the right of adopted children to inherit from adoptive parents unless a will is made. The two predominant religions on the island, the Roman Catholic and the Sanito (Mormon), oppose adoption in principle, although the Catholic Church encourages it if gains for the Church, such as conversion, are expected. The Sanito church stresses family stability and preaches that everyone must take care of his own children.

> Sanito pastors fight vigorously against premarital and postmarital sexual freedom. Without doubt, they want to discourage, in an indirect way, accidental or experimental unions, which are so much easier when there is no difficulty in placing the children of these unions.[61]

In the past, adopted children had the same status as natural children, and most of them inherited from their adoptive parents. This is more rare now because there is always "trouble" with the natural heirs. A few adopted children in the past were registered under the name of the adoptive parent rather than under that of the natural parent, so that they would be fully incorporated into the group of consanguines. This practice protected the adoptee from litigation by natural children of the adopter, although it was illegal according to French law.

Properties thus remained familial properties, the management of which remained within limits neatly defined by the culture and under the control of all the siblings. By contrast, the adopted beneficiary of a formal legal bequest inherits complete individual rights subject to the control of no one. This is quite contrary to Tuamotuan norms.[62]

Adopters prefer to adopt close relatives, especially nephews and nieces, which results in a "strengthening of the 'opu' by distributing the children among the siblings' families and preventing an inequality of patrimony division in the second or third descending generation."[63] Generally, conflicts about inheritance occur only between cousins or adoptive children who are not raised together.

Nukuoro[64]

Adoption has traditionally been common in Nukuoro, but the rate is declining. The status of adopted children is ambiguous, and there is a great deal of social anxiety about the institution of adoption. Many people consider it a "bad custom" that has a detrimental effect on adopted children. The realities of adoption rarely conform to the social ideal of what it should accomplish, except when childless adults adopt. The most explicit and formal adoption occurs to replace an heir who has died, or to provide an heir for barren couples. A child adopted under these circumstances is the least likely to return to his natal family under his own volition. Other adoptions are ambiguous and are easily revoked. Carroll believes that they occur as a form of psychological reassurance that one is in good favor with kin who frequently do not treat each other as kin should.

On Nukuoro there has been continuous contact with Europeans for almost one hundred years, the Christian religion has been established, copra production has necessitated the use of money. It is now American Trust territory. Land is privately owned.

> Thus the system of land tenure does not allow for the expression of norms of kin-group solidarity in day-to-day cooperative use of jointly-owned property. Expressions of the unity of the kin-group must find another outlet.[65]

One such outlet is adoption. Despite the cultural norms of kin-group solidarity,

> most individuals absorb a great deal of information from the thoughtless acts of their kin from which it is possible to conclude that no one cares about them. They are, in a word, "insecure."[66]

In the pre-World War II period, wealth and status were stabilized in the hands of a few.

> It was not uncommon for all of the natural children of an important person to be adopted, and for that person to adopt many children from others.[67]

Wholesale trading of children seemed to be the norm. Parental responsibility has always been shared by many kin, and there is much fosterage of children among kin—"an obligation of kinship which everyone accepts willingly."[68] Although society expects an adoptive parent to take full responsibility for a child, including inheritance rights, in practice many adopted children return eventually to their natural parents. Adoptive parents often leave only a token of land to adoptive children if the children fail to live up to expectations, although they would never disinherit natural children. Many adoptees do not inherit anything from adoptive parents. Adoptees who return to their natural parents are less likely to inherit from their adopters. Adoptees can be disinherited by the adopter claiming that they are not "really" the children of their adopters.

> Parents can never be sure that the adopter of their child will leave him land, and adopters can never be sure that the natural parents of their adopted child will *not* leave him land.[69]

On the other hand, a child may inherit from each of his natural parents as well as each of his adoptive parents. Nothing is certain about inheritance or the status of an adoptee. Despite shared parental authority over children, "Nukuoro notions of consanguinity imply that there is *no* possible substitute for one's natural parents."[70] The natural parents are ultimately responsible for a child's welfare. There is a great deal of anxiety about keeping land in the family, and many people attempt through adoption or otherwise to get land from other families. Although familial siblings inherit land from their parents, they tend more and more to work the land separately even though they still regard all land as belonging to "their family."[71]

Kapingamarangi[72]

This island is United States Trust Territory in the Eastern Caroline Islands. Despite many changes brought about by contact with English, Germans, Japanese, Americans, and Micronesians, the society retains much that is traditional, including frequent adoption. In former days, adoption was a means of having a member of the "sacerdotal class" in the family of the "nonsacerdotal class." Adoption is now sometimes done to reap material benefits, and the children of people with more land, the people who own retail stores, and salaried government officials are

> consistently adopted by people of various degrees of kinship who stand to profit by the liberal extension of credit at the local store or by gifts of food or clothing. This is especially apparent in the Ponape community where the Kapinga must depend to a great extent on a money economy for their subsistence, and where people are usually competing to adopt the children of those with a regular source of income.[73]

The adopters are most often unmarried women with children, without men to support them.

The sibling set is the basic societal unit, and holds land corporately, except for *taro* plots, which are owned individually. There are frequent land disputes, which engender bitter passion. Competition for affection is especially keen among high-status people, and their children are especially desired as adoptees. Adoption involves a transfer of parental status among kin. "The norms of behavior regarding utilization and disposal of land are at the same time norms of kinship behavior."[74] There are ownership rights and use rights to land. Use rights depend upon close kinship and warm personal relationships. Adoption can strengthen use rights. Adopted children may inherit from both natural and adoptive parents. The actual validation of adoption is accomplished by willing land or taro plots. Adoption functions as a "message" that natural parents and adopters are kin and should act accordingly. Adoption is also done to compel fulfillment of obligations, not only by affection but by land. It is used as a means of social replacement, whereby a relative is adopted with a view toward inheritance of land and taro plots. It is also a means of social control of children, since an adopter may withhold land from his own children in favor of an adoptee.

Ponape[75]

One of five island groups in the Caroline Islands, Ponape, is United States Trust Territory. Adoption and other forms of fosterage have remained a common practice. Ponape provides an interesting example of how a society both resists and adapts to foreign cultural importations. The main cultural influences of major world powers have been as follows: American and other Western whalers and traders from about 1835 on; American and other Protestant missionaries from about 1850 on; the Spanish Colonial government from 1885 to 1899, during which Catholic missionaries became permanently established; the German colonial government from 1899 to 1914; the Japanese military and mandate government from 1914 to 1945; the American military and Trust Territory government from 1946 to date. Despite all these influences, Ponapeans have retained their native language, matrilineages and matrilineal exogamy, much of the native mythology despite a general conversion to Christianity, and the feast and title systems. Because of frequent shifts in policy by colonial administrators, Ponapeans have tried to hold on to a stable native culture. Although some customs evoked more concern by colonial administrators than other customs, the custom of adoption was of interest to both missionaries and administrators. Neither the Protestant churches nor the Catholic Church gives ritual acceptance to adoption; in fact they have discouraged it when the natural parents are alive and in good health. Fischer says:

> Some missionaries have seen a connection, correctly, I think, between the frequency of adoption and the emphasis on sibling ties as opposed to martial ties, and they regard adoption as a renunciation of the responsibility and importance of marriage on the part of true parents.[76]

The economy of Ponape is subsistence, based mainly on yams, breadfruits, bananas, coconut, and taro, augmented by some wage-labor and production of copra. Most people live on isolated small farmsteads. There are no village clusters, although there may be a hamlet or an extended family cluster around a village chief. Most families are nuclear families, except for important people or chiefs, who may have young married relatives living with them. Ponape has a somewhat greater emphasis on individual achievement and the nuclear family than do many Oceanic societies. However, ties between parents and adult children are strong, as are ties between adult siblings. The family does not consider the tie between a junior member and his spouse as important as sibling ties. Although there is a strict hierarchical order of inherited rank according to birth order and the mother's birth order, industriousness and public service is also valued, and a person's work is ranked by the village chief. The husband is in competition with other men, and the wife's status depends largely on her husband's status. Ultimate authority over lineage matters is generally in the hands of the senior male. Although Ponapeans believe that all children should have land of their own, they generally give older children a larger share of the inheritance. Most adopting parents are childless when they adopt, but if they give birth to a child subsequently they are likely to prefer the true child and to favor him in inheritance. This is considered acceptable by many Ponapeans, as is preferential treatment of some children over others in general. This fits in with an achievement orientation, since a successful child will probably care for aged parents better than an unsuccessful one will. Disputes about family property are likely to arise between true and adopted children after the death of the adoptive parents.

The Japanese, during their period, granted an adopted child equal inheritance rights if the adoption had been officially registered. The Japanese, during part of their rule, also tried to enforce their custom of adopting a son-in-law to inherit the land for his wife; but this is no longer true. In 1957 the American administration decreed that an adopted child would be considered as younger than any natural child, "except that the oldest adopted son, older than [the] real son, shall be entitled to one-third of the value of the estate. . . ."[77] Since it is more common to give younger, rather than firstborn children, for adoption, these children would inherit less from their parents anyway, because of the practice of primogeniture, which fits in with both the Ponapean tradition of emphasizing birth order and with the German land reform which prescribed patrilineal primogeniture. Fischer says that a preference of adoptive parents for boys as adoptees may be related to German and Japanese efforts to introduce patrilineal descent, although there is no definite knowledge about this. There is some preference for sons in the culture, and there is an indulgent father-son relationship.

Ponapeans are permissive about sexuality. Adoption is often used as a means of prolonging the premarital state of "sliding into marriage." Although illegitimacy is not stigmatized morally, and may even be valued as proof of a woman's fertility, illegitimate children are sometimes a deterrent to marriage and a woman may give her child for adoption to a childless couple. Both Catholic and Protestant missionaries, and especially Catholic, tried to discourage divorce. However, divorce is fairly common, and two or three marriages in youth is rather common. Divorce is one important source of children for adoption, and may be related to the high value on sexual freedom, i.e., giving one freedom to pursue extramarital affairs. A divorced man's mother or sister may adopt his children. Traditionally, marriage among the nobility was marked by ceremony and was considered stable, although the nobles could practice polygyny. The common people were permitted only one wife at a time and were married by simply declaring themselves married and publicly living together. Many marriages still begin this way, and are formalized by church ceremony only after they have been tested.

Ponapeans are attached to their native places and have an affection for the land they have worked, an attitude which prevailed even before the German land reform, which, in turn, attempted to substitute "private" ownership for ownership by the chiefs. Even before then Ponapeans apparently had effective control over the land they planted and tended. Because of this feeling for the land, reinforced by mythology, it is important—not only from the standpoint of subsistence, but also because of affectionate feelings—for a Ponapean to have a personal successor to live in the community when he is gone. A common reason given for adoption is to "have someone to inherit my land." Fischer says,

> This reason for adoption is one which is strong and widespread in Oceania, but might be weaker in societies with less settled political organization or with less settled subsistence activities, such as herding societies.[78]

Fischer says that one of the main functions of adoption in Ponape is to prevent the grossly uneven accumulation of land through random irregularities in genealogy. The society is composed of small, stable units that are able to work out stable sociopolitical arrangements. An optimum population level is reached in a few generations, and adoption maintains a stable population. There is a rough redistribution of land in each generation. Adoption also provides personal care for the aged. Women take pride and apparently gain status from child-rearing, and adolescent children are useful for work.

Rotuma[79]

Britain gained control over Rotuma in 1881, and in 1898 the British forbade an adopted child to share in an adopter's inheritance "unless the person adopting it shall be the last of the family or sole owner of such land."[80] In the past, one of the main functions of adoption was for commoners to gain higher status by adopting a boy of chiefly rank. However, this is no longer done, and adoption has become "an exclusively domestic affair" without any significance for land tenure. Adoption is not formalized and is usually between close relatives, most often the grandparents. People refer to adopted children by the same term as grandchildren, which probably had its origins in the custom of sending children to their grandparents for weaning. The maternal grandmother is considered the only direct mother substitute. The majority of adopted children comes from unmarried mothers and dissolved families. People sometimes consider children from families dissolved by death or divorce a burden and they care for them grudgingly.

No distinction is made, even in the language, between adoption and fosterage. There is a great deal of child-sharing in the community. Children are valued commodities greatly indulged, adopted children especially so, "so they will not think of their real mother and father."[81] It is considered a disgrace if an adopted child complains about his treatment and chooses to return to his natal home. Lineage is bilateral and attached to a house site and land use rights. Economically the most significant social unit is the individual household. The main occupations are farming, cutting copra, and fishing. Some people engage in wage-labor in Fiji, and in Fiji more people in the parents' generation, rather than the grandparents' generation, adopt. Due to a dramatically declining death rate, the rate of adoption is declining.

Conclusion

The "child welfare" function of adoption was a fairly recent development, begun about the middle of the nineteenth century and fully developed in Britain and North America after World War I. I use quotes around "child welfare" because I believe that the main function of this form of adoption is to provide children for childless middle-class and upper-class couples, despite the efforts of adoption agencies to reject applicants whom they consider inadequate as parents. If child welfare were the primary function of adoption, adoption agencies would be investing most of their resources into finding adoptive homes for all children legally available for adoption, and working to change laws so that children would not grow up in the limbo of foster care. Most agencies are not doing this. It is rare to find a report in the literature of an agency that focuses its adoption home-finding process on finding homes for specific children in foster homes.[82] Instead, most agencies strive to fulfill the fantasies of the adoptive parents regarding the kind of child they want to adopt. If the agencies are unable to do this, the adoptive applicants wait for the "right" child or withdraw their application.

The adoption policies of the most advanced Western capitalist countries, Britain, the United States, and Canada, have developed the farthest toward insuring full inheritance rights for adopted children from adoptive parents, and excluding biological kinship ties. There are vestigial remnants of ties to the biological family in the incest taboo evident in some laws which forbid intermarriage between adopted children and their biological kin. This incest taboo could hardly serve any practical function, since adoptive children are kept from any knowledge of the identity of their biological family, and are often placed far away from the natural parents so that they will not meet by chance. In the more advanced industrialized countries, the concern shifts from anxiety about disinheriting biological heirs to a desire for exclusive possession of children, unencumbered by claims of natural parents. I believe that one of the main social functions of adoption agencies has been to pose an institutional and almost impenetrable barrier between natural parents and the adopted child. In Hawaii, for example, where kinship ties have traditionally been strong and most adoptions have occurred between relatives because of greater trust between relatives, those kinship ties are now beginning to weaken, and adoption through agencies is becoming more popular because of fear of the stranger. Similarly, in urbanized, industrialized societies, high mobility has weakened family and community ties. To obtain children, the middle and upper classes are more likely than the working and lower classes to turn to adoption agencies rather than to relatives or informal community contacts. The adopted children come not only from strangers, but frequently from poor strangers and from unmarried mothers, who have a stigmatized social status. In a polarized class society, the middle and upper classes do not want contact with poor or "deviant" people—and they most certainly do not want contact with the poor or the stigmatized parents of their adopted children. In fact, they do not want to discuss the background of the natural parents with their adopted children and many of them do not want to tell the children that they are adopted.

To develop this thesis more fully, I discuss in the next chapter the relationship of social stratification to the forms of substitute care of children.

Notes to Chapter Two

1. T. Richard Witmer, "The Purpose of American Adoption Laws," Chap. 1 of *Independent Adoptions*, Helen Witmer et al., (N.Y.: Russell Sage Foundation, 1963), p. 23.

2. United Nations Department of Economic and Social Affairs, *Comparative Analysis of Adoption Laws*, ST/SOA/30, 1956, p. 23.

3. Jack Goody, "Adoption in Cross-Cultural Perspective," *Comparative Studies in Society and History*, vol. 11 (N.Y.: Cambridge University Press, 1969), pp. 55–78.

4. Ibid., p. 73.

5. Margaret Kornitzer, *Adoption in the Modern World* (N.Y.: Philosophical Library, 1952), p. 267.

6. Romans 8:14–17; Galatians 4:5–7; Exodus 2:10, and Esther 2:7.

7. Meir Horowitz, "Child and Youth Legislation," in *Child and Youth Welfare in Israel*, ed. by Moshe Smilansky (Jerusalem: Henrietta Szold Institute for Child and Youth Welfare, 1960), p. 262.

8. Goody, op. cit., p. 62.

9. Ibid., p. 59, citing J. A. Crook, *Law and Life of Rome*, London, 1967, p. 111.

10. Goody, pp. 60–61.

11. Gerald R. Leslie, *The Family in Social Context* (N.Y.: Oxford University Press, 1967).

12. Ibid., p. 174.

13. Ibid., p. 175.

14. Goody, p. 64.

15. Ibid., p. 65, citing J. D. Mayne, *A Treatise on Hindu Law and Usage*, London, 1892, p. 102.

16. Ibid., citing J. P. M. Derrett, *Introduction to Modern Hindu Law*, Bombay, 1963.

17. A. L. Basham, *The Wonder That Was India*, (N.Y.: Grove Press, 1959), p. 160.

18. David G. Mandelbaum, *Society in India*, vol. 1 (Berkeley: University of California Press, 1970), pp. 96–97.

19. Personal communication.

20. Goody, p. 66.

21. Ibid., citing Liu, Hui-Chen Wang, *The Traditional Chinese Clan Rules*, Monographs of the Association for Asian Studies, no. 7 (N.Y., 1959), p. 76.

22. Leslie, p. 119.

23. Ibid., p. 114.

24. Ibid., p. 119.

25. This process is analyzed by Wilhelm Reich, *Sexual Revolution* (N.Y.: Orgone Institute Press, 1951), pp. 153–267; and Leon Trotsky, *The Revolution Betrayed* (1937) (N.Y.: Pathfinder Press, 1972), chap. 7, "Family, Youth and Culture," pp. 144–185. Reprinted by permission.

26. David and Vera Mace, *Marriage East and West* (Garden City, N.Y.: Doubleday, Dolphin Books, 1960), p. 279.

27. Witmer, p. 23.

28. Ibid., citing Pollock and Maitland, *History of English Law*, vol. 2, 2d ed. (Cambridge, Eng.: The University Press, 1898), p. 300.

29. United Nations, *Analysis*, p. 2–3.

30. Witmer, p. 30.

31. Ibid., p. 24.

32. Ibid., p. 25.

33. Ibid., p. 32.

34. United Nations, *Analysis*, p. 2.

35. Ibid., p. 3.

36. Kornitzer, p. 218.

37. Ibid.

38. United Nations, *Analysis*, pp. 4–5.

39. Ibid., p. 3.

40. Kornitzer, p. 328; United Nations *Analysis*, p. 23.

41. Witmer, p. 20.

42. Ibid., p. 28.

43. United Nations, *Analysis*, p. 4.

44. Ibid.

45. Ibid.

46. Kornitzer, p. 263.

47. Ibid., p. 331.

48. Ibid.

49. Ibid., p. 336

50. Ibid., p. 343.

51. Alan Howard et al., "Traditional and Modern Adoption Patterns in Hawaii," in *Adoption in Eastern Oceania*, ed. by Vern Carroll (Honolulu: University of Hawaii Press, 1970), p. 29.

52. Ibid., p. 26.

53. Anthony Hooper, "Adoption in the Society Islands," in *Adoption in Eastern Oceania*, pp. 52–70.

54. Ibid., p. 58.

55. Ibid., p. 56.

56. Ibid.

57. Ibid., p. 68.

58. Ibid., p. 59.

59. Ibid., p. 61.

60. Paul Ottino, "Adoption on Rangiroa Atoll, Tuamotu Archipelago," in *Adoption in Eastern Oceania*, pp. 88–118.

61. Ibid., p. 93.

62. Ibid., p. 111.

63. Ibid., pp. 105–106.

64. Vern Carroll, "Adoption on Nukuoro," in *Adoption in Eastern Oceania*, pp. 121–157.

65. Ibid., p. 153.

66. Ibid.

67. Ibid., p. 137.

68. Ibid., p. 156.

69. Ibid., p. 144.

70. Ibid., p. 146.

71. Ibid., p. 137.

72. Michael D. Lieber, "Adoption on Kapingamarangi," in *Adoption in Eastern Oceania*, pp. 158–205.

73. Ibid., p. 195.

74. Ibid., p. 163.

75. J. L. Fischer, "Adoption on Ponape," in *Adoption in Eastern Oceania*, pp. 292–313.

76. Ibid., p. 303.

77. Ibid.

78. Ibid., p. 306.

79. Alan Howard, "Adoption on Rotuma," in *Adoption in Eastern Oceania*, pp. 343–368.

80. Ibid., p. 368.

81. Ibid., p. 353.

82. For a description of one such project, see "Adoption of Real Children," Joan Shireman and Kenneth W. Watson, *Social Work*, vol. 17, no. 4 (July 1972): 29–38. See also, "New hope for the 'hard-to-place' child," *Boston Sunday Globe*, 2 January 1972. This describes the program of the Massachusetts Adoption Resource Exchange (MARE).

CHAPTER THREE
SOCIAL CLASS AND SUBSTITUTE
CHILD CARE

This generation of children will get the food and the education it needs when the parents have enough money to take care of them.

Cesar Chavez[1]

The social position of the family and of children changes as the relationships of production change. Philippe Ariès,[2] the French historian, traces a change in the status of the child during the decay of feudalism in Western civilization. In the Middle Ages, children were considered small adults without any separate status from adults. The family was not separated from work and community life. Although there were great disparities in wealth, the poor were not outcast from the total community and there were no social classes in the modern sense. The architecture of the homes was geared to communal functioning rather than to a separation of family functions. The moral training of children, their psychological development, and their intellectual education were not matters of special concern to the adults. As the social structures of feudalism broke up and gave way to the nation-state and polarized classes in a mass society, children were given a distinct status. The Church took over the responsibility for the education and the moral training of children, and the children were virtually imprisoned in their schools. In the twentieth century, the child became a focus of intense psychological and sociological interest.

Kornitzer summarizes the changing status of poor children during and after the Middle Ages:

> In feudal and even later medieval times there appear to have been no unwanted children in the modern sense. The feudal lord had duties as well as privileges, among them being responsibility for all his people. The State was a pyramid of little societies, with the village life of the manor at its base. In the shadow of the keep, family life on the grand scale took care of all children—legitimate, orphans, base-born. If children were sometimes neglected or ill-treated they were never outcast.
>
> Feudalism took six hundred years or so to decay completely; Elizabeth's Poor Law recognized the partial breakdown of society, the Industrial Revolution gave the *coup de grace*, and the nineteenth century inherited the under-the-surface chaos into which the breakdown of the wider family had cast children. While the young of the well-to-do were nurtured in a bleak self-saving individualism, the children of the poor became industrial slaves.[3]

The children of the poor have been a political issue since the beginnings of the Industrial Revolution, but only in recent years have they been recognized as such now that the class struggle has forced issues critically important to children: income maintenance, education, health, housing, and substitute child care. Child labor was economically useful to developing industrialized societies until the beginning of the twentieth century.

> ... for 350 years or so—from Henry the Eight's first Poor Law in 1530— the problem of the unwanted child solved itself in three ways, through child labour and the poorhouse apprentice, through infant mortality, and through baby-farming of the grossest kind. Society might be worried about the morals of the parents, but not about the disposal of the hundreds of thousands of children spewed into the gutters every year. These died or paid their way.[4]

Among the earliest settlers to the United States were children recruited from the almshouses of London by the Virginia Company of London and sent to Virginia under apprenticeship contracts. "As in England, the idea of trade-training and self-support for poor children was combined or confused in the minds of colonial leaders."[5] The economic usefulness of child labor declined as industrialization reached an advanced stage and as the nation became more urbanized. Child labor laws put an end to large-scale economic exploitation of children. It is interesting to note that child labor laws have again become a political issue in the 1970s, as the corporations are experiencing a declining rate of profit and welfare recipients are scapegoated. The sociologist Edward Banfield [6] advocates abolishing child labor laws. Some mothers who receive AFDC payments have told me that they favor the abolition of child labor laws so that their 12- and 16-year-old sons might support them. Probably their wish coincides with Banfield's policy recommendations. Conservatives suggest that the current economic crisis could be solved by cutting back on welfare payments.

Kadushin [7] says that indenture probably became unconstitutional in 1865 with the adoption of the Constitutional Amendment forbidding involuntary servitude. Billingsley [8] points out the relationship between the abolition of slavery and the abolition of the indenture system, which was principally for white children, since most black children were slaves. In the latter half of the nineteenth century, the indenture system was supplanted by the "free" foster home. The beginning of foster care as an organized system of caring for dependent children combined two social functions: (1) social control of "deviants," i.e., masses of vagrant children in New York City whom Charles Loring Brace described as children of the "dangerous classes"[9] ; and (2) providing labor for farmers and small tradesmen in the West, Midwest, and South. The New York Children's Aid Society, organized in 1853 by Charles Loring Brace, found foster family homes for about 100,000 children between 1854 and 1929.[10] Some of the children were sold at auction when they arrived at their destination. Children who had one or both parents living had to break their ties with these parents, and fosterage became in effect either a form of pseudo-adoption or another form of indenture.

The families of these children—all poor, many immigrants—were regarded as "unfit parents," and foster care was conceived as a means of "rescuing" the children from their parents.

Western states began to object to having children "dumped" on them; the Catholic Church objected to children being placed in Protestant homes; the closing of the frontier reduced the need for child labor; and professional child welfare workers objected to "the wolf of the old indenture philosophy of child labor in the sheepskin disguise of a so-called good Christian home."[11] The semi-indenture system of "free" boarding homes (paid for by the child's labor) evolved during the 1920s into the foster boarding home system, where foster parents are paid for the child's board. There are still a few work homes for adolescents and unmarried mothers, primarily in rural areas. Child welfare professionals have to the present time given a low priority to services to children in their own homes, including adequate income maintenance, despite the official rhetoric begun at the First White House Conference of 1909, which encouraged measures to help a child remain in his home.[12]

While the indenture system changed to the "free" foster home and later to the foster boarding home, the almshouse gave way to the orphanage in the first half of the nineteenth century. Billingsley and Giovannoni [13] describe how this was accomplished by relabeling the inhabitants of the almshouses. Since it was hard to mobilize public sympathy and money for paupers, the reformers relabeled the inhabitants of the almshouses to make their plight seem more worthy. Thus "paupers" were separated into the "insane," the "lame," the "blind," the "aged," the "orphaned." This process of "deviance labeling" later distinguished between "delinquent" and "dependent" children, with "dependent" the higher status label. "Dependent" is the twentieth century replacement for the label "orphan."

The almshouse kept children who were too young for indenture, and indentured them when they were old enough to work. Most of the children in orphanages also graduated into an indentured position. Despite the term "orphanage," many of the children were from poor families who could not maintain them. Orphanages were racially segregated, and present-day institutions for dependent children still resist full integration. As a result, the majority of dependent black children are either in foster care or they are in correctional institutions with the lower-status label of "delinquent."

With the passing of the indenture system, orphanages gradually were called institutions for dependent and neglected children or for emotionally disturbed ones. During the twentieth century, foster care came to be preferred over institutional care for dependent children. In 1923, 64.2% of the dependent children in the United States were in institutions; however, in 1969, only about 18% of the children in placement were in institutions, whereas about 67% were in foster homes, and 13% were in adoptive homes.[14] Billingsley and Giovannoni say that foster care served black children better than institutional care because then black children were cared for by black foster parents rather than by white middle-class and largely segregated institutions. Foster care, however, is more likely to sever children's kinship ties than is institutional care. Maas and Engler [15] point out that black foster children are less likely than white children either to return home or to go into an adoptive home. In large cities a disproportionate number of minority group children are in foster care.[16] Foster care represents a political choice to "rescue" poor children from their parents, as opposed to providing money and social services to children in their own homes. The process is circular. White middle-class rescue fantasies toward black children intensify as the poverty and ghettoization of black children increases. Social agencies, which express in some circuitous way the "will of the people," are reluctant to do what needs to be done on a large scale to help the parents keep the children, although they are willing to place black children in black foster homes. It is similar to the "relief in kind" or "relief in cash" debate which preceded the passage of the 1935 Social Security Act. The "relief in cash" forces won with public assistance, but the "relief in kind" forces are still dominant in child welfare. Can the poor be trusted to care for their own children if given the resources, or must the middle class supervise the poor children's care? The debate is resurfacing in its full political rancor during the 1970s.

Research on foster care confirms that foster children come from "the more socioeconomically deprived sectors of the population."[17] The only exception to this are the handicapped and emotionally disturbed children, who come from a wider range of socioeconomic backgrounds. The most frequent reason for short-term care is the mother's illness. The most frequent reasons for long-term care are the child's disturbed behavior or physical problems, or the parents' death, divorce, desertion, or inadequate income. Parental marital problems, combined with inadequate income, often lead to child neglect or abuse.[18] Foster care involves mostly lower-class children cared for by working-class foster parents and supervised by middle-class professionals. In recent years, a few middle-class people have made a career of child care in agency-owned small group homes. They are among the few foster parents who are paid a living wage. Board payments for most agency-supervised foster parents throughout the United States range from a median of $64 to $80 a month.[19] The private child welfare agencies, which are increasingly turning over their foster care functions to public agencies, are directed by upper-class boards of directors.

Institutional care is also stratified by class.

> Emotionally disturbed children from families with higher income, educa-
> tion, and occupational status [are] more frequently placed in specialized
> institutions than in foster homes. The reverse [is] true for children from
> more deprived backgrounds manifesting the same difficulties.[20]

By and large, the middle-class child stands a better chance of being in a higher-prestige treatment institution, while the poorest—including a disproportionate number of minority group children—are most often in institutions geared to custodial or "correctional" care. Rich children are sent to expensive boarding or military schools; poor children are sent to public or private (usually sectarian) charitable institutions. The professional and administrative staff of treatment institutions are middle class; the child care staff include largely upper-lower or lower-middle-class couples and middle-class youth who stay at the job for a brief time and move on in search of more permanent and better paid careers. The older child care workers tend to stay on the job longer since they are often untrained for any other kind of work. There is a high turnover rate among middle-class child welfare personnel in both institutions and foster care agencies. Foster parents complain of the transitory nature of agency personnel, which subjects the foster parents to frequently shifting policy interpretations and to supervision by inexperienced young professionals and social work students.

Working-class people are more likely than middle-class people to adopt relatives rather than nonrelatives. With the middle class, it is the other way around. The rise of the middle class in advanced industrialized societies has contributed to the increased popularity of nonrelative agency adoptions. Agencies handled 57% of nonrelative adoptions in the United States in 1960, and 77½% of them in 1970. In 1960, about 58,000 nonrelative adoptions were completed; in 1970, about 89,000. Until 1969, the absolute numbers increased but the rate of increase declined until there was no increase between 1969 and 1970 (the last date for which figures are available).[21] Of the total number of children adopted by nonrelatives, the proportion of blacks, however, has remained at a fairly constant 9-10% over the years, which is of course lower than their 11% representation in the population as a whole.[22]

The middle class rose with an achievement orientation. The high mobility required for this achievement, and for the move from a predominantly rural to a predominantly urban society, resulted in a loosening of kinship ties. The family serves the important function of helping to achieve and secure social status.[23] Whyte [24] documents the importance of having children in an achievement-oriented suburban community populated largely by workers and managers in large corporations and civil service workers. Infertile couples usually adopted children in order to maintain their status within the community. Maas and Engler [25] hypothesized that

> agency adoption tended to go with the achievement orientation, with the impersonal or contractual orientation, and with the interdependent orientation in a community culture.

The more traditional communities studied by Maas and Engler were less likely to break parental ties either through adoption or through removal of children from their parents. They were also more likely to use sectarian institutional care than foster care, and to return even involuntarily placed children to their parents than were the more achievement-oriented and professionalized communities. In the southwest metropolis of "King City," a

> more anchored upper class . . .—visibly identified by wealth and place of residence—functioned as standard setters. This segment adopted children through a high-status agency located elsewhere in the state. The middle-class suburbanites of the community tried to emulate, in many ways, this upper segment.[26]

In the even more traditional southern community of "Jamestown," the same process took place, while

> Adoption below the upper stratum . . . (proceeded) on the basis of a separating placement within a social category, made by persons known and trusted personally by the adoptive family, in which heredity of the child was of much importance.[27]

When the gap between the social classes is widest, the upper class may not even want to adopt children of the poor or of another social category, Thus in "Brighton," a traditional and highly stratified New England community, "the rejection of the dependent child from the lower class was greatest."[28] The same thing occurred in "La Paz," where the upper-class Anglos were widely separated from the dependent Spanish.

McKinley points out that the lower class, as compared to the upper-middle class, places a heavier emphasis on ascriptive roles such as familial and kinship roles. "This seems to be true for the mother, and we see the prominent figure of 'mom' in the lower levels of society. . . ."[29] Maas and Engler found this in "Brighton," where

> children still tended to be cared for by extended families and neighbors or within the facilities of a specific church or ethnic group. The "lowest" classes, particularly, seemed to absorb their own dependents, while the "upper" classes either had none or absorbed them in private care.[30]

Michel [31] discusses the communal life style developed by some French working-class families living close together in furnished hotels. About 40% of the parents in her study place one or more of their children in foster homes because their living space is too small. Those children who remain with their parents, however, receive a great deal of their care from neighbors. Because of the close proximity of families, neighbors help care for each others' children, and sometimes serve as godparents. Borrowing of money is widespread. "Proximity creates relationships such that mutual assistance between neighbors is more frequent, more 'familiar' one might say, than with even the closest parents."[32]

Adoption in the United States is related in complex ways to inheritance, family lineage, property relationships, and social status. Since there has been little awareness of this fact, there is little research on it. Adoption in the United States seems more related to status than to direct effort to continue the lineage, although continuing a family line is still important to more traditional cultures and to the upper class. Kirk [33] speculates that the higher frequency of adoption of girls than boys may be due to adoptive parents' narcissistic hurt over not being able to continue a biological lineage; by adopting girls they may be denying the importance of a "blood line." It is interesting in this connection to note that agencies generally de-emphasize the importance of heredity, except in cases of incest. The achievement orientation tends to de-emphasize the importance of a "blood line" and kin. The traditional and ethnically stratified community of "Brighton" was the only one of the nine communities studied by Maas and Engler where adoptive parents preferred boys to girls, by a ratio of two to one, perhaps because ascriptive roles and blood lineages were important. Their preference for boys was not determined by children available since there was an equal number of boys and girls in foster care.[34] Jaffee and Fanshel found, in their follow-up study of 100 adoptive children, that the Catholic families, which were in a lower socioeconomic stratum than the Protestant or Jewish families, were less likely to express a preference for girls.[35] Perhaps this preference also stems from more traditional values. On the other hand, among middle-class families, girls are apparently preferred.

Kings, Commoners, and Children

Some people hearken back nostalgically to the Middle Ages, when the king was responsible for the welfare of the commoners and all statuses were fixed. There was poverty, but there were no "paupers." The Enclosure Act of 1489 drove the commoners off the nobles' and king's lands by giving it to the sheep owners, and the commoners joined the swelling ranks of paupers. Wool was profitable for the mercantile companies, and King Henry VII helped them take the land from the commoners. There are still remnants of the sovereign's responsibility for the people in some United States laws. For example,

> By the common law of England which our fathers brought with them to this continent, the title to the sea bottom was in the king and extended from high water mark to an imaginary line three miles at sea.[36]

Under that law, all the inhabitants of the land were allowed to use the beaches. Massachusetts and Maine (which were parts of the same state until Maine became a separate state in 1820) framed laws in 1641 called the Body of Liberties, which declared that the proprietor of the land adjoining the sea shall own the beach, and has the right to forbid trespassers.[37] Massachusetts' early preoccupation with private ownership of property is probably reflected in its first adoption law (1851), which protected the adoptee's right of inheritance.

In the history of many Polynesian societies, there is a similar pattern of sovereign responsibility for the commoners. A chief might have "owned" all the land, but the commoners had effective use rights. Polynesian societies reveal the process of stratification including the changes which take place in adoption and fosterage as stratification increases. How has the evolution toward stratification affected adoption, fosterage, and child care in Polynesia? The answer seems clear in the island of Mokil, which has apparently been highly stratified for a long time.[38] There has been a shift from traditional adoption practice, which generally involved transfer of property and inheritance rights, to a form of adoption that does not involve transfer of property, but is done to obtain child labor. This shift occurred when the Mokilese economy changed from a subsistence basis where the products of the land were shared in a semicommunal way to an economy based partly on trade, and, in the interest of trade, land was restricted exclusively to its owners.

The acceptance of trade and of Western concepts of land use also created the need for extra-familial labor among the few who emerged with large holdings of land. Instead of taking over the Western custom of wage work to meet this need, however, the Mokilese developed the exploitive form of adoption.[39]

It might be more accurate to say that the Mokilese began to change "true" adoption into indentured labor—a form of fosterage common in England and the United States during the developing stage of capitalism. The Mokilese traditionally distinguished between true or honorable adoption (*sheri shoyshoy*), where the adopted treats the child as if he were his own child, and *shotay* adoption, which is translated with a sneer as "working man." A *shotay* is a dependent who works with servantlike status for his adopted parents for subsistence and without hope of inheriting land or receiving rewards beyond the bare necessities of life. An adopter may mistreat a *shotay* in various ways without incurring adverse public opinion.[40]

Since land is both acquired only through kinship and becoming scarce, *sheri shoyshoy* adoption is used increasingly as a device to acquire more land. On the other hand, poor parents with many children often agree to *shotay* adoptions, hoping the children will receive better care than they can provide.[41] Under present economic pressures, many *sheri shoyshoy* adoptions degenerate into *shotay*-like relationships.[42]

Another Polynesian society, Nukuoro, [43] has also been highly stratified for a long time and has changed land tenure from kin-based corporate ownership to private ownership. The status of an adoptive child has become so ambiguous that many adoptees return to their natal family. Anxiety about land, personal relationships, and adoption is high. The only unambiguous adoptions are of the form most similar to adoption in the United States, i.e., adoption by childless adults. Adoption in Hawaii is also beginning to take the same form as adoption in mainland United States.[44]

Kapingamarangi [45] is an example of a society where stratification and a heavier reliance on a money economy for subsistence is changing former adoption practice into fosterage for child labor. Where child labor is the chief motivation for adoption, as in all cases of adoption of a child by his great-grandparent, the adoption often begins as a fosterage arrangement.[46]

Ponape provides another example of the generally lower status of foster care than adoption. One form of Ponapean fosterage which is simply labeled "foster child" includes

> orphaned children of remote and junior relatives or of immigrants without local family ties who are sometimes cared for by wealthy families without becoming full-fledged adopted children. These people when they become adults would be regarded as "servants or retainers," *lidu*.[47]

It seems to be a general rule in all societies that nonrelated orphans or dependent children are likely to be relegated to a second-class status unless childless couples adopt them.

On the island of Rotuma [48], commoners once gained higher status by adopting a boy of chiefly rank. However, adoption is no longer tied to land tenure. There are now strong similarities to adoption in the United States, in that most of the adopted children come from unmarried mothers and dissolved families, even though adoption is still done between close relatives. This, too, is similar to adoptions among the lower and working classes in the United States: as the Rotumans tend to prefer to adopt relatives independently of a social agency.

Hawaii and Tahiti provide examples of the psychological effects of extreme stratification. Howard et al.[49] and Levy [50] describe the people in both societies as having a high degree of anxiety and deep unsatisfied dependency needs. Both societies place a high value on cooperativeness and selflessness. In Hawaii, young children are highly desired as objects of affection and are greatly indulged until they are 2 or 3 years old. When they become more mobile and more verbal, however, their demands for attention are sharply rebuked and they are punished for dependency. Adolescent boys spend an increasing amount of time with their peers and away from home. Their relationship with peers is intense but unstable, easily broken when dependency needs are not met. Girls, on the other hand, spend a great deal of time at home helping with housework. They are socialized early into the housewife role, the only role in which they are consistently encouraged. Therefore, Hawaiian women are strongly motivated to have children.

> Although men are not so directly socialized into the nurturant role, they, too, find babies to be the safest creatures in an unpredictable world and are motivated to have some in their household.[51]

Hawaiians have always valued the nurturing role highly. People were always expected to take care of those in need, and prestige accrued to the generous. This may be related to the traditional reciprocally dependent relationship of commoners and chiefs. Each had responsibilities toward the other. Howard et al. suggest that the reason for the continued popularity of adoption is the need to express dependency needs through having babies. A high proportion of older women adopt after their own children have passed through the dependency stage. Howard et al. suggest that similar motivations for adoption may apply to the Tahitians and other Polynesian societies.

Levy says that Tahitians cultivate casual, tentative relationships and discourage intense feelings and relationships. He hypothesizes that adoption functions purely as a psychological message that *all* relationships are tentative and contingent, rather than categorical. There is no assurance that anyone is required to care for a child, not even the natural parents. Levy denies that adoption in the Tahitian community which he studied had had any relationship to economic factors. My own hypothesis about both Hawaii and Tahiti is that long-standing and extreme stratification has created widespread anxiety about having one's needs fulfilled, so that all relationships reflect this anxiety.[52] Similar psychological factors are evident in highly stratified industrialized societies. The kind of anxiety about having one's dependency needs met which is characteristic of Tahitians is an anxiety also characteristic of foster children and their natural parents in the United States. There is also a good deal of anxiety among foster parents, who are neither paid a living wage nor given much psychological support by most agencies.

Fosterage of High Status Children

There is an exception to the general rule that fosterage denotes lower status than does adoption for the child. This is when the foster parents care for the child of a higher-status family. One example is ancient Ireland, where foster parents cared for children of upper-class families with the objectives of training children and forming close bonds between families to promote social cohesion.[53] Another example is the Northern Gilbert Islands,[54] where the institution of fosterage grew out of the relationship between aristocratic and commoner descent groups. The aristocratic descent group held "residual" (permanent) title to land, whereas commoners held "provisional" (use) rights to land, sometimes in perpetuity. In return for the use of the land "they owe certain goods or services to the donors."[55]

> *All* commoners tend to behave as though in some sense they were the guardians of their superiors. . . .[56]

Guardianship seems to be similar to the relationship between grandparent and grandchild, and "the ward is treated with even greater indulgence than the grandchildren are."[57]

The ward does not inherit from his guardian, but inherits from his parents. Becoming a guardian is one way for a person to obtain land, since the ward's natural parents give property to the guardian. "All of the members of a child-giving group are considered superior in rank to the guardian."[58] The closest comparable system of child care in Western societies might be the expensive private boarding schools or the nursemaid of a rich family, although she does not inherit property from the family and the child continues to live with his natural parents. In fact, the modern paid servant of the rich family is a typical product of a society where there is little or no social concern about promoting social cohesion between families of different social classes and where the classes are quite polarized. In Ireland and the Northern Gilbert Islands, there was still concern about social cohesion between the aristocracy and the commoners, while in the United States today there is little institutionalized concern about social cohesion between classes.

Are the Affluent Better Parents?

I ask the question because there is so little debate about it in child welfare circles, and because so many child welfare professionals assume that the answer is an automatic yes. The question is a slippery one. What is "better"? Do we know enough about child-rearing to set objective criteria? The research findings are ambiguous and often contradictory, both internally and externally (in comparison with each other). Researchers too have their middle-class biases, and sometimes find their data uncomfortable to live with if it does not fit their biases. The honest ones at least give the data, and we can make our own hypotheses. I wish that workers would do studies so that their biases could compete on the open market with the middle-class biases.

A good many middle- and upper-class parents are having serious problems with their children, and the rich as a class are reluctant to admit that although they have the power, they also have serious problems. Money can't buy you love, and neither can the achievement motivation. Bronfenbrenner [59] believes that the enforced inutility of children in our society and the segregation by age both work to produce feelings of alienation, indifference, antagonism, and violence among children of all classes. Children raised in an atmosphere of "cold democracy" and isolated individualism, says Bronfenbrenner, may succeed in developing cognitive and competitive skills, but they may in the process lose some capacity to feel and to love.

Research on adoptive and foster parents gives hints that the achievement motivation may sometimes be more of a hindrance than a help in caring for other peoples' children. In considering the class composition of foster parents and adoptive parents, one should bear in mind that they are not strictly comparable. Foster parents come predominantly from the skilled working class and the lower-middle class, with some unskilled workers; adoptive parents include more middle- and upper-class people, with some from the lower-middle class and skilled working class. An examination of the origins of this situation tells a good deal about class attitudes. V. George says that when foster care began in England, upper-class women, who were in charge of finding foster homes, believed that they themselves should be of a higher social class than foster parents in order to command respect from foster parents. Yet they did not want them too "low": they considered lower-class homes inadequate, and prohibited anyone who was or who had been on relief from becoming a foster parent. Middle-class foster parents were less accepting than working-class parents of close supervision by the boarding-out committees. Therefore, the people chosen as foster parents were mainly from the skilled working class.[60]

George believes that the same rationale did not apply to choosing adoptive homes because there was no lengthy supervision of adoptive homes. I think this is only part of the reason. More importantly, childless upper- and middle-class people wanted children. They established private sectarian adoption agencies in order to get them and entrusted this job to middle-class professionals. Foster parents, on the other hand, were sought out by agencies responsible for the care of poor children. Foster parents were not clients of the agency, even though they usually have been treated as clients rather than as colleagues. The professionals in adoption agencies have the dual job of pleasing their clientele and of finding homes for children. They are aware of the class differential between the families of the adoptees and the adoptive families, and probably implicitly take this into account in making placement decisions. The British social worker Kornitzer, more candid than her American colleagues, says that practice wisdom dictates that a child should be placed one up (in social class), "never one down, but *only one up!*"[61] (Emphasis in the original.)

Child welfare professionals share at least one characteristic in common with family service professionals: they prefer to work with middle-class clients.[62] Purvine and Ryan [63] studied the intake of a total child welfare agency network in a metropolitan community of two million people. Inquiries from applicants of high occupational status were more likely to be accepted for service. Adoption workers are more likely to give the "blue-ribbon baby" (the trade euphemism for a white, healthy infant) to more affluent families, and to give the child whom they consider "second-rate" (older, physically or emotionally handicapped, racially mixed or of a racial minority) to the families whom they consider "marginal." These "marginal" families are likely to be older, married longer, less affluent, and less well educated.[64] The reasons for this apparently lie not only in the biases of middle-class social workers, but also in the greater tolerances of working-class over middle-class couples. More affluent adoptive couples are likely to insist on having a "perfect" infant.[65] White-collar parents have a very low tolerance for children with below-average intelligence. In the more prosperous communities studied by Maas and Engler, adoptive parents placed a high value on having a physically perfect child. Farm and blue-collar parents seem more accepting of older children than do professional and white-collar parents.[66] Jaffee and Fanshel found that Catholic homes of a lower socioeconomic status had adopted more older children, while Protestant and Jewish families of a higher socio-economic status usually had adopted infants.[67] Some studies indicate that adoptive parents are actually more tolerant of differences in children than are agency professionals, [68] and professionals do not explore the possibilities that exist for adoptive homes for the "hard-to-place" child.

Follow-up studies of adopted children's adjustment show either that socioeconomic status makes no difference or that children of higher socioeconomic status are slightly less well adjusted. Witmer's study of independent adoptions in Florida concluded that social class made no difference. Her families, however, included mostly lower-middle or working-class parents.[69] Wittenborn found that the educational and occupational status of the adoptive home was not related to acceptance of the child.[70] Brenner, on the other hand, found in her study of fifty adoptive families that the median income of families whose adoptees made a less favorable adjustment was substantially higher than those in the more positive outcome categories.[71] Nemovicher compared thirty adopted boys with the same number of nonadopted boys and found that the adopted boys differed significantly from the controls in being more hostile, tense, dependent, and fearful. Most of these adopted boys were from prosperous Jewish families in New York state.[72] Ripple found that among the adopted children she studied "small but persistent differences in the white sub-sample showed higher education and economic status to be less favorable" to a good adjustment.[73] She speculated that this may reflect workers' inappropriately favorable evaluations of the applications of the more articulate and sophisticated. Kornitzer found in her study of adopted children that lower business and professional adoptive couples were apt to be less successful as adoptive parents than were working-class couples.[74]

Jaffee and Fanshel's follow-up study of one hundred children who had been adopted between 1930 and 1940 is probably the most rigorous follow-up study extant. Their findings on the influence of socioeconomic status on adjustment are ambiguous, but I believe that a careful study of them throws a great deal of light on the question. The researchers measured socioeconomic status considering three factors: (1) income, (2) occupational prestige, and (3) amount of parents' education. They divided the one hundred children into three outcome categories, with about an equal number in each group: (1) Group I, low-problem; (2) Group II, middle-problem; and (3) Group III, high-problem. The median income of the low-problem group was higher than the other two groups. However, the highest income category—$40,000 and over—included 3% of the low-problem group, 9% of the middle-problem group, and 12% of the high-problem group. On the factor of occupational prestige, there was an insignificantly higher mean ranking in the high-problem group (5.6 as compared to 5.5 for each of the other two groups). The striking difference is on the educational factor, where high-problem adoptive families had much more education than the other two groups. More than one-half the fathers of high-problem adoptees had completed college and one-fourth had professional or graduate education. By contrast, less than a third of the fathers of adoptees in each of the other two groups had completed college, and fewer had entered professional or graduate education. Only 12% of the fathers in the high-problem group had failed to get any high school education, while 15% of the middle-range group and 24% of the low-problem group had not had any high school education.

Jaffee and Fanshel conclude, *on the basis of a combined mean score*, that there is a "relatively weak linkage" between socioeconomic status and outcome. They repeat this conclusion later in their book, yet, in their statistical correlations of adoptive parents' socioeconomic rank with outcome variables and with global interviewer rating, they show that

> children raised in higher social class families tended to encounter more personality problems over the years than did their lower social class counterparts, and study interviewers were rather clearly predisposed to assign negative rather than positive ratings to higher SES (socioeconomic status) families. . . . The social relations of higher SES adoptees were somewhat likely to be more problematical in nature, and adoptive parents of higher socioeconomic standing were more inclined than their lower SES counterparts to express dissatisfaction with their adoptive experience.[75] [The latter two correlations were not statistically significant.]

Religious affiliation was related to socioeconomic status. The four agencies studied were the Catholic Home Bureau (all Catholic families); the Chapin Nursery/Spence Alumnae (all Protestant); the Free Synagogue Committee (all Jewish); and State Charities Aid (mostly Protestant, a few Catholic, and a few mixed marriages). A predominant number of higher SES families came from the Free Synagogue Committee and the Chapin Nursery/Spence Alumnae agencies, and these had a high representation in the high-problem group.

Protestant families who comprised approximately two-fifths of the total sample are somewhat overly represented in the high-problem outcome group, where they make up almost half of the total. The pattern of distribution is even more exaggerated for the Jewish families who are especially heavily concentrated in the middle-range and high-problem outcome groups. By contrast, our Catholic families are more than well represented in the low-problem group and underrepresented in the high-problem group.[76]

Perhaps the most striking finding of the study, according to the authors, was the high number (78%) of the high-problem parents who reported that their children had not fulfilled their expectations regarding education.[77] Parental dissatisfaction with the child's education was a more important factor to the child's total adjustment than was the amount of education the child received. These facts seem quite significant, in view of the fact that high-problem families included more fathers with advanced education. High-problem adoptees included a higher number of less-educated children, and more of their parents were dissatisfied with the children's educational achievement. An "excellent-to-good" educational adjustment characterized 61% of the low-problem, 32% of the middle-range, and 18% of the high-problem group. A "below average or very poor" educational adjustment characterized 3% of the low-problem, 18% of the middle-range, and 43% of the high-problem group. Of the ones who went to college, a higher proportion in the high-problem group performed at below-average level. Fewer parents in the low- and middle-problem groups made any special effort to promote school achievement. Five high-problem children had been sent to a boarding school for help with academic problems, as compared to one each in the low- and middle-problem groups. "Parents of high problem adoptees had tended to promote the school achievement of their children in a variety of ways."[78] Boys fared less well than girls in educational adjustment, and girls showed a slight tendency to be freer of personality problems.[79]

Parents of high-problem adoptees were also less satisfied with the adoptee's friends, heterosexual relationships, personality, vocational adjustment, methods of handling finances, and living standards.

Three-fifths of the high-problem adoptees were boys. Fathers of the high-problem group were more likely to be the chief disciplinarians, as compared to the other two groups, where the mothers were more likely to be the chief disciplinarians. The fathers were especially likely to be strict with male adoptees. The only parents who said they often gave their child severe spankings were in the high-problem group.

Where adopters requested boys, adoptees tended to have encountered problems in their educational pursuits and were likely to be experiencing a less than satisfactory economic adjustment at the time of the study. Adoptive parents were somewhat inclined to express dissatisfaction with the adoption experience.[80]

The authors were surprised to find "that the socioeconomic level of the adoptive parents was but a weak indicator of how adoptees would tend to fare in later years."[81] Judging from the way they presented their data, I assume they expected to find that affluent parents were better parents. I suggest an alternate hypothesis which they did not propose. I think that the strength of the parents' achievement motivation and the level of their socioeconomic aspirations for both themselves and their children were critical factors in the child's adjustment. There would not necessarily be a direct correlation between amount of income and level of aspiration, but there would probably be a close correlation between the parents' level of satisfaction with the adoptee's educational achievement and vocational adjustment, and parental satisfaction with the child's overall adjustment and personality.

I suggest that this is the reason for the "most striking finding" of the study, i.e., a large number of high-problem adoptees whose parents were dissatisfied with their educational adjustment. The parents had high expectations of the children, especially of the boys, because male educational and vocational achievement is considered critical in this society. I suggest, further, that this was related to the greater number of severe spankings in the high-problem families, the greater strictness of the fathers, and the more problematic adjustment of boys than girls. In support of this hypothesis, I use Leonard Pearlin's findings that the father's satisfaction with his job and the nature of his job helps to structure the way both parents treat their children. Pearlin found that prosperous parents encourage self-control and independence, value a college education more highly than do poor parents, and favor professional occupations for their young males. Boys are spanked more often than girls in both middle-class and working-class families because "there may be an element of urgency in parents' aspirations for boys that is absent in those for girls."[82] Middle-class parents with lower aspirations spank less because they feel less urgency about getting their children into college— needing less achievement to uphold the family status. Middle-class parents of sons associate long-range goals with self-denial and delay of gratification.

> The severity of the measures they use (with their sons) is commensurate with the importance they place on future achievement.[83]

In both classes, parents expecting that their child will not realize their aspirations use corporal punishment more than parents without such an expectation.[84] Middle-class fathers who see the delay of rewards as necessary to their work are more likely to use corporal punishment with their sons, at least as an auxiliary control, than are those who do not.[85]

I suggest, therefore, that people with a less highly developed achievement orientation may be more effective adoptive parents. If this is true, it poses a problem for the field of adoption since a strong achievement orientation may, according to Maas and Engler, be a critical motivation to adopt nonrelatives in the first place.

My hypothesis may also apply to foster parents, although their situation is different from adoptive parents. They are not taking a child to be a permanent part of their family. While a successful foster child reflects favorably upon the foster parents, the child's success is not as critical a factor to the family's status and self-esteem as it is with adoptive parents. Nevertheless, there is some evidence that people who place a higher value on ascriptive rather than achieved status may be more accepting of other people's children. Most foster parents "come from large clannish families and the foster mother's interests revolve around homemaking and child care. . . ."[86] Fanshel hypothesized that foster parents from clan-type families are more willing to accept the physically handicapped and mentally retarded child.[87] Trasler found no relationship in his study between social class of foster parents and outcome, while Parker found that "the lower the socio-economic class of the foster parents the more successful a placement is likely to be."[88] On the other hand, Cautley found that although the range of socio-economic levels of the families she studied was rather narrow, families with higher incomes were more successful.[89] Trasler's and Parker's studies were done in England, while Cautley's was done in the United States. I suspect, without being able to prove it, that foster parents' overall socioeconomic status in the United States might be more marginal than that of foster parents in England. A comparison of the unskilled and the skilled working-class performance in foster care would probably show a different picture than would a comparison of middle-class and working-class foster parents. None of the studies on foster care has made the fine distinctions regarding occupations and aspirations as Pearlin made in his study of natural parents.

Kadushin concludes, in his review of the research,

> Given the somewhat limited educational background and rural, folk-oriented ideology of foster parents, there is apt to be a discrepancy in child care attitudes as expressed by foster parents and social workers.[90]

This statement points up one of the most persistent problems in foster care: the conflict between the middle-class social worker and the working-class foster parent. The transcription of a foster parents' group meeting reproduced in Appendix A deals with the role of the foster parent in the child care system. Is the foster parent a client, a colleague, a substitute parent, or a child care specialist? Do foster parents inevitably shut out the natural parent in their zeal to prove themselves good parents? In Chap. 4, I analyze the fate of the natural parent whose child is in foster care.

Notes to Chapter Three

1. In "La Causa and La Huelga," *Community Organizers and Social Planners*, ed. by Joan Ecklein and Armand Lauffer (N.Y.: John Wiley & Sons, 1972), p. 47.

2. *Centuries of Childhood: A Social History of Family Life* (N.Y.: Vintage Books, 1965).

3. Margaret Kornitzer, *Child Adoption in the Modern World* (N.Y.: Philosophical Library, 1952), p. 4.

4. Ibid., p. 6.

5. Grace Abbott, *The Child and the State* (Chicago: University of Chicago Press, 1938), p. 89.

6. Edward Banfield, *The Unheavenly City* (Boston: Little, Brown, 1970), p. 245.

7. Alfred Kadushin, *Child Welfare Services* (N.Y.: Macmillan, 1967), p. 357.

8. Andrew Billingsley and Jeanne M. Giovannoni, *Children of the Storm* (N.Y.: Harcourt Brace Jovanovich, 1972), p. 24.

9. Kadushin, *Child Welfare Services*, pp. 357–358.

10. Ibid., p. 358.

11. Henry Thurstone, *The Dependent Child* (N.Y.: Columbia University Press, 1930), p. 136.

12. Often, even though a social worker might prefer to provide home-maker services and money to better the child's care in his own home, laws and governmental funding encourage the recommendation of foster care placement.

13. Billingsley and Giovannoni, pp. 31–33.

14. *Children under Institutional Care*, 1923, U.S. Department of Commerce, Bureau of the Census, 1927, p. 18; *Child Welfare Statistics*, 1969, N.C.S.S. Report CW-1 (69), U.S./DHEW, p. 1. Cited by Billingsley, p. 70.

15. Henry S. Maas and Richard E. Engler, Jr., *Children in Need of Parents* (N.Y.: Columbia University Press, 1959), p. 345.

16. Shirley Jenkins and Elaine Norman, "Families of Children in Foster Care," *Children*, vol. 16, no. 4 (1969); David Fanshel, "The Exit of Children from Foster Care: An Interim Research Report," *Child Welfare*, vol. 50, no 2 (February 1971): 65–81.

17. Alfred Kadushin, "Child Welfare," in *Research in the Social Services: A Five-Year Review*, ed. by Henry S. Maas (National Association of Social Workers, 1971), p. 46.

18. Ibid., p. 46.

19. *Board Rates for Foster Family Care* (N.Y.: Child Welfare League of America, 1970), p. 9.

20. Kadushin, "Child Welfare," p. 35.

21. *Statistical Abstract of the United States 1972*, U.S. Department of Commerce, Bureau of the Census, Table 497, p. 305.

22. Kadushin, "Child Welfare," p. 15.

23. Kingsley Davis, "Intermarriage in Caste Societies," in *The Family*, ed. by Rose L. Coser (N.Y.: St. Martin's Press, 1966), pp. 105–127.

24. William H. Whyte, *The Organization Man* (N.Y.: Simon and Schuster, A Clarion Book, 1956), p. 355.

25. Maas and Engler, p. 291.

26. Ibid., p. 234.

27. Ibid., p. 296.

28. Ibid., p. 298.

29. Donald Gilbert McKinley, *Social Class and Family Life* (N.Y.: The Free Press, 1964), p. 92.

30. Maas and Engler, p. 298.

31. Andrée Vieille Michel, "Kinship Relations and Relationships of Proximity in French Working-Class Households," in *A Modern Introduction to the Family*, ed. by Norman W. Bell and Ezra F. Vogel (N.Y.: The Free Press, 1968), pp. 311–318.

32. Ibid., p. 313.

33. H. David Kirk, *Shared Fate* (N.Y.: The Free Press, 1964), pp. 123-145.

34. Maas and Engler, p. 346.

35. Benson Jaffe and David Fanshel, *How They Fared in Adoption: A Follow-up Study* (N.Y.: Columbia University Press, 1970), p. 109.

36. Stanley King, "Sand Dunes and Sea Law," *The Dukes County Intelligencer* (Edgartown, Mass.: Dukes County Historical Society, Inc.), vol. 3, no. 1 (August 1961).

37. Ibid., unpaginated.

38. J. E. Weckler, "Adoption on Mokil." Weckler does not give the history of stratification on Mokil, but indicates that it has a long history: "The Mokilese today, and probably far back in their past, tend more to rally around a powerful man and seek his favor than to smite him in support of the weak." Reproduced by permission of the American Anthropological Association from the *American Anthropologist* 55:563 (566, 567), 1953.

39. Ibid., p. 563.

40. Ibid., pp. 556–557.

41. "No parent who is able to provide for his family will permit his child to enter a *shotay* adoption" (p. 567).

42. "Nearly every adoptee sooner or later returns to the *paneyney* (patrilocal residence) of his birth, often in an atmosphere of bitterness and recrimination. . . . An institution that formerly functioned entirely to increase social solidarity, today often produces discord and dissension" (p. 567).

43. Vern Carroll, "Adoption on Nukuoro," in *Adoption in Eastern Oceania*, ed. by Vern Carroll (Honolulu: University of Hawaii Press, 1970), pp. 121–157.

44. Alan Howard et al., "Traditional and Modern Adoption Patterns in Hawaii," in *Adoption in Eastern Oceania*, pp. 21-51.

45. Michael D. Lieber, "Adoption on Kapingamarangi," in *Adoption in Eastern Oceania*, pp. 158–205.

46. Lieber gives an example of the distinction between fosterage and adoption:

> The wife of a Kapinga store owner living in Ponape needed help with housework and the care of several children. She wanted a girl about ten or eleven years of age. Her husband's brother's son had thirteen children. The husband took the ship to Kapingamarangi to talk with his nephew and came back with the nephew's eleven-year-old daughter. He originally wanted to foster the girl, but as he was relatively wealthy his brother's son subtly but firmly pressured him into adopting the child [p. 179].

47. J. L. Fischer, "Adoption on Ponape," in *Adoption in Eastern Oceania*, p. 296.

48. Alan Howard, "Adoption on Rotuma," in *Adoption in Eastern Oceania*, pp. 343–368.

49. Howard et al., pp. 21-51.

50. Robert I. Levy, "Tahitian Adoption as a Psychological Message," in *Adoption in Eastern Oceania*, pp. 71–87.

51. Howard et al., p. 48.

52. Two valuable discussions of the evolution of stratification in Polynesia are Irving Goldman, "The Evolution of Polynesian Societies," in *Culture in History*, ed. by Stanley Diamond (N.Y.: Columbia University Press, 1960), pp. 687-712; and Morton H. Fried, "On the Evolution of Social Stratification and the State," in *Culture in History*, ibid., pp. 713-731. Goldman classifies Polynesian societies into traditional, open, and stratified. Traditional societies were organized around the village and lineage type of land tenure. Open societies do not have economic stratification, but have social stratification. Stratified societies had dispersed settlements formed by groupings of people around estates of leading chiefs and war leaders. The key change leading to a stratified society is the change in land tenure, creating a clear distinction between landed and landless. This created a social cleavage "that the Polynesians themselves began to regard as unbridgeable and in some instances it made subsistence itself an issue in political conflict" (p. 696). Goldman regards Tahiti and Hawaii as representing the culmination of Polynesian political evolution toward highly stratified socieites, in which administrative divisions have replaced more traditional organization of lineage and tribe. Tahiti still retains the traditions of hereditary rank and great deference for the aristocracy. It had a class of chiefs who were the ruling aristocracy, a landed middle class of nobles, and—at the bottom of the social scale—the commoners, who constituted the majority of the population. The commoners were "not only landless, but to all intents and purposes a caste" (pp. 696–699).

Goldman says that "Ranking gives to all descent groups a potentially unstable character simply because human beings do not tolerate social inequality too well. As a consequence, no known hierarchical society has been able to devise more than temporary measures to insure its stability" (p. 690). Fried points out that in stratified societies, some members have unimpeded access to strategic resources and others have impediments. "It was the passage to stratified society which laid the basis for the complex division of labor which underlies modern society. It also gave rise to various arrangements of socio-economic classes and led directly to both classical and modern forms of colonialism and imperialism" (p. 722). The state which emerges with a stratified society organizes power on a supra-kin basis. It takes on the task of maintaining the general order, "but scarcely discernible from this is its need to support the order of stratification" (p. 728). Its principles of organization include "the idea of hierarchy, property, and the power of the law" (p. 728).

53. Sanford N. Katz, *When Parents Fail* (Boston: Beacon Press, 1971), p. 90.

54. Bernd Lambert, "Adoption, Guardianship, and Social Stratification in the Northern Gilbert Islands," in *Adoption in Eastern Oceania*, pp. 261–291.

55. Ibid., p. 263.

56. Ibid., p. 272.

57. Ibid.

58. Ibid., p. 262. The system of guardianship may be peculiar to societies which are progressing from kin-based to more highly stratified class societies where the state takes over the parenting function without regard for kin ties. Guardianship

may represent a midpoint system of substitute care between communal clan-based societies where children are the property of the community, and class societies where children are the possessions of nuclear families. In the process of such a transition, foster care and adoption seem to become separate systems of child care. For example, see Roger M. Keesing, "Kwaio Fosterage," *American Anthropologist*, vol. 72, no. 5 (October 1970). Adoption in Kwaio differs from fosterage in that adopted children sever all natal relationships and rights, although the natal parents remain known to the child and genealogies are not amended. I can hear echoes of the Child Welfare League of America guidelines for assessing foster parents in Kwaio, where a guardian chooses a foster parent from among the kin who volunteer. The guardian (who is the sponsor of the father's marriage) is responsible for supervising the care of the child, and for placing the child with another foster parent if the child is mistreated. The rights and duties of a foster parent seem exactly the same as the rights and duties of a United States' foster parent. The guardian in Kwaio retains jural rights to the child, whereas in the United States the guardian is likely to be the state or an agency acting for the state. One significant difference between Kwaio and United States guidelines for choosing foster parents, however, is that the foster parent in Kwaio must live near enough to the child's own kin so that he can visit freely with kin who are interested in him.

Another form of guardianship, the custom of *compadrazgo* as practiced in Mexico and godparenthood as practiced in Jugoslavia, is found in more traditional societies and cultures where kin relationships are strong. Godparenthood in the United States is probably most common in traditional cultures and among propertied families. It seems a far superior form of substitute care to fosterage as it is practiced in the United States. See Eugene A. Hammel, "Some Aspects of Godparenthood in Southern Jugoslavia," paper presented to a colloquium of the Center for Slavic and Easter European Studies at Berkeley, 9 March 1964; Leo Grebler et al., *The Mexican American People: The Nation's Second Largest Minority* (N.Y.: The Free Press, 1970), p. 358.

59. Urie Bronfenbrenner, *Two Worlds of Childhood* (N.Y.: Russell Sage Foundation, 1970), p. 163.

60. V. George, *Foster Care* (London: Routledge & Kegan Paul; N.Y.: Humanities Press, 1970), pp. 16, 19, 94, and 204.

61. Kornitzer, p. 103.

62. Richard Cloward and Irwin Epstein, "The Case of Family Adjustment Agencies," in *Social Welfare Institutions: A Sociological Reader*, ed. by Mayer N. Zald (N.Y.: John Wiley & Sons, 1965), pp. 623–43.

63. Margaret Purvine and William Ryan, "Into and Out of a Child Welfare Network," *Child Welfare*, vol. 48, no. 3 (March 1969): 126–135.

64. Jaffee and Fanshel, *How They Fared*; Henry Maas, "The Successful Adoptive Parent Applicant," *Social Work*, 5: 14–20 (1960); Lillian Ripple, *A Follow-up Study of Adopted Children* (Chicago: University of Chicago, 1968); Alfred Kadushin, "A Study of Adoptive Parents of Hard-to-Place Children," *Social Casework*, vol. 43, pp. 227–33; Trudy Bradley, "An Exploration of Case Workers' Perceptions of Adoptive Applicants" (N.Y.: Child Welfare League of America, 1966).

65. Jaffee and Fanshel, *How They Fared*; Maas, *Social Work*; Kadushin, "Child Welfare."

66. Maas, *Social Work*, pp. 14–20.

67. Jaffee and Fanshel, *How They Fared*, pp. 251–252.

68. Maas, *Social Work*; Bradley, *An Exploration*; Jaffee and Fanshel, *How They Fared*; Billingsley and Giovannoni, *Children of the Storm*.

69. Helen Witmer et al., *Independent Adoptions* (N.Y.: Russell Sage Foundation, 1963).

70. J. R. Wittenborn, *The Placement of Adoptive Children* (Springfield, Ill.: Charles C. Thomas 1957).

71. Ruth F. Brenner, "A Follow-up Study of Adoptive Families" (N.Y.: Child Adoption Research Committee, Inc., 1951).

72. J. Nemovicher, "A Comparative Study of Adopted Boys and Non-adopted Boys in Respect of Specific Personality Characteristics" (Ph.D. diss., School of Education, New York University, 1959).

73. Lillian Ripple, "A Follow-up Study of Adopted Children," *Social Service Review*, vol. 42, no. 4 (December 1968): 486.

74. Margaret Kornitzer, *Adoption and Family Life* (N.Y.: Humanities Press, 1968), pp. 13–14.

75. Jaffee and Fanshel, *How They Fared*, p. 259.

76. Ibid., p. 55.

77. Ibid., p. 210.

78. Ibid., p. 82.

79. Ibid., p. 250.

80. Ibid., p. 256.

81. Ibid., p. 261.

82. Leonard I. Pearlin, *Class Context and Family Relations* (Boston: Little, Brown, 1971).

83. Ibid., p. 109.

84. Ibid., p. 109.

85. Ibid., p. 113.

86. Kadushin, "Child Welfare," p. 47.

87. David Fanshel, "Specialization Within the Foster Care Role, Part II," *Child Welfare*, vol. 40, no. 4 (April 1961).

88. R. A. Parker, *Decision in Child Care* (London: Allen & Unwin, 1966), p. 69.

89. Patricia Cautley, *Successful Foster Homes—An Exploratory Study of Their Characteristics* (Madison, Wisc.: Dept. of Public Welfare, 1966).

90. Kadushin, "Child Welfare," p. 47.

CHAPTER FOUR
PARENTS' RIGHTS AND
CHILDREN'S RIGHTS

Soon the state people were making plans to take over all of my mothers' children. . . . A Judge McClellan in Lansing had authority over me and all of my brothers and sisters. We were "state children," court wards; he had the full say-so over us. A white man in charge of a black man's children! Nothing but legal, modern slavery—however kindly intentioned. . . . I truly believe that if ever a state social agency destroyed a family, it destroyed ours. We wanted and tried to stay together. Our home didn't have to be destroyed. But the Welfare, the courts, and their doctor, gave us the one-two-three punch.

Malcolm X[1]

Parents' Rights

As the state expands its control over substitute care of children, it increasingly excludes parents from decision-making and from contact with their children. As the states' rights to children expand, parents' rights contract.[2] Uruguay is an extreme example of this. There the child's natural parents are legally "killed off" when the child is adopted, and the adopted parents are not *allowed* to mention the child's parents. In the United States, many adoptive parents psychologically "kill off" the natural parents by not discussing them with the children, despite social workers' advice to do so.[3]

In foster care, the foster parents seem more inclined than ever to "freeze out" natural parents in their efforts to be "better parents" to their foster children. A 1970 study [4] revealed that almost half of the foster parents questioned the very right of natural parents to visit their children, and 95% believed that foster parents should deprive the natural parents of visiting privileges if such visits made the child unhappy. In contrast to this, a 1963 study [5] found 90% of foster parents affirming visiting rights of natural parents and less than one-third denying visiting privileges if they made the child unhappy. The contrast was similar in regard to major areas of decision-making for children, such as giving permission for an underage marriage. Ninety percent of foster parents in the 1963 study believed parents should have this right, compared to forty-nine percent in 1970.[6] A big change in attitude over a period of only seven years.

The state restricts rights of poor parents by denial of legal rights, by economic exploitation, by racial discrimination, and by sexual oppression. I shall discuss these areas separately.

Denial of Due Process

A curious thing happened to the benign visions of the early twentieth-century reformers. They agitated for taking children out of the adult criminal courts and they won the Children's Courts, which based their procedures upon "enlightened" social investigation, informal hearings before a judge, and indeterminate sentences to "correctional" or "therapeutic" institutions. But the reformers' dream became a nightmare. Decades later Gerald Francis Gault and his lawyer protested to the Supreme Court that he had been denied the due process of the law by an informal hearing, that his indeterminate sentence had become interminable, and that the "correctional" institution was cruel.[7] In its capacity of *parens patriae* to children, the Juvenile Court oppressed children and parents, and helped to render parents powerless.[8]

Similarly in the child welfare field, the early social reformers envisioned institutions and foster homes as partial solutions to the problems of poor children from "inadequate" homes. Decades later it became clear that institutions and foster homes can neglect children more seriously than do parents.[9] In at least some respects, the neglect perpetrated by the foster care system seems to be getting worse.[10] In neglect cases, as in delinquency cases, reformers of the early twentieth century believed that a "welfare" philosophy would guarantee children more humane treatment than would legal adversary proceedings. However, "welfare" treatment has resulted in the loss of many legal rights for the poor, including the right to a jury trial and other due process, and the right to standards of justice equal to the standards used for the middle class and the rich.

Most neglect cases are not granted the right to jury trial, but are tried before a single judge. In the best of circumstances—an enlightened judge with plenty of time, a well-staffed court, skilled and adequate social services—informal proceedings could benefit a child. In the worst of circumstances, a judge's proceedings can evoke the horror of Nazi Germany. The shadow of the concentration camp lurks in the following statement of a California judge to an unmarried pregnant Mexican-American woman:

> The County will have to take care of you. You are no particular good to anybody. We ought to send you out of the country—send you back to Mexico. You belong in prison for the rest of your life for doing things of this kind. You ought to commit suicide. That's what I think of people of this kind. You are lower than animals and haven't the right to live in organized society—just miserable, lousy, rotten people.
>
> There is nothing we can do with you. You expect the County to take care of you. Maybe Hitler was right. The animals in our society probably ought to be destroyed because they have no right to live among human beings. If you refuse to act like a human being, then you don't belong among the society of human beings.[11]

Most juvenile judges, like most people, are neither brilliant and inspired nor fascists. They are almost always white, usually male, and always middle class. They have biases about illegitimacy, sexual permissiveness, housekeeping standards, money management, life styles, personality attributes, and child-rearing practices—biases which profoundly affect the lives of children and their parents. The probation officers or social workers who investigate the facts and report to the judge also have biases. Even if they have a graduate degree—which most of them do not—child-rearing is still an art rather than a science, and graduate schools in the human services are staffed by middle-class teachers, largely white, with little direct experience of slum life or minority group culture. The public welfare workers and the clinic staff who are most likely to come in contact with poor families and who often file neglect charges are similarly biased. Among the biases of many of these middle-class professionals are a lack of respect for kinship ties [12] and, often, paternalistic or contemptuous attitudes toward the poor and minority groups. "Child neglect is a value-loaded concept clearly based on class factors." [13]

Most parents do not have legal counsel during neglect charges; and most parents do not appeal a court's decision to take their children away. Vague neglect statutes allow wide latitude for interpretations, do not require a written opinion by the judge, and do not encourage appeal. These neglect statutes

> provide the judge with a vehicle for imposing his own preferences for certain child-rearing practices and his own ideas of adult behavior and parental morality. These statutes . . . sometimes appear to be a means of policing the poor, especially parents on public welfare, and other parents, often young, who do not conform either in dress, life-style, or child-rearing practices to dominant middle-class norms. Here the interests of the child become secondary to the desire to punish. . . . [14]

The middle and upper classes also abuse and neglect their children, materially as well as psychologically. However, the upper and middle classes assume parental competence among themselves. When their children show massive disaffection through drugs, run-aways, or rejection of parent values, the parents call this a "social problem," and do not take each other to court on neglect charges. Their child-rearing practices are obscured from community view in the privacy of their homes. The poor, on the other hand, are more visible and more subject to social control through the agencies they deal with such as welfare, courts, and hospital clinics.

A different standard is applied to the poor. Their sexual practices, their housekeeping, their money management, their child-care practices are scrutinized and chastised assiduously. Rich parents may send their child off at an early age to a military school where he is harshly treated, but no one will object.[15] No one objects when rich parents drink themselves to a stupor, practice adultery, swap mates, go into debt, turn over the daily care of the children and the house to someone else. No one will even know the details, because the rich generally do not open their lives to inspection by researchers. Poor people answer the researchers' questions, seldom realizing that they have a choice.[16] Poor women have been charged with neglect and have had their children taken from them for writing bad checks and "mismanaging" money;[17] for having more than one illegitimate child;[18] for raising their children in unpopular religions;[19] for having "loose morals";[20] for drinking in a tavern;[21] for being poor;[22] and for allowing a friend or neighbor to care for a child without official state sanction.[23]

> Most neglect hearings proceed on the assumption that there are no opposing sides, that all parties share in a common desire to promote the child's welfare.[24]

The judge has generally assumed the role of protector of the child's interests, and many states therefore do not allow for the appointment of legal counsel for parents or children. A "child welfare" philosophy has given great power to social agencies and judges, and has taken away parents' legal rights to challenge agencies and courts. This happens the most when the welfare world of social agencies permeates the legal world. Judges are less likely to sever legal parental ties in communities where welfare agencies have relatively little influence on the judge.[25] If a parent who cannot afford a lawyer lives in a state which will not appoint one, she has no way to fight a legal decision.[26]

Neglect statutes are generally broad and unspecific, giving agencies and judges great leeway in interpretation. Because interpretations of neglect are broad, social workers empowered to investigate neglect complaints are often vague and ambiguous in their dealings with "neglectful" parents and "neglected" children. This increases parents' anxiety and works against an honest relationship between parents and social workers. A social worker in a child welfare agency where I once worked dropped in unannounced at breakfast time to see what a mother was feeding her child. The worker, who was investigating a neglect complaint, asked the mother ambiguous leading questions about how she fed and dressed the child, what recreation the child had, and so on. The worker reported the mother's evasive answers in an "aha, she's hiding something" tone of voice. I suggested that anyone might be evasive under the circumstances. What parent is completely confident about her parental competence and secure about subjecting it to offical scrutiny?

When parents attempt to regain custody of a child, they have a difficult time proving that they have become "fit" parents.[27] Social workers and judges are reluctant to change their minds about parents once they have declared the parents "unfit" and have taken the children into care. I have the impression, however, based on my child welfare practice, that parents who retain a lawyer have a much better chance of getting their children back than parents who do not. Most child welfare workers subscribe to a personality theory that assumes the possibility of change; yet, ironically, they neither give very much help to parents, nor encourage much contact between parents and children, nor make it easy for parents to get their children back. The children continue indefinitely in the limbo of foster care, with the sanction of the courts.

Economic Exploitation

Public assistance has been used to "regulate the poor" since the beginnings of the welfare system. Bell, [28] Piven and Cloward, [29] and Ritz [30] (among others) document how public assistance has been used to enforce work at low wages, to insure a supply of cheap labor, and to intimidate low-paid workers who are not on welfare. Perhaps the most terrifying of the threats used against Aid to Families of Dependent Children mothers by public officials is the threat to take away their children. Many of the mothers feel that to lose their children is to lose the only wealth they have, and sometimes to lose their only reason for living.[31] Parents and children are helpless victims of welfare witch hunts conducted periodically by various government officials. Under the guise of "protecting the children," various state and local officials at various times have cut off AFDC grants of unmarried mothers, threatened to cut off the grant if a woman had more than one out-of-wedlock child, threatened to place out-of-wedlock children in foster homes or adoptive homes (and have sometimes done so), forced AFDC mothers to work at cheap labor.

The litany of foster care is the litany of poverty: unemployment and underemployment, inadequate public assistance grants, poor health and medical care, mothers carrying the burden of child care alone. The families at the bottom of the economic ladder contribute most of the child abuse and neglect that is detected by the state.[32]

The most striking feature of neglecting parents is the

> level of poverty in which they live. By almost any economic scale, these parents are poor. Not surprisingly, a high proportion are supported by either private or governmental funds. Substandard housing, lack of good health and educational facilities, and little opportunity for recreational diversions appear to be the standard way of life. These parents are indeed part of the "other America."[33]

A study of the families of 624 children who entered foster care in New York City for the first time in 1966 showed that 57% received some form of public assistance; for 45% it was the chief means of support. The 43% who earned wages or salaries earned less than the citywide average. Mothers from a lower socio-economic level said they were nervous and worried more often than did the mothers who were not as poor. Most of these parents were alienated, distrustful, and angry. Puerto Rican parents were the most alienated of all. While the majority thought agencies were helpful, about 15% of them on the lowest socioeconomic level thought agencies were usurpers and believed that "agencies act like parents have no rights at all—they think they own the children."[34] When asked what they would want if they had three wishes, about half answered, "to have my child back" and "to have a home with my family all living together." Many of them wished for mental or physical health, a good spouse to get "off welfare," and to "find happiness." After studying the families of children in foster care, Jenkins urged that philanthropic funding organizations give high priority to changing radically the foster care system. She called for parents to organize:

> If parents whose children were taken into foster care against their wishes chose to exercise strong organized efforts with regard to parental rights, they might have a substantial impact on the entire field.[35]

Racial Discrimination

In a survey of foster care in New York City, some Puerto Rican and black parents expressed the belief that their children had been "taken by the whites."[36] Malcolm X was not alone in seeing foster care as a system of legalized slavery. In the nine communities studied by Maas and Engler, the child of minority ethnicity (Negro, Spanish-speaking, American Indian, Portugese, French-Canadian, or mixed) "was more likely to remain in foster care than to be adopted."[37] These children, however, less frequently exhibited psychological disturbance and experienced fewer moves than the majority child. (The two facts are probably related, since psychological problems of children in foster care increased with the number of different moves they made.) Mothers of these children had less coopera-tive relationships with agencies. In the New England coastal town of Brighton, a highly stratified community, no black children were adopted. In the segregated Southwestern metropolis of King City, black people went to out-of-town agencies to adopt in order to avoid the stigma associated with welfare agencies in the community. Maas and Engler describe the caste divisions in La Paz, a Southwestern community of 28,000, of whom 60% had Spanish surnames:

> La Paz always presented a picture of a "we" group caring for a "they" group in its health and welfare programs. It was Anglo money, Anglo medicine, and Anglo welfare programs that took care of the "Spanish needy," and the gulf between the givers and the recipients seemed quite wide.[38]

Billingsley and Giovannoni [39] argue, convincingly, that the needs of black children in the substitute care system will be better served by agencies controlled by black people. There is no doubt that agencies controlled by white people have discriminated against minority groups. Forer, a lawyer who works in the juvenile court system, tells how this works in the juvenile "correctional" institutions:

> A number of white mothers on the fringe of poverty launch active campaigns to get their children sent to (private) correctional institutions. These children are usually committed to predominantly white, private, church-controlled institutions.[40]

These private institutions have an unwritten but carefully observed *numerus clausus* (racial quota). As far as Forer knows, no judge or organization has challenged this system.[41]

Billingsley and Giovannoni argue from the perspective of the 1960's and 1970's thrust toward Black Power and community control. Oddly enough, support for their argument comes from one of the most blatantly racist Southern communi-ties studied by Maas and Engler. Jamestown, a town that fairly drips with the traditions of the Confederacy, completed adoptions for proportionately as many black children who came into care as white children—because agencies were segregated and black children were placed through black agencies. This was in sharp contrast to the "liberal" city of Westport, a progressive metropolis on the West Coast, where 91% of the adopted children were white, although only 65% of children in foster care were white. Not one black child in Westport returned home, and few black children were adopted. Forty percent of the children who attained their majority in foster care in Westport were black, although only 18% of the foster care population was black. Blacks in Jamestown had a median income of $839 in 1957, as compared to $1,701 for the total population.[42] Despite the poverty of black families, however, Jamestown authorities were less ready to take black children into care than were Westport authorities. Although blacks in Westport made up only 4% of the total population, they comprised 18% of the foster care population. In Jamestown, on the other hand, blacks comprised 49% of the total population and only 20% of the foster care population. One can only speculate about which situation proved to be better for black children in the long run—staying in the limbo of foster care in Westport, or growing up with parents in poverty in Jamestown. Jamestown was not a "progressive" community. No doubt the authorities were reluctant to spend money on black families. Institutions were racially segregated and the law forbade interracial adoption. Most people were far from embracing all men as brothers, despite their strong allegiance to Christian institutions. Yet they were reluctant to sever family and community ties. When children in Jamestown were adopted, they were adopted by their own sectarian or ethnic group. Close family ties and close community ties were valued more highly by Jamestown residents than was upward mobility.

Sexual Exploitation

An Iowa legislator once compared lobbying AFDC mothers to his hired hands. A federal Congressman once called a group of demonstrating AFDC mothers "brood mares." Both legislators want welfare recipients to be subservient; both think of welfare recipients as menial laborers; and both resent recipients' sexual and reproductive behavior. With monotonous regularity, welfare witch hunts reveal the economic and sexual anxieties of the dominant class. Promiscuity and illegitimacy seem to be the stuff of which antiwelfare legislators' recurring nightmares are made. Often their reflexive remedy is a threat to punish mothers of illegitimate children by discontinuing welfare grants and/or putting the children in foster homes.[43] *Putting the children in foster homes does not save the state money. In fact, it increases the taxpayer's load tremendously since the cost of raising a foster child to the age of 18 is about $122,500, as compared to $34,464 for raising a child in a natural home to the age of 18.*[44] Discontinuing the grant does not reduce the illegitimacy rate; it increases it.[45] Therefore, the legislators' actions clearly do not solve the "problem" of illegitimacy. Nor do the legislators generally seek to find out if their actions are solving the "problem." Why, then, do they behave in this apparently irrational way? To understand this, I think we have to look to the theories of Wilhelm Reich.

Drawing on the studies of the Trobriand Islanders by Bronislaw

Malinowski,[46] Reich attempted to carry Engels' theories on the origin of the patriarchal nuclear family further into a consideration of the function of sexual pleasure and the relationship of sexual repression to economic oppression.[47] Reich believed that "the natural ethics of primitive matriarchal society, characterized by sexual freedom, were immeasurably superior to the morality of the capitalist era."[48] The transition of the matriarchal classless society to a patriarchal class society was marked by increasing sexual repression enforced by a rigid morality. The function of this repression, according to Reich, was to deprive people of self-confidence and thus to insure subservience to the ruling class:

> Sexual oppression is among the ruling class's key ideological resources in holding down the working population. . . .[49] A moralistic type of sex instruction is linked in human history to the interest of private property. . . .[50] The advance in technology was paralleled by a decline in sexual culture. . . .[51] Possessory interests and greed increased in proportion to the degree that sexual interests had to be suppressed.[52]

Here Reich diverged from Freud, who believed that sexual repression arose from instinctual conflicts and was fundamental to the development of all human society. Reich argued that an analysis of history showed that instinctual conflict was

> a result of a clash between primitive needs (hunger, sexual needs) and the conditions of existence (economy, natural influences, technology). . . .[53]

In an economy of private ownership of the means of production, sexual repression is necessary to maintain compulsory monogamy and the patriarchal family.

> While material privation encompasses only the dominated class, sexual privation is a phenomenon which encompasses all ranks of class society, but which is rooted in the material laws of class society.[54]

Society maintains authoritarian control through the authoritarian institutions of Church, state, school, and family.

> It requires children to obey their parents, and prepares for the later obedience of the adults to the authority of the state and capital by producing fear of authority in all individuals in society.[55]

Therefore, since the dominant class feels sexual freedom to be a threat to its very existence as a class, it fights the poor on two levels: the material level of economics and the ideological level of sexual repressiveness. "Man in the house" welfare laws, which both prohibited an AFDC mother from having a boyfriend in her house and spawned detective units in welfare departments to spy on women's sexual practices [56] served two functions: to insure that welfare payments would not be paid to men whom legislators believed should be forced to work, and to suppress the women's sexuality. South Africa imposes similar restrictions for the same purposes when it breaks up families of poor black laborers.

Many of the social workers whose job it is to judge parental fitness have assumed that a premarital or extramarital sexual affair constituted prima facie evidence of "unfit" parentage. There is a good deal of evidence to the contrary. An outstanding case example is the mother of Malcolm X who, according to Malcolm X, was happier when she had a boyfriend, and more accepting of the children, than at any other time in his childhood that he remembered. On the level of clinical theory, Wilhelm Reich postulated a close correlation between healthy sexual functioning and being a healthy parent. While Masters and Johnson did not specifically study the relationship of parental functioning to sexual functioning, one would hardly conclude from their study that chastity was a healthier state for an adult than a satisfying sex life.[57]

Children's Rights

The Right to a Permanent Home

"You can take the child away from the parent, but you can't take the parent out of the child," runs an old child welfare adage. It does not, however, reflect the practice of a majority of child welfare workers. Probably the majority of child welfare workers subscribe to the following formulation of the professional rescue mission:

> One of the purposes of residential treatment is to neutralize or inactivate temporarily the influence of the child's parent and simultaneously to put the child under the care of adults who can become—partially and temporarily at least—substitute parental figures.[58]

The assumption is, of course, that "bad" parents made the child sick, so the obvious treatment is to keep the parents away from the child and give him "good" parents. Does it work? Work for what? It probably made a small contribution toward turning Malcolm X into a revolutionary. Removing a child from his parent most certainly does not guarantee that the "bad" parent will be replaced by a stable set of parents who will accept him categorically for a life time. Malcolm X believed that his rights as a child were synonymous with his mother's rights as a mother. Yet children are seldom asked how they define their rights and, since the child care system began, professionals have kept children from their parents in the name of "children's rights."

Let us say, for the sake of argument, that a child's most basic need—beyond mere physical survival—is to have at least one person who is committed to giving attention and love until the child grows up. Some people argue that the principal remaining function of the nuclear family is to provide the security of stable kinship ties to children. Maas and Engler proceed from this premise when they indicate that one of the most important of children's rights is the right to a permanent home. By this criterion, none of the nine communities they studied

> approached the problem of children in foster care as, literally, problems of children in need of parents and permanent homes.[59]

Paradoxically, the communities described by Maas and Engler as being most committed to a "children's rights" philosophy did the worst job of providing foster children with permanent homes, except for the healthy white infants who were likely to be adopted. The communities that subscribed to a "parents' rights" philosophy, such as Jamestown, were reluctant to break parental ties. Jamestown placed fewer children in adoptive homes than any of the nine communities and had more children under study returned home than in adoptive placements. A greater proportion of dependent children in Jamestown retained affectionate ties to their parents than in any of the nine communities save one. Jamestown relied heavily on institutional care, which was usually requested by the parents; parents continued to have contact with the child after placement—more so with institutionalized children than with children in foster care.[60] A smaller percentage of Jamestown children (56%) were reported to be confused about their worth, place, and direction, than of Centralia children (67%). (Centralia was the community rated highest on the "children's rights" continuum.) More of the children in Jamestown returned home rather than stay in the limbo of foster care, as they did in Centralia. In Jamestown one child in five placed involuntarily returned home, as compared to none of the involuntarily place children in Centralia who returned home. Children were in care for a shorter time in Jamestown than in Centralia.

Maas and Engler evaluated communities on a parents' rights–children's rights continuum. From a legal point of view, I suggest that a more accurate way to conceptualize the continuum is parents' rights–states' rights. When parents lose legal rights over their children, it is not the children who gain more legal rights, it is the state. Let us begin to consider this by looking at children as property. The concept of parents' rights to their own children may have been created for economic reasons during the feudal period, when custodial rights had a commercial value and were subject to transfer and sale. A child was primarily a financial asset to his father, and a custodial right was essentially a property right.[61] The indenture system was a continuation of children as property, and as late as 1957 in the American city of Jamestown children could be deeded by parents as a piece of property. When property is as jealously guarded as it was by the Southern Bourbons, intrusion by the state is resisted for fear of the state encroaching upon property rights. An Episcopal minister in Jamestown, commenting on the citizens' attitude toward government, said:

> People prefer the private to the state but would defend the state to the Federal Government. If the Federal Government is out of the picture, however, they will turn against the state. And they would throw out county government to get local government.[62]

Now let us consider children as new property, as dealt with by the modern middle class. In order to do this, I shall discuss two of the communities studied by Maas and Engler which were populated by a growing middle class: Centralia, a midwestern city with a population of 100,000, and Westport, a West Coast metropolis with a population of about 750,000. Both of these communities were high on the "children's rights" continuum. Centralia operated under a legal "Children's Code." Both communities were more geared to achievement and upward mobility than were the "parents' rights" communities. Religious ties were weakening and secularism was taking precedence over sectarianism in child care. The Juvenile Court judge in Westport viewed with alarm the tendency toward children being "sovietized" by public agencies, and he objected to the juvenile judge becoming a "mere arm of the welfare department."[63] Both communities were moving toward more achieved homogeneity and impersonality in relationships, i.e., the anonymous mass society. Both communities emphasized adoption rather than the return to home. Following is a comparison of Westport to King City, a racially segregated Southwest metropolis which is of comparable size more traditional in a "parents' rights" emphasis:

> Figures on all those leaving care in a six-month period showed that 36 percent went into adoption in [King city], compared to 52 percent in [Westport], while 57 percent returned home in [King City], compared to 39 percent in [Westport].[64]

While healthy white babies were likely to be adopted in Westport, older foster children and minority children were not faring as well. In this most highly professionalized of all the nine communities, foster children had fewer affectionate ties to their parents than in any other urban community; twice as many parents had lost legal rights to their children than in King City, but Westport foster children were more often confused about their identity than were King City foster children. "The dependent child in Westport reflected the indeterminacy of his unstable position in that community."[65]

Similarly, in Centralia, where agencies were highly professionalized and collaborated with each other a good deal, most children in care were not moving toward the permanent, improved home situations desired for them and more were confused about their identity than in Jamestown. Centralia had a lower proportion of voluntary separation than did any of the other communities. Most of the children were cared for in foster families rather than in institutions. Fewer parents of children in care had continuing relationships with agencies. Centralia had one of the three highest adoption percentages among the nine communities, and one of the lowest return home rates.

To return to the concept of children as property, I suggest that the property of the achieving middle class includes children—one's own if possible, otherwise adopted. Therefore social agencies, which are sponsored and partly funded by white affluent people, give a high priority to meeting the needs of white affluent couples for "perfect" white babies to adopt. The children whom the white middle class does not want to "own"—older children, children with handicaps, children of minority groups—stand a good chance of being left in foster care as the "unwanted surplus." The state pays as little as possible to maintain them, yet the state is reluctant to return them to their parents. The ideology of the professionals who see themselves as "better parents" prevents the children's return home. "Child welfare" is often a euphemism for control of the poor by the middle and upper classes. Juvenile court judges and welfare agencies act as the arm of the state to achieve this control. The child welfare system has become a dumping ground for the children of the dispossessed. In child welfare as elsewhere, "the trend is toward the bourgeois-smug."[66]

The Right to a Stable Identity

There is a continual tension in the foster care system about whether, and how often, children should have contact with their natural parents. Social workers are of two minds about it, although they are more likely than foster parents to allow parental contact. Most often they act as brokers to negotiate frequency and location of parental contact. They seldom allow foster parents to make these arrangements on their own, and almost never allow the children to do so. Most social workers display a remarkable lack of curiosity about the long-range effects of parental contacts on children's developing identity. Rather, social workers generally react to foster parents' anxieties, or to parents' or children's entreaties— performing constant ad hoc balancing acts between foster parents and parents. The situation is simpler when a child is in an institution, since child care workers do not have as intense an emotional investment in children as do foster parents. Foster parents are more likely to be in competition with parents for the child's affection. This is one of the reasons that parents often prefer institutional care to foster care and are more likely to request it voluntarily than they are to request foster care.

Research findings on the identity of children in foster care are scanty, but seem to lean toward the conclusion that maintaining natural kinship ties of children older than infants serves children better than cutting off such ties. When parents cannot care for their own children, relatives apparently do a better job of it than either foster homes or institutions, according to one study done in Scotland.[67] Jenkins and Sauber recommend paying relatives and friends, if any are available, to care for children, rather than placing children in foster care.[68]

Are children in foster care and institutions better off if they continue contact with their parents, even if they do not return home? The evidence is mixed, but leans in the direction of an affirmative answer. Weinstein asked the children themselves (a rather unusual practice in foster care research). He studied the self-image of sixty-one children in foster care, and concluded that

> continuing contact between the child and his own parents had an ameliora-
> tive effect on the otherwise detrimental effects of long-term foster care.
> The average well-being of youngsters whose parents visited them regularly
> was significantly higher than children who did not have contact with their
> natural parents. This was true even when the children had been in foster
> care for long periods.[69]

Children who identified with natural parents rather than with foster parents had the highest well-being ratings of any group in the study, while those who identified most with foster parents or who had mixed identification achieved significantly lower ratings. Trasler [70] found that the major cause of breakdown of foster placement was the child's emotional reaction to previous rejection, and suggested that this could be alleviated by encouraging parental contact and by helping the child to talk often about his separation experiences. Murphy [71] found that a foster mother's hostile attitude toward the natural mother was associated with a poor placement outcome. Pringle and Clifford [72] interviewed housemothers in English residential institutions to determine what factors led to "notably stable" and "notably unstable" adjustments of the children. They found a strong link between good adjustment and continued contact with relatives or family substitutes. Contact with parents was also associated with a higher learning ability.

On the other hand, George [73] found no relationship between frequency of parental visits and outcome of foster placement. Few of the children in his study were visited frequently. Mech [74] found more anxiety among children visited by their parents, especially among the girls. The mere presence of anxiety, however, should not necessarily be taken as a bad sign. Foster parents often ask to have parental visiting stopped or limited because "it upsets the children." I believe that the foster parents who are more sensitively attuned to children's feelings recognize that these upset feelings are necessary and desirable. This is illustrated by the foster parents' discussion of 5-13-69 in Appendix A. One of the most serious things that happens to foster children is their repression of grief and rage, which results in a state of "emotional deep freeze" that can stunt the child's personality development for life.

The Right to Share in Decisions Affecting Their Lives

Foster children are often moved about from one home to another as casually as pawns on a chess board. They are often not consulted about their wishes or given any reason why they are leaving a home, nor are they often given any choice about the home to which they move. More often than not, they have not met their new foster parents before they move.

A good deal of foster care work by social workers, especially in public agencies, consists of reacting to emergencies. A foster mother calls to say that she will not care for a child another day; the worker frantically searches among other foster parents for another home; she drives out to get the child and his belongings, and the child leaves one home in an atmosphere of bitterness, and enters another with fear and trembling. Some social workers will argue that, given the shortage of funds and staff, they cannot do differently. They are partly right. The federal government and the states do not allocate enough funds to care for children adequately.[75] Yet, even under the present miserable working conditions, social workers would save themselves trouble with a child in his future home if they insisted upon taking the time to do careful work with the child around his feelings of loss, rage, and guilt, and if they insisted upon several preplacement visits and careful preparation for the next home. Several studies show that children can accept separation and loss better when they have some clear idea of why they are in foster care and of what will happen to them in the future, and if they are consulted about plans made for them.[76] Perhaps a good deal of this clarification can be accomplished best by working with foster children in groups, where they can get peer support. Peterson and Sturgies give a good description of one such group.[77] I once worked with a group of adolescents at a public welfare department in Colorado, and was impressed with how much the youth supported each other, and how much courage this group support gave them to challenge the welfare department on important issues affecting their lives. The group was requested spontaneously by the youth, as an outgrowth of their foster parents meeting as a group to discuss common issues.

We do not know much for certain about how to help people, but one of the most certain findings of research is that people feel better when they have a say in what happens to them. This is as true of children as of adults. Children are by definition relatively helpless and powerless. They cannot get much power by themselves because they are under the control of their parents in small private family units, they are unorganized, and they do not vote. Therefore they do not get their fair share of society's resources and they have little say in what resources they want or how they may use them.[78] Judges consider a child's own feelings toward parents or his environmental conditions as relatively unimportant and often irrelevant.[79]

> The law has not yet formally recognized in its procedure a child's competency to express its own feelings or to know its own best interests, save in isolated instances.[80]

Social workers claim to be attuned to the child's wishes, yet generally do not offer a child an informed choice of whether to go into placement, or a choice among different homes. An *informed* choice would involve much discussion, several preplacement visits, perhaps to more than one home, and intensive follow-up work. State agencies usually do not have the time and money for this; private agencies often do not either, and if they do, may not consider it important. The situation was quite different in Samoa and Tikopia when Mead [81] and Firth did their studies; there a child chose the person he wanted to stay with, and left home temporarily when pressures were too great. In most of the Oceanic societies where adoption is common, the burden of winning a child's love is on the adoptive parents, and the adoptive or foster parents show great respect for the child's wishes. In some of these societies, it is the adoptive parents who are disgraced if the child chooses to return to his natal family. In American society, on the other hand, it is the child who bears the brunt of stigma if he runs away from home. If he runs, he generally runs to no one in particular; there is no institutionalized escape from the family.

It would be difficult, if not impossible, to devise such an institutionalized escape without changing American values and norms about children being the exclusive possession of their parents. This shift in values toward children probably will not come unless there is a shift in property relations—from private ownership to communal ownership and citizens' control of the means of production and of community services. I do not mean state control, whether it is called communism, capitalism, or social democracy. State control of the means of production involves some state control of children, the future producers. Such state control—always and everywhere—means control of the many by the bureaucratic few.

The Hegemony of the Professionals

It is hard to escape the conclusion that social workers benefit most from the foster care system, through the jobs it provides them. The jobs do not pay very well, but nevertheless they are jobs. Foster parents also benefit, but less than social workers since they are paid so poorly. There are complex reasons for perpetuating a dysfunctional system, but in sorting the reasons, one should not overlook the obvious fact that it *does* generate jobs for the staff. Possibly this is why social workers were given the job of administering the categorical welfare system after the 1935 Social Security Act was passed; the middle class needed jobs. A dramatic illustration of this occurred in Massachusetts recently, when citizens' groups and legislators tried to close three county training schools that cared for truant children. From any enlightened point of view the schools were dysfunctional: antiquated in concept, expensive, badly staffed, and cruel to children. But political patronage was rampant in staffing and maintenance, and the resistance by staff and their political friends to closing the institutions was incredibly fierce.

While it would be simplistic to say that such vested interests are the only reasons that a bad system continues, there is no doubt that the power of the professionals over foster children *is* expanding, and the professionals inevitably define their job according to their particular perspective on what is good for children. Most child welfare professionals have not seriously come to grips with the issue of kinship and its relationship to emotional security and social status. The theory that guides social workers (when they are guided by any theory) is more individualistic and intrapsychic than sociological. Most agencies muddle through on the kinship issue. When an agency stops muddling through and takes a clear stand on kinship, it is likely to go in the direction of cutting off ties from the natal family. An extreme example of this is the Iowa Children's Home Society, which is experimenting with what they call the "parental force" theory.[82] The basic concept in this philosophy, which grew out of Rankian theory, is that the agency becomes the parent of the child it accepts for care—either by a direct release from the parents or through court action. Each child has two case workers: one the "parental force" worker, who behaves as a parent, and the other, the therapist. The foster parents in the home and the child care workers in the institution are directed to act not as either parent or therapist, but simply as caretaking and loving people. The agency claims that this division of functions clarifies a child's status, reduces the child's anxiety, and shortens the time in care. Foster parents, social workers, and child care workers may come and go, but "the agency is the entity the child can accept as the secure, unchanging force in his life. . . .[83]

Research is continuing on this project, and perhaps it is too soon to pass judgment on it. It raises a critical sociological question: "Can an institution be an adequate substitute for parents?" The usual sociological definition of the family assumes a face-to-face primary group of people in continuous intimate contact with each other. How does an institution as parent fit into the customary sociological model of the family, and how does it shape a child's developing identity? The foster parent is apparently granted limited autonomy in reacting spontaneously to a child's emotional outburst, as evidenced by this example narrated by a foster mother:

> She had this crying spell—"I wish my mother and father were back together again, and I wish we could all be together as a family—this would make me happy!" And I agreed that it would and that I was sorry this couldn't be. She really cried—she sobbed and cried, and I gave her affection and kept repeating that I did understand. She asked me whether I had a happy childhood. *I evaded that question. Then I said, "Now you want to remember this is what you want to talk with your caseworker about when you see her."*[84] (Emphasis added.)

"Parental force" not only deprives the parents of their rights: it also deprives the foster parents of some of their spontaneity. It gives social workers and physchiatrists total control. It may be an improvement over the usual ambiguous status of a child in foster care, and it has the advantage of clarifying a child's status, but it has the insidious possibility of further institutionalizing the "rescue" mission of middle-class professionals acting for the state. When parents are excluded and child care workers are stripped of their autonomy, the balance of power in the child care system shifts still more toward the professionals acting for the state. This represents a political choice, although it is called "treatment."

Notes to Chapter Four

1. *The Autobiography of Malcolm X*, Grove Press, N.Y., 1965, pp. 20–21.
2. The stated function of foster care is primarily to provide short-term care for children during family crises, or to care for children who have been legally relinquished by their parents until the children are adopted. Social workers are supposed to help the family surmount the crisis or "rehabilitate" itself while the child is in care so that the child can return home. For the child available for adoption, social workers are supposed to find the adoptive home. In practice, foster care becomes long term for a majority of the children. Those who stay in care longer than a year are likely to grow up in foster care. In the communities studied by Maas and Engler, most child welfare workers had little or no regular contact with the natural parents of the children in foster care. If the parents changed for the better, they changed themselves. The agencies did not ask for financial contributions from most of the parents. Helping to pay for foster care gives parents some concrete way of holding on to their children, and agencies seem to want this less now than they did in 1954.

The expanding role of the state in foster care is shown by the increased proportion of state funds as compared to private funds and parental contributions in the past two decades. In 1970, natural parents provided as much as 5% of the foster care budget for 37% of public and voluntary agencies, as compared to parental contributions of over 5% of the budget in 55% of agencies surveyed in 1954. Purchase-of-service payments from public agencies in 1970 made up 53% of voluntary agency budgets, which means that the majority of foster children are supported by the state rather than by the natural parents and private funds, even when they are placed by private agencies. [*Board Rates for Foster Family Care* (N.Y.: Child Welfare League of America, 1970), pp. 4–5.]

 A comparison of public and voluntary agency foster care between 1933 and 1969 also shows the expanding role of the state. In 1933, 46.7% of foster care was done by public agencies and 53.3% by voluntary agencies. In 1969, 82.3% was public and 17.7% private. The proportion of public and private institutional care remained about the same; 16% public and 84% private in 1933; 16.7% public and 83.3% private in 1969. (*Child Welfare Statistics*, NCSS Report CW-1 (69) US/ DHEW, SRS, 1969, table 24, p. 30.

 3. Both specialists and laymen disagree on whether and when adopted children should be told of their origins. Social workers have traditionally urged early and full sharing of information about adoption, but some psychiatrists believe the child should be past the Oedipal stage when (s)he is told. Studies on "telling" are contradictory—partly, I believe, because few studies seek the opinions of the children themselves. Jaffee and Fanshel's follow-up study interviewed only adoptive parents and concluded that "telling" was not critical to a child's adjustment (pp. 263–268). Studies that interview the adopted children after they are adults, however, all conclude that the children want their adoptive parents to "offer sufficient information for them to obtain some sense of their origins," and they consider it the parents' responsibility to initiate the discussion. [Alfred Kadushin, "Child Welfare," in *Research in the Social Services*, ed. by Henry Maas (N.Y.: National Association of Social Workers, 1971), p. 19.] Paton postulates that when adoptive parents are not threatened by the child's search for natural parents and sometimes even help in the search, the child resolves his anxieties about adoption more easily than does the child whose parents are threatened by the search. [Jean Paton, *The Adopted Break Silence* (Acton, Calif.: Life History Study Center, 1954).] Only a small percentage of adopted children do conduct a search for their parents, as evidenced in Scotland, where an adopted child aged 17 and over is allowed to apply to the Register House for information about his biological parents from the original birth certificate. About 3% of adopted children conduct the search, usually when the adoption had been very unhappy. "That the knowledge can be made available as a right is said often to be sufficient to satisfy the needs of an adopted person." [Standing Committee of Agencies Registered for Adoption, "Adoptees' Right to Know," *Child Adoption*, no. 53, (1968): 30–31.] Paton, however, says that many children want to conduct the search but refrain for fear of hurting their adoptive parents' feelings.

 4. Benson Jaffee and Draza Kline, *New Payment Patterns and the Foster Parent Role* (N.Y.: Child Welfare League of America, 1970), p. 46.

 5. Martin Wolins, *Selecting Foster Parents* (N.Y.: Columbia University Press, 1963).

 6. Some of the foster parents in the 1970 study worked for an agency whose explicit purpose was to create a kind of "psychological adoption" for foster children, an objective that probably encouraged excluding natural parents.

However, the same trend toward excluding parents was evident in the agencies that did not try to create an adoptionlike placement situation. The main thrust of reforms in the foster parent system is toward creating a quasi-adoptive relationship between foster children and their foster parents, rather than involving the natural parents more fully [see, for example, *Foster Care in Question* (N.Y.: Child Welfare League of America, 1970); Alfred Kadushin, "The Legally Adoptable Unadopted Child," *Child Welfare*, vol. 37, no. 18 (1958): 19–25.] The efforts of Child and Family Services of Hartford, Conn., to engage foster parents in work with natural parents were atypical in the field, but demonstrate that at least some foster parents are able and eager to work with natural parents.

7. The 1967 Gault decision by the Supreme Court (In Re Gault, 387 U.S. 1) "did not restore juveniles to the rank of 'persons' guaranteed all the protection of the Constitution," but it did grant juveniles four procedural rights in hearings: (1) the right to notice of charges; (2) the right to confront witnesses and the privilege against self-incrimination; (3) the right to appeal, and (4) the right to counsel. [Lois G. Forer, *"No One Will Lissen"* (N.Y.: Grosset and Dunlap, Universal Library Edition, 1971), p. 32.]

8. For a discussion of the state's role in infantilizing parents of juveniles, see Forer, Chap. 11, "Parental State: Infantilized Parents," pp. 220–233.

9. Maas and Engler found that in the New England town of Brighton, foster children became more psychologically disturbed while in foster care than when they first came into care. Sixty-one percent of the foster children were confused about their identity. The children who returned home, however, were less likely to have psychological symptoms than were the children who stayed in foster care.

10. A recent Seattle study showed that more than 6 of 10 foster children had undergone four or more moves. Half had been moved from four to seven times, and 12% had between eight and seventeen different placements. Only 5% remained in one home. (Jaffee and Kline, *New Payment Patterns*, p. 46.) Such dismal statistics clearly put the burden of proof upon the state to demonstrate that the state is, in fact, the better parent. Earlier studies showed somewhat fewer moves for children. [Helen R. Jeter, *Children, Problems, and Services in Child Welfare Programs* (Washington, D.C.: U.S. Government Printing Office, 1963); Henry Maas and Richard Engler, *Children in Need of Parents* (N.Y.: Columbia University Press, 1959), p. 422.]

11. Sanford N. Katz, *When Parents Fail* (Boston: Beacon Press, 1971), p. 63.

12. Leichter et al., *Kinship and Casework*, Russell Sage Foundation, N.Y., 1967. Cited by Scott Briar and Hnery Miller, *Problems and Issues in Social Casework*, Columbia University Press, N.Y., 1971, p. 197.

13. Katz, p. 42.

14. Katz, p. 65.

15. The following two statements illustrate the discrepancy between an official perception of a military school, and a student's perception:

"A real military academy is appealing to almost every young red-blooded American boy."
Brochure, General Douglas MacArthur Military Academy
"Nobody wants to be here. We're here because we were put here."
—Cadet, Lake Elsinore Military Academcy

(From "Military Prep Schools in Decline" by William Endicott, *The Los Angeles Times*, reprinted in *Boston Sunday Globe*, 9 May 1971, Sec. B-1.)

16. This is changing. Recently the Roxbury community of Boston refused to allow Harvard researchers access to their black children, reasoning that the community would not benefit from the findings—whatever they were—in the present repressive political climate.

17. Katz, p. 56.

18. Ibid., p. 68.

19. Ibid., p. 69.

20. Ibid., pp. 87–88.

21. Ibid., p. 76.

22. Ibid., p. 78.

23. Ibid., p. 24.

24. Ibid., p. 41.

25. Maas and Engler, p. 315.

26. "An empirical study conducted by the *Columbia Journal of Law and Social Problems* revealed that in 1966, 76 percent of all respondents (parents) in neglect cases of the Kings County (Brooklyn) Family Court did not have counsel at any hearing. . . . 'Representation in Child-Neglect Cases: Are Parents Neglected?' 4 *Columbia Journal of Law and Social Problems* 230, 1968." Cited by Katz, p. 51.

27. Katz, p. 77.

28. Winifred Bell, *Aid to Dependent Children* (N.Y.: Columbia University Press, 1965). This is a thorough documentation of the political manipulation of ADC mothers and children by welfare officials and state legislators. Much of this manipulation was an expression of racism, since repressive policies were directed most heavily against black people, especially in southern states. Bell discusses the vague "suitable home" laws enacted by many southern states which led to welfare officials removing children from homes of ADC recipients despite evidence of good parental care.

29. Frances Fox Piven and Richard Cloward, *Regulating the Poor* (N.Y.: Vintage Books, 1971).

30. Joseph Ritz, *The Despised Poor: Newburgh's War on Welfare* (Boston: Beacon Press, 1966), is a discussion of how City Manager Joseph Mitchell of Newburgh, N.Y., used the welfare issue in an attempt to advance his own political career. Mitchell threatened to place in foster homes out-of-wedlock children born to AFDC mothers if they had more than one out-of-wedlock child.

31. I discuss the totalitarian features of the welfare system, including the threat to remove children, in my two-part article, "Welfare and Totalitarianism," *Social Work*, January and April 1971.

32. Shirley Jenkins and Elaine Norman, "Families of Children in Foster Care," *Children,* vol. 16, no. 4, July–August (1969).

33. Katz, p. 25.

34. Jenkins and Norman, p. 158.

35. Shirley Jenkins, *Priorities in Social Services: A Guide for Philanthropic Funding*, Vol. 1, Child Welfare in New York City, Praeger Special Studies in U.S. Economic and Social Development (N.Y.: Praeger Publishers, 1971).

36. Jenkins and Norman, p. 88.

37. Maas and Engler, p. 354.

38. Ibid., p. 87.

39. Andrew Billingsley and Jeanne M. Giovannoni, *Children of the Storm* (N.Y.: Harcourt Brace Jovanovich, 1972), p. 24.

40. Forer, p. 230.

41. Ibid., p. 231.

42. Maas and Engler, p. 150.

43. For thorough documentation of these practices, see Bell, *Aid to Dependent Children*.

44. *New York Times*, 13 February 1972, citing a study by David Fanshel and Eugene B. Shinn, "Dollars and Sense in the Foster Care of Children: A Look at Cost Factors."

45. Bell, pp. 182–183, cites the only follow-up study done on families affected by the "suitable home" laws which cut off ADC assistance. Before ADC was discontinued in Mississippi between 1954 and 1956, 41.5% of the children of ADC recipients were illegitimate; when the families were interviewed in 1957, 91.4% of the children born in the intervening period were illegitimate. Most parents had found only sporadic, poorly paid, seasonal employment.

46. Bronislaw Malinowski, *The Sexual Life of Savages* (1929) (Harvest Book, paperback ed., 1969).

47. "The Imposition of Sexual Morality" (1932; 2d ed., 1935), From Sex-Pol: Essays 1929–1934, by Wilhelm Reich, edited by Lee Baxandall, Copyright © 1966, 1971 by Lee Baxandall. Reprinted by permission of Random House, Inc.

48. Ibid., p. 227.

49. Ibid., p. 101.

50. Ibid., p. 127.

51. Ibid., p. 227.

52. Ibid., p. 230.

53. Ibid., p. 231.

54. Ibid., p. 237.

55. Ibid., p. 245.

56. "Man in the house," laws were declared unconstitutional in 1968 by the U.S. Supreme Court in the case of King v. Smith, which denied the right of a state to refuse assistance on the grounds of a mother's relationship with a male who was not her husband.

57. William H. Masters and Virginia E. Johnson, *Human Sexual Response* (Boston: Little, Brown, 1966).

58. Morris Fritz Mayer, "The Parental Figures in Residential Treatment," *Social Service Review*, vol. 34, no. 3 (1960): 273.

59. Ibid., p. 284.

60. Institutions were privately owned, while the state handled foster care. When the state handles substitute care, it is much more likely to place children in foster homes than in institutions. The reason most often given for this is that a foster home more nearly duplicates the natural family. I think another reason is that foster care is much cheaper than institutional care. A cost analysis of substitute care in New York City in 1970 showed that foster care costs an average of $10.08 a child a day, as compared with $15.09 for an agency-operated boarding home, $20.52 for a group residence, $20.88 for large-scale institutional care, and $25.32 for a residential treatment facility. (*New York Times*, 13 February 1972. Citing Fanshel and Shinn.) Of course, one reason that foster care is so cheap is that the

foster parents are paid so little. They have been isolated and unorganized, and therefore have not agitated as a group for higher pay or better working conditions. Organization of foster parent groups has begun recently, aided by the Child Welfare League of America.

61. Katz, p. 4. Katz gives a good discussion of parental rights from a legal point of view.

62. Maas and Engler, p. 158.

63. Ibid., p. 245.

64. Ibid., p. 269.

65. Ibid., p. 284

66. Günter Grass, *The Tin Drum* (Greenwich, Conn.: Fawcett Publications, 1967), p. 326.

67. T. Ferguson, *Children in Care—and After* (London: Oxford University Press, 1966).

68. Shirley Jenkins and Mignon Sauber, *Paths to Child Placement*; Family Situations Prior to Foster Care (N.Y.: Community Council of Greater New York and New York City Department of Welfare, 1966).

69. Eugene Weinstein, *The Self-Image of the Foster Child* (N.Y.: Russell Sage Foundation, 1960), p. 17.

70. Gordon Trasler, "A Study of Success and Failure of Foster Home Placements" (Ph.D. diss., London University, 1955).

71. H. B. M. Murphy, "Foster Home Variables and Adult Outcomes," *Mental Hygiene*, 48 (1964): 587–599.

72. M. L. Kellmer Pringle and L. Clifford, "Conditions Associated with Emotional Maladjustment among Children in Care," *Educational Review*, vol. 14, no. 2 (1962): 112–123.

73. V. George, *Foster Care* (London: Routledge and Kegan Paul, 1970), pp. 185–186.

74. Edmund Mech, "Manifest Anxiety in Foster Home Children" (Master's thesis, Bryn Mawr College, 1959).

75. Most of the public funds for foster care are paid by the states. The federal government pays only about 10% of foster care expenses, as compared to paying one-half to three-quarters of the expenses for the disabled, aged, handicapped, and other programs for the disadvantaged. Children in foster care receive less federal financing than any other major group of the federal government. [Joseph H. Reid, "Patterns of Partnership" (Unpublished mimeo. N.Y.: Child Welfare League of America, 8 November 1969).]

76. Carolyn B. Thomas, "The Resolution of Object Loss Following Foster Home Placement," *Smith College Studies in Social Work*, vol. 36, no. 3 (June 1967); Robert Holman, "The Foster Child and Self-Knowledge," *Case Conference*, vol. 12, no. 11 (March 1966): 295–298; Weinstein, "The Self-Image of the Foster Child."

Parker found that placements preceded by more than five pre-placement visits were slightly more successful than placements where there had been fewer than five pre-placement visits. [R. A. Parker, *Decision in Child Care* (London: Allen and Unwin, 1966).]

77. J. B. Peterson and C. H. Sturgies, "Public Welfare: Group Work with Adolescents in a Public Foster Care Agency," in *The Practice of Group Work*, ed. by William Schwartz and Serapio Zalba (N.Y.: Columbia University Press, 1971).

78. A striking example of this is the distribution of resources for children in the Massachusetts Department of Mental Health. While children comprise 40% of the state population, they receive from only 4 to 13% of the resources of the Department of Mental Health. [*Suffer the Children: The Politics of Mental Health in Massachusetts* (Boston: Task Force on Children Out of School, Inc., 1972), p. 98.]

79. Katz, p. 59.

80. Ibid., p. 60.

81. Margaret Mead, *Coming of Age in Samoa* (N.Y.: Mentor Book, New American Library, 1949); Raymond Firth, *We, The Tikopia* (Boston: Beacon Press, 1963).

82. Edith Zober and Merlin Taber, "The Child Welfare Agency as Parent," *Child Welfare*, vol. 44, no. 7 (July 1965).

83. Ibid., p. 389.

84. Ibid., p. 390.

Addendum

As we went to press, the *New York Times* published some interesting facts about adoptees searching for their natural parents. A private detective, Ed Goldfader, president of Tracer's Company of America, reported that, beginning last year, adoptees searching for their natural parents constituted a large new clientele for his agency:

> In 1972, we received 1,514 requests from adoptees wanting to trace their natural parents. Most of the requests came from women. Some were concerned about the possibility of passing hereditary illnesses on to their own offspring. Many had waited until their adoptive parents had died, because they didn't want to hurt their feelings. But all of them expressed a great curiosity about their biological identities and reported feelings of insecurity and of going through an "identity crisis." (John Culhane, "The Cases of the Runaway Wives," *The New York Times Magazine*, 10 June 1973, p. 90.)

CHAPTER FIVE
THE STATUS OF WOMEN IN
CHILD WELFARE

*Let us, then, no longer sit idly by, and allow men to take the
sole or chief management in the education of destitute children,
of whose needs they are not the most competent judges. Let us
come to the rescue of the little ones.*

Mrs. Hannah Archer, "To the Rescue," in *Now-a-Days*, July 1869[1]

As I write about the child welfare system, the pronoun "she" usually
comes to mind rather than the conventional "he." That is not because of a feminist
effort of will to demasculinize the language: it is because most of the people I
have known in child welfare agencies were women—except for the children,
administrators, and psychiatrists. Of the seven child welfare agencies where I have
worked in the United States and Canada, women comprised the majority of
adoption workers [2], and all of the workers who saw unmarried mothers. Four of
the directors were men. Most of the parents I saw were mothers; most of the foster
parents I worked with were foster mothers. I did not do adoption work, but
adoption workers seemed to see the woman and the man of the applicant couple
with about equal frequency. If one was seen more than the other, it was the
woman.[3] By an overwhelming majority, women staff the line ranks of the child
care system and husbandless women supply the children for it. The differential
status of women and men is evident at every level of the child care system, and
each position in the system reveals another facet of these status differences in
society. I shall examine several positions in the system.

The Unmarried Mother

Unmarried mothers supply most of the children for adoptive couples. The
number of their children available for adoption is decreasing because both contra-
ceptive devices and abortions are easier to get, and because there is less stigma
attached to keeping illegitimate children—at least in some circles. Current attitudes
toward adoption are much more accepting than were attitudes in the late nineteenth
and early twentieth centures, when legislators resisted adoption because it would
make it easy for an unmarried mother to get rid of the "fruits of her sin." The
legislators feared that providing such a social outlet for giving up babies would
encourage more "sinning," and ultimately undermine the structure of the family
and of society itself. This is the same concern voiced by missionaries and administrators in Rangiroa Atoll and Ponape. In those islands, the Western moralists saw

adoption as linked to permissive sexuality, and they resisted both. As late as 1948 in England, adoption societies were still being accused of encouraging immorality. The Princess Alice, Countess of Athlone, reassured adoption workers that their work was Christian and not immoral.[4]

Nineteenth-century legislators in England were so afraid of the possibility of adoption undermining the family that they required a probation period of about six years to avoid fraud.[5] The fraud they feared was the possibility of adoptive couples willing their estate to other than "legitimate" heirs. In the face of these (male) fears, the English adoption societies of the early twentieth century were among the first to tell the public that even "quite nice girls" got into trouble and produced babies who were a "social problem."[6] Adoption was, in fact, a woman's liberation program of the early twentieth century, along with the drive for woman's suffrage. The first adoption agency in England, established in 1912, was the Adoption Committee of the Cambridge Branch of the Church League for Women's Suffrage. Their aim was to "rehabilitate" unmarried mothers and to turn unwanted into wanted children.[7]

As late as 1952, the British adoption specialist Margaret Kornitzer still revealed some squeamishness about the possibility of adoption encouraging immorality:

> Nor has the mother of an illegitimate child the *right* to get it adopted. In fact most champions of a good adoption code are anxious that adoption should not in any way be considered an easy means of getting rid of the results of sin. There is some evidence that a mother relieved of one illegitimate child may soon have others, and to say that adoption is good for the child is not the same thing as saying that it is good for the mother.[8]

Kornitzer goes on to say, however, that social conditions are against the mother who wants to keep her baby, and if the mother gives up the baby for adoption she must accept that

> everything possible is done—in practice as well as in law—to dismiss the natural mother utterly from the child's life.[9]

Otherwise, she claims, the adoption will not succeed. She advises against grandparents adopting the child, and says that the putative father will not be considered as an adopter, except in unusual circumstances as when he is married and his wife consents to the adoption.

When social workers advise an unmarried mother to give the baby up for adoption and advise against the mother's relatives adopting, and when laws prevent the father from adopting, children are more likely to be adopted by strangers. I suspect that such "treatment" prescriptions by social workers mask the most important function of nonrelative adoptions: to provide babies for childless couples. In the United States at least, fears about adoption encouraging immorality have receded in the face of middle- and upper-class couples' desire for children.

Adoption workers would deny that their first priority is finding babies for couples. They claim to be concerned primarily with the best welfare of the unmarried mother and her child. They are no doubt sincere in this disclaimer. However, the workers who see unmarried mothers often also work with adoptive applicants. Even when different workers see the mother and the applicants, they are almost always in regular contact with each other and coordinating their work in the same agency. The pressure of adoptive applicants for babies is great, and the workers must please the applicants as well as the unmarried mothers. Adoption agencies, unlike most agencies, traditionally have often had some recipients of service (adoptive parents) on their boards of directors. Board members sometimes pressure the agency to give special attention to friends who want babies. Whether or not the agency complies—and most agencies probably do not comply in any obvious way—they cannot be impervious to their sources of funding. Therefore, it is not surprising when workers emphasize the social difficulties an unmarried mother will encounter in keeping her baby, rather than the possible advantages of keeping the baby.

In terms of concrete services offered to the unmarried mother, an agency is far more likely to have for unmarried mothers a residence home where the women can get good prenatal and obstetrical care than a day nursery, homemaker service, or home nursing for a mother who keeps her baby. The residence home will help to insure that the baby will be healthy and properly delivered and that the social worker can be in close contact with the unmarried mother. These homes for unmarried mothers have served relatively few minority group women, and in the South they have been racially segregated.

The adoption picture regarding black adoptable babies gives further evidence that agencies have been more intent on providing white couples with babies than on meeting needs of all unmarried mothers. Adoption workers often told themselves and others that many black children were not adopted because black mothers prefer to keep their babies, due to their particular cultural values. Billingsley and Giovannoni [10] laid that myth to rest by showing that black babies are adopted when agencies attuned to the black community take on the job of finding black adoptive couples. Agencies run by white middle-class staff have made many black adoptive applicants feel so uncomfortable that they withdraw their application after one interview.[11]

The sexual revolution and the women's liberation movement are forcing changes in the kinds of services agencies offer. Recently in Boston the Florence Crittendon Home, formerly only a prenatal residence, opened a clinic to perform abortions. In the process of making the shift, it encountered a good deal of resistance from some board members and some sectors of the community. United Community Services, the centralized funding agency, withheld funds from the Crittendon Home when it announced plans to perform abortions. The American Civil Liberties Union fought the UCS action by urging people to earmark their contributions to the Crittendon Home. As a result, the Crittendon Home received more money than they would have with UCS funding. Such are the morality struggles in Boston.

The Illegitimate Child

The illegitimate child derives its status from the status of its unmarried mother. The stigmatized social status of the bastard [12] bears out Engels' thesis that the patriarchal family serves the function of keeping property within the family. In medieval times, the feudal system of land tenure was based on the family. Only children born in wedlock could achieve the status of legitimacy.[13] The illegitimate child had no recognized kin and was known as *filius nullius*, the child of nobody, or *filius populi*, the child of everybody. Although the "blood" relationship between the child and his natural parents was not ignored, the child was nobody's child when it came to inheriting property. Inheritance in the Middle Ages involved not only property, but also status associated with entrance to the trade guilds and corporations, open to legitimate sons of freemen, but closed to illegitimates.[14] The natural parents were not responsible for the child's support, and had no right to his custody. A court-appointed guardian granted consent for marriage when the child was a minor. After the Reformation,

> the statement that the illegitimate child was a stranger in blood to his own kin was taken literally and applied across the board. . . .[15]

Gradually the child's kin ties to the mother were reestablished, but only for the purposes of support, in order to avoid burdening the parish with his support. By 1872 in England, the mother was allowed to sue the father for support up to five shillings per week. Even when the father could be sued for support to recover costs for the parish, however, the mother was never relieved of her primary liability for the child's support. The father might give partial support, but he could not gain custody if the mother wished to keep the child. Nor could the child inherit from the father.

> Indeed, at this time, the child could not acquire a father for all purposes except by a private Act of Parliament. No other method of legitimation was available; even the subsequent marriage of the natural parents, recognized by the church as sufficient to give the child legitimate status, was not recognized by the common law. It was truly said of English law at this period, that "once a bastard, always a bastard, and nothing but a bastard."[16]

The sociologist Kingsley Davis says that this law, called by him the "rule of noninheritance" from the father, is to protect the father's legal family.[17] The "rule of nondescent" decrees that an illegitimate child can begin a family line but cannot continue one. The child will be attached to the one that is not lineally significant. Society faces a conflict between the need to separate the child from his procreators and the need to attach the responsibility of his support on to the parents. However, strict laws would defeat the principle of paternal nonattachment to the illegitimate child, so there are many legal loopholes. Davis argues that the only way to eliminate illegitimacy would be to eliminate marriage and the family. This method, he says, would also abolish society since the the family is the basic institution of society. Obviously he is not in favor of that. Therefore, illegitimacy, he adds, cannot be abolished and must be condemned by society, because failure to condemn it would result in unfavorable attitudes toward the system.

Precisely! To abolish illegitimacy would create serious inroads into the family as the basic unit for maintaining private property through the system of inheritance. After the Russian Revolution, the Bolsheviks did away with all legal distinctions between legitimate and illegitimate children. During the Stalinist regime, however, the family was strengthened and the attitude toward illegitimate children changed, so that children carried the mother's name rather than the father's name and the unmarried mother could not hold the father for support. The law which codified this

> adopted the principle of the Code Napoléon: *"La recherche de la paternité est interdite."*[18]

Davis claims that all societies condemn illegitimacy. This is not true. Tahitians attach no social stigma to illegitimacy, although French law under which they now live does, and neither do Ponapeans. The reason for this, I think, lies in different traditions of property ownership and kinship. Tahiti and Ponape have a tradition of communal ownership of property and of children, while France has a tradition of private ownership of property and children.

Most states in the U.S. have "mitigated more or less the rigors of the common law and conferred upon illegitimate children rights which that law denied."[19] In many states, legitimation may be effected by the putative father acknowledging the child. Some states require open and public acknowledgment.[20] Some states provide for legitimation by the father receiving the child into his family, with the consent of his wife, and treating it as a legitimate child.[21] Generally the father's domicile prevails, not the mother's.[22] Usually legitimation equalizes children born out-of-wedlock with legitimate children.[23] For purposes of inheritance, the common law recognizes that an illegitimate child has a mother. Statutes in almost all states at least allow an illegitimate child to inherit from the mother,[24] but some courts do not allow inheritance from the mother's ancestors or collateral relatives.[25] Some courts allow inheritance by illegitimate children only when there are no legitimate children.[26]

> Common law disabilities of the illegitimate are relaxed or removed only to the extent that the legislature has seen fit to remove them, and no rights of inheritance can exist in any case which is not within the statute.[27]

Some states place limitations on the right of the father to give property to illegitimate children, at least when he has a lawful wife and children or descendants.[28] If illegitimate children are not declared heirs by statute, they are rarely entitled to inherit a gift unless the will includes them.[29] The common law rule is that the word "child" or "children" in a will means a legitimate child.[30]

The legal distinction between adoption and legitimation is

marked and in some contingencies far-reaching. Legitimation, as distinguished from adoption, refers to persons between whom a blood relation exists.[31]

Some statutes providing for legitimation use the term "adopt" instead of "legitimate." A court may render a decree for adoption with the capacity to inherit without legitimating the child.[32]

In matters of custody, until 1972,

> all jurisdictions of the U.S. recognize that the mother, if a suitable person, is the natural guardian of her bastard, and, as such, has a legal right to its custody, care, and control superior to the right of the father or any other person unless it is otherwise expressly provided by statute.[33]

This law had interesting repercussions when a father wanted to gain custody of a child which the mother has relinquished for adoption. Such a situation occurred recently in Massachusetts. The father and his lawyer reported formidable legal barriers to securing custody of the child from the agency that planned to place the baby for adoption.[34] However, unmarried fathers recently gained legal rights to custody of their children in a decision handed down by the United States Supreme Court on April 3, 1972, in the case of *Stanley v. Illinois*. The Court ruled that Mr. Stanley, an unmarried father, was entitled to the same rights as a father of children born in a legal marriage. This decision makes it mandatory for the unmarried father to be involved in any adjudications about the custody of his children.[35]

Kay points out that most California cases of legitimation have been based on an 1872 statute, still unknown in English law, called "conduct legitimation." The five conditions of this law are (1) biological paternity, (2) illegitimacy, (3) public acknowledgment, (4) reception into the family, and (5) treatment as legitimate. Courts have varied in their interpretation of whether these conditions have been met, and each case is decided upon its individual merits, but the legal trend in California is toward narrowing "the wide gulf between legitimate and illegitimate."[36]

> The California courts, in dealing with cases involving the claims of a child born illegitimate to be treated as legitimate, have worked out a family system based upon the common residence pattern of father, mother, and child and upon the factual performance of the roles of parent and child within this setting between persons not biologically related. . . . Just as the eighteenth century saw the prerogatives of the eldest son fall into disuse in favor of an equal treatment of all children, so the nineteenth and twentieth centuries are witness to slow attainment of equal legal status by the illegitimate child. If the legal development progresses toward greater ease in abolishing the distinction between legitimates and illegitimates, it may be predicted that its force will affect the pace of social acceptance for illegitimate children. As the civil rights struggle has demonstrated most recently, the attainment of legal rights leads merely to a more intense effort to translate legality into reality.

Whether the legal abolition of distinctions between legitimate and illegitimate children, if that occurs, would "practically abolish also the marital relation and thus destroy the home" as Justice Van Dyke feared in 1904 depends ultimately on the strength of the social institution of marriage. . . .[37]

In the course of the debate about illegitimacy, some judges and social workers have revealed their fears about the possibility that liberalizing illegitimacy laws may destroy the family, "the backbone of any civilized country."[38] Fears of uncontrolled and uncontrollable sexual promiscuity are revealed in a statement by a California judge in 1942, responding to the efforts of a father to gain custody of an illegitimate child. The father lived with the child and its mother, although he was legally married to another woman from whom he had been separated for seventeen years. The judge said:

> If the rules are relaxed or misconstrued to the extent here sought we will unsocialize our system beyond description. The terms "home" and "family" will have no meaning other than designating sheltered centers for sex promiscuity. A man could start out in a marriage relation and when established therein even to the extent of a large family could begin to branch out as his capacity permitted. At each stop he could remain long enough to make public acknowledgment of an incidental paternity and then roam on to the next stop and in these days of easy transportation could cover much territory. If each one of these landings could assume the dignity of a home and each group become a family within the law then the chaotic conditions would require complete abandonment of all the sane notions we entertain and encourage.[39]

The same fears were expressed by a professional social worker in 1960 when, as the director of a fact-finding commission on illegitimacy, she recommended to the Maryland legislature that illegitimate children should be removed from their home because such a home

> fails to supply a stable moral environment [and rears] children in an environment which will likely condition them for the same type of immoral and anti-social conduct as that in which their parents have indulged.[40]

The social worker warned that if the state does not take as firm a stand against illegitimacy as it once took against tuberculosis and venereal disease, even though such a stand may be unpopular,

> we are powerless to uphold the Judaeo-Christian concepts of sanctity of marriage, standards of family life, and concern for the welfare of children.[41]

In 1968 a lower court in Maryland, applying a neglect law which defines a neglected child as one who is living in a home "which fails to provide a stable moral environment,"[42] removed three illegitimate children from their home.

Their mother was a welfare recipient. The case was appealed and won on the argument that

> ... Neither the inherent powers of an Equity Court nor its powers of *parens patriae* allow an imposition by the court of its own ideas of policy and morals.[43]

A dissenting judge, quoting the 1960 Report of the Commission on Illegitimacy, argued that the children should not be allowed to stay in a home

> where promiscuity and nonconforming patterns of family life become the accepted standards of living for the children to emulate.[44]

The Adoptive Mother

Sociologists describe childless women as "role handicapped":

> Both the biological structure of woman as childbearer and the social roles that have almost universally accrued to her as childbearer make her intensely role handicapped when the capacity to fulfill this pattern is lacking.[45]

Men can more easily fulfill social expectations through their work, whereas women are looked down upon to some degree if they do not have children. Society considers paid work a secondary role for women, marginal to their primary occupation of child-rearing and housework. Therefore, "involuntary childlessness represents a serious crisis for women."[46] In a study of how adoptive couples felt when they first learned of their infertility, the terms used by wives in describing their feelings had "an emergency quality."[47] Men were more likely to say they felt disappointed, regretful, anxious, incomplete, concerned about their wives' feelings, or that they had failed their wives. Women, on the other hand, reported feeling despair, bitterness, desperation, depression, inferiority, yearning, "absolutely heartsick," "not a whole woman," "a flop as a wife and woman." One woman said, "I think it was my biggest disappointment. I was completely miserable." Her husband reported the milder feeling of being "disheartened."[48]

Kirk points out that the ideology of marriage which is taught to children simply does not allow for the possibility that one may not be able to have children. Girls especially are continually reminded that they are expected to be mothers when they grow up. Therefore it is a severe shock when they face the possibility of being unable to live out this social prescription. Adoption is one solution to this dilemma, even though it is usually considered less desirable than bearing one's own children. Since having children is more important to women, women are more eager to adopt than men. Kirk argues that men's reluctance to adopt may be related to kinship sentiments,

> most likely derived from a patrilineal kinship system in which male heirs are needed to carry on the family line.[49]

It is important to study how women deal with society's definitions of them, especially important at this juncture of history. The Women's Liberation movement contends that women should participate with men in the work world as equals, and that women and men should share child-rearing and housework equally. Women's Liberation, among other factors, has also helped to reduce the supply of adoptable babies, particularly white babies. There are more black babies available, but Black Liberation groups insist that only black couples should adopt black children.[50] There are no answers now—only questions. If women were participating in the work world as equals with men, would they have less need to adopt when they are childless? Will helping to care for other peoples' children satisfy the need most people have for contact with children? Will adoption agencies consider working women less desirable as mothers than women who stay home? I understand that agencies are becoming more accepting of working mothers, but agencies generally change their policies slowly, and traditionally they have frowned upon mothers who work—except for black women, who always had to work more than white women. Kornitzer was unequivocal in 1952 in her condemnation of married working mothers:

> . . . the spinster or widow—even the working one, who is often an admirable parent—seems to me a better proposition for the child than the married couple where the wife goes out to work. The former do not adopt unless they have the money and the will to arrange for the child's adequate care, and they give unlimited unselfish devotion. But there is almost always a strong vein of self-interest in the married woman with young children who persists in going out to work even where there is no absolute need for her to do so.
>
> Many social evils, in fact, are traceable to the working mother with neglected children, and not all the day nurseries or baby-sitters in the world will solve the problems she raises. Adopted children, who suffer more than most from a sense of insecurity, need to be very sure of their new parents. Mother must be there when they want her. . . . An adoption society will always inquire if the wife is working and will not place a baby with her unless she promises to give up her job.[51]

I hope that Kornitzer has changed with the times since 1952; certainly England has changed, as has the United States. The 1950s were times of almost aggressive domesticity. Studies on working mothers certainly do not show that "many social evils" emanate from working mothers. The 1970s are a time of demands for day-care centers, for access to worthwhile jobs, and for equal pay for equal work. Will adoptive mothers be made to feel guilty about wanting the same things that other mothers want? I hope not.

The Adopted Girl

Adoptive couples for the past several decades have preferred girls to boys by a small margin (about 54%). Kirk speculates that this is because the narcissistic injury sustained by men when they find themselves unable to continue a family line is abated when they adopt a girl, since a girl will not carry the family name into subsequent generations.[52]

If adoptive parents choose a girl as a "second-best" compromise solution to their childlessness, one would expect that they will feel different about her and treat her differently than they would treat a boy. One might logically guess that she would be treated as "second-best." If she is, however, it does not show up in follow-up studies of adjustment: girls seem to be adjusting better than boys. Before I go into the studies, let me first sound a note of caution about studies of adjustment. Researchers generally consider that a child is adjusting well if the child's family and teachers are satisfied with the child's behavior. "Adjustment" means adjustment to the status quo. Resistance to the status quo is generally considered a bad "adjustment." To my knowledge, there is no research on whether, for example, an adopted girl is fighting for freedom and equality, or on how competent she is to rebel against irrational authority.

Adopted girls in the United States seem to please their parents better than do adopted boys. Jaffee and Fanshel's study showed more boys than girls in the high-problem group.[53] A study of independent adoptions in Florida showed the same thing.[54] A study of fifty-six adopted children seen at psychiatric clinics showed 41% of them to be female. (Among the 537 nonadopted children seen at the clinic, 28% were female.)[55] On the question of sex preference of parents as it relates to outcome, Jaffee and Fanshel found that a high proportion of their low- and middle-problem groups had preferred a girl (36%), while only a small proportion of the high-problem group had stated any preference (18%).[56]

The situation may be different in England, according to a Kornitzer study that showed adopted girls with a far larger proportion of negative adoption outcomes than boys. Kornitzer believed that this is because both the girls and their adoptive parents are apt to be concerned with a possible repetition of the natural mother's out-of-wedlock pregnancy, and that this fear contaminates the relationship between the female adoptee and her parent.[57] Edwards said, regarding English adopters:

> Many adopters want a perfect child: female, of course beautiful, clever, a social success, who will pass examinations with ease and marry young into the aristocracy. . . .[58]

Kornitzer, in 1952, did not see the intelligence of the girl as a critical factor in adoption success. Suggesting that educated people are not necessarily the best bets for adoptive parents, she explained that

> Educated people like a bright child, and in a borderline success are less likely to tolerate a dull one (at least a boy: a girl can get away with being intellectually dull if she is pretty and has social gifts).[59]

Both of the above British statements may point the direction to one reason for sex differences in outcome between England and the United States.

There is no aristocracy for girls to marry into in the United States; there is instead a large middle class dedicated to achievement and upward mobility. Since boys are expected to achieve more than girls, they may be seen as failures if they do not live up to their parents' expectations. Girls may be considered successful if they are relatively docile and obedient and don't get pregnant out-of-wedlock. I know of one case where the adoptive mother considered that she had raised her adopted girl successfully when the girl did not get pregnant before marriage. The fear of illegitimacy may be stronger in England than in the United States; at least England's laws about it were slower to change than in most of the United States. In 1874, the California legislature provided that "a child born before wedlock becomes legitimate by the subsequent marriage of its parents."[60] English law did not arrive at this result until 1926.[61]

> And even then, children who were born in adultery, the so-called adulterine bastards, could not be legitimated by the subsequent marriage of their parents until the Legitimacy Act of 1959.[62]

California, on the other hand, had achieved this in 1872 by its Code of Conduct Legitimation, which is still unknown in England.[63]

I believe that adoptive parents' feelings about illegitimacy, and about sexuality in general, have a profound influence on their adopted children. If the parents have strong moral feelings against illegitimacy, they probably are not able to empathize with the child's mother; they are probably reluctant to discuss the mother with the child; and they probably fear a repetition in their own adopted daughter. Research shows that one factor contributing to success in an adoption is the adoptive parents' ability to empathize with the child's natural parents.[64]

The Foster Mother

Fostering has always involved mainly the foster mother. The foster father was seldom mentioned in the nineteenth and early twentieth century foster care literature.[65] This has not changed very much up to the present time. Taking care of other peoples' children is still considered primarily a woman's job. Most foster fathers are content with this division of labor, although there are some foster fathers who share enthusiastically in the care of foster children, and others who share half-heartedly. Most foster mothers accept the division of labor without much question, and some resist letting their husbands in on what the women see as their own job.

The majority of successful foster mothers are older women who are either childless or whose children are grown up or no longer demand their mother's full attention. (This is similar to Hawaiian women who adopt because they need children to care for.) Many foster mothers in American and England grew up in large families, and feel that a small family is incomplete. By and large, the most successful foster mothers live in the country or the city rather than in the suburbs, according to a study in Montreal. This study showed that suburban families were not as successful with either "poor risk" or "good risk" children as were urban and rural families. Foster mothers who preferred boys, older children, and who were willing to take several children at once were much more successful than the rest with "poor risk" children, though not necessarily with "good risk" children. With "poor risk" girls, foster mothers older than the natural mother's age were especially successful. The researcher concludes that the "poor risk" child needs a home where ambitions are limited and the level of expectation is low. Suburban families in Montreal evidently demand more of children than most foster children can achieve.[66]

Agencies today employ a more refined version of the nineteenth century system of supervision called the "Paul Pry System." The social workers still inspect homes and children (although they don't strip the beds or the children as they did in the nineteenth century). The researchers nowadays inspect with psychological tests. There are numerous research studies on the motivations of foster parents for taking foster children. Board payments to foster parents are so low that social workers can't imagine themselves taking on such a difficult job for so little pay. Therefore, the social workers rather suspect that foster parents must have some queer mental quirks. Just as social workers who took pay were looked upon with some suspicion in the early days of the profession, so have foster parents been subjected to the same suspicions of mercenary motives. It is a classic case of "Blaming the Victim." Social agencies and the government, like most employers, try to get labor as cheaply as possible. People in power do not want to spend much money on poor children. Thus foster parents too often find the work more aggravation than it is worth, and thus the children keep moving from one home to another unless they find a saint or a masochist who can put up with the demands that these very needful children make upon adults.[67]

The Foster Girl

Research on differential treatment of boys and girls in foster care is scanty and sometimes contradictory, but gives hints that there is some difference. Summarizing foster care research between 1948 and 1966, Dinnage and Pringle ask:

> Why is the proportion of boys being fostered smaller than girls, and why is the rate of foster home breakdown lower for girls? Are both phenomena simply part of the general (and also still unexplained) pattern of boys showing a higher incidence of emotional maladjustment or are additional factors involved?[68]

In the nine communities studied by Maas and Engler boys outnumbered girls 3:2 in foster care.[69] Two of the rural communities (Norden and Granger) showed greater imbalance on sex distribution than did any of the other communities. Boys comprised 70% (almost 5:2) of the foster care population in Norden.[70] In the big cities of Westport, King City, and Centralia, boys in foster care only slightly outnumbered girls.[71] In those cities, however, boys were more likely than girls to return home. Girls outnumbered boys in foster care only in the community of La Paz. The authors wondered, "Was this a reflection of ethnic preferences or disfavor?"[72] (A large proportion of the foster children had Spanish surnames.)

As for foster parents' sex preferences, Etri found that the "least adequate" foster parents in her study preferred girls.[73]

The most revealing information on the differential effects of foster care on girls and boys comes from Meier's follow-up study of 75 adults (30 men, 45 women), aged 28–32, who had spent at least five years in foster care in Minnesota and who had not returned to their natural homes.[74] About half had been placed before 5 years of age; they had had an average of nearly twelve years in care, and an average of five of six placements. All but one were white.

The first interesting finding was that three times as many men as women refused to answer the interviewers' questions. All 45 of the women had married and 38 were still with their husbands. (In the general population, 10.9% of this age group is unmarried.) Men, on the other hand, had an average rate of marriages but a very high rate of separation. For both men and women, the families of their partners appeared to be important as parent surrogates.

Seven of the women had ten illegitimate children; six had relinquished the children for adoption. (This was a higher illegitimacy rate than in the general population.) Fifteen women had a total of thirty-two still-births and miscarriages—a very high number compared to the average among the general population. Many women expressed doubts about their own competence as mothers, although most children appeared happy and healthy. The women were good housekeepers; some were compulsively neat. Fifty-seven percent of the women's husbands earned over $100 a week; yet only 47% of the men in the control group earned over that amount. Five of the women's husbands were professional men; only one of the men who had been in foster care was professional. Many of the women lacked confidence in themselves—much more so than the men—and they compared themselves unfavorably with their foster mothers. A slightly higher proportion of women than men were ill or felt under physical strain. In general, both men and women performed better in most areas than they felt they did. Women were more likely than men to lack a "sense of well being." Some men and women felt defensive about their background, but women appeared more aware of their problem, and less restricted by it. Men were more bothered about having been born illegitimate than were women.

I conclude from these findings that women tended to flee anxiously into domesticity—if compulsive housecleaning and problems with pregnancy can be taken as evidence of anxiety—while men tended to flee *away* from domesticity after they had tried it. Women, however, were less likely to deny their anxiety than were men.

The Mother of the Foster Child

Attitudes toward foster care have not, alas, changed very much since the days of the Poor Law in England. Some people in the middle nineteenth century feared that the boarding-out system would encourage poor working-class parents to desert their children. People also feared that boarding out illegitimate children would "fatally undermine the morality of the community."[75] Some people in twentieth century America feel the same way. Foster care is still for the children of the "Poor Law" (now AFDC) and other poor children. Boarding out in the nineteenth century was for orphaned or deserted children; foster care in England and the United States now is mainly for children whose parents are separated or widowed.[76] Studies show remarkably similar findings—only between 19% and 25% of the foster children have both parents living together.[77]

Many of the mothers are ill, either physically ill, in the hospital having another baby, or mentally ill. Most of the mothers are poor. In the general population, more women than men are poor, by a ratio of 8:5, and the mothers of foster children reflect the lower economic status of women. The women who place their children in foster care are less likely to have relatives who can help them, and are more likely to have husbands who are unwilling to help with the children.[78] Many of their husbands are unemployed or sporadically employed. Mothers are likely to feel guilt about the placement, while fathers are more likely to feel shame. Many of them are angry at society and at social agencies.[79] Twenty-four percent of the mothers in one study were either unaware of or opposed to the decision for placement; 15% were unaware of or opposed to the agency's placement plan.[80] Members of minority groups are especially alienated from agencies, and especially discriminated against by society. These women and their children are the victims of a class society.

The Social Worker

"Rescuing the little ones" was a form of Women's Liberation in England during the second half of the nineteenth century. Upper middle-class women with leisure time on their hands expressed a philanthropic concern for the welfare of Poor Law children "that has no equal in the history of the child care service."[81] In those days, the "Ladies of England" were expected to

> "play the pianoforte and visit the poor as a matter of course." It was taken for granted that a young lady straight from the schoolroom was "qualified to deal with every form of distress and poverty, because she has the kind heart with which all women are credited in right of their sex."[82]

Even before the creation of "boarding out" as a child care system, beginning in the sixteenth century, women had cared for orphans and deserted children. Children of the Poor Law below apprenticeship age were boarded with nurses in the suburbs of London.[83]

Mrs Hannah Archer was the first person in England to publicize effectively the advantage of boarding out, especially for girls aged 2 to 11, because, she said, the workhouse contracted their minds and affections and made them "unfitted for being placed out" in respectable employment.[84] Boarding out was seen as especially desirable for girls, who were trained for domestic employment and who were in danger of getting pregnant in the workhouse. Boys could more easily get technical training in an institution.[85]

The rich ladies were the nineteenth century equivalent of the social workers today. They were "people of standing" who volunteered their time, at least until the twentieth century. They found foster homes and supervised them. They made surprise visits to inspect the house and the children; often they stripped the beds and inspected the children's naked bodies for bruises and dirt. Some foster parents grumbled about this "Paul Pry system" of investigation, but the Local Government Board believed that foster parents would accept inspection from someone of a higher class than themselves but not from someone of a similar class. The local officials considered it important to maintain this status differential. Some of the more gracious ladies, however, also gave picnics and steamer trips to the foster parents and foster children. The same gracious ladies took foster girls into their homes for "domestic training" before sending the girls into the world as domestic workers.[86] Some of the ladies, on the other hand, were accused of being more interested in supplying parishoners with foster children's labor than with the welfare of foster children, e.g.,

> "Squires in some parishes paid their labourers no wages, but promised them instead five or six boarded out children from the workhouse. The parson assisted in this with all his influence, because it enabled the charity-school managers to obtain a larger Government grant."[87]

Both men and women believed that women were far better than men in supervising foster homes, since a foster mother could talk freely to another woman about things she would not discuss with a man and

> "It must be patent to all that there are numberless little matters in the rearing and training of children that come particularly under female observance."[88]

The Boarding Out Order of 1911 in England specified that every foster child should be supervised by a woman, but for the first time it encouraged hiring paid staff rather than relying entirely on volunteers. This was the beginning of the entry of middle-class women into the child care system, working as paid staff. Gradually, middle-class women took over the staff work of foster care, and upper-class women became members of boards of directors and organized fund-raising events for private agencies. There is always some tension between the two groups; the social workers do not always agree with the policies of the boards, and the leisured rich women sometimes want more contact with the children than the social workers allow. The uneasy balance is maintained, however, because the social workers believe that they need rich people on the board and the rich women do not need to work and do not want the responsibility of a full-time job.

Women have done child care work as they have done teaching, partly because caring for children is considered "women's work." Their bid for acceptance as boarding-out supervisors in nineteenth century England was a bid to enter the work world in a "respectable" role. Having won their place in the child care system (but not, proportionate to their numbers, as administrators of the system) they settled in and accepted their "place" too easily. They proceeded to help the men who ran the society to regulate the poor. They won a limited freedom in the work world, but they won it, to some extent, at the expense of poor women and children. Let the modern Women's Liberationists take heed!

With only a few exceptions, women in the foster care system have been too polite to challenge the basic premises of the system. I propose that we women who know the system best free ourselves and the foster children from century-old definitions of "child welfare" and "come to the rescue of the little ones" in a new way, appropriate to the latter half of the twentieth century.

Notes to Chapter Five

1. Cited by V. George, *Foster Care* (London: Routledge & Kegan Paul, 1970), p. 9.

2. In Bradley's study of 87 adoption caseworkers, all but two were women. Forty-seven percent were currently unmarried, and only 37% had reared at least one child. [Trudy Bradley, *An Exploration of Caseworkers' Perceptions of Adoptive Applicants* (N.Y.: Child Welfare League of America, 1967).]

3. To digress a bit for an observation on worker behavior, I also noticed that adoption workers sometimes had meals with adoptive applicants, while foster care workers seldom dined in foster homes, and workers with unmarried mothers never dined with their clients. I suspect this is because adoption workers felt on a more equal status level with adoptive applicants than did foster care workers with foster parents or workers with unmarried mothers with their clients.

4. Margaret Kornitzer, *Child Adoption in the Modern World* (N.Y.: Philosophical Library, 1952), p. 64.

5. Ibid., p. 320.

6. Ibid., p. 65.

7. Ibid., pp. 60-61.

8. Ibid., pp. 46-47.

9. Ibid., p. 49.

10. Andrew Billingsley and Jeanne M. Giovannoni, *Children of the Storm* (N.Y.: Harcourt Brace Jovanovich, 1972).

11. Bradley shows that a high proportion of Negro applicants who were rated by caseworkers as good prospects for an adoptive placement withdrew their application after an initial interview. (Ibid., pp. 60-62, 173-174.)

12. The legal term "bastard" is, of course, in popular usage a derogatory swear word.

13. R. H. Graveson, *A Century of Family Law: 1857-1957* (London: Sweet and Maxwell, Ltd., 1957). (Cited by Herma Hill Kay, "The Family and Kinship System of Illegitimate Children in California Law," *The Ethnography of Law,* ed. by Laura Nader, vol. 67, no. 6, part 2. Reproduced by permission of the American Anthropological Association from the American Anthropologist, 1965.

14. The family still functions to help place the child in society. Even if there is little real property to inherit, the family connections may help a child

get into a union, get a job, get into college, and so on. Of course the family income also helps the child in social placement.

15. Kay, p. 59.

16. Ibid.

17. Kingsley Davis, "Illegitimacy and the Social Structure," *American Journal of Sociology*, vol. 45, no. 2 (1939): 215–233.

18. Lewis A. Coser, "The Case of the Soviet Family," in *The Family, Its Structure and Function*, ed. by, Rose L. Coser (N.Y.: St. Martin's Press, 1966), p. 531. This article discusses the shifts in official Soviet attitudes and laws toward the family as the totalitarian state seeks to control the people, partially through control of the family structure.

19. *American Jurisprudence, State and Federal*, 2d ed., vol. 10 (Rochester, N.Y.: The Lawyers Cooperative Publishing Co., 1963), p. 849.

20. Ibid., pp. 880–881.

21. Ibid., p. 882.

22. Ibid., p. 887.

23. Ibid., p. 886.

24. Ibid., p. 949.

25. Ibid., p. 956.

26. Ibid.

27. Ibid., p. 949.

28. Ibid., p. 939.

29. Ibid., p. 941.

30. Ibid., p. 942.

31. Ibid., p. 877.

32. Ibid., p. 878.

33. Ibid., p. 889.

34. Courtesy of the *Boston Sunday Globe*, 6 August 1972, p. B-1.

35. Rita Dukette and Nicholas Stevenson, "The Legal Rights of Unmarried Fathers: The Impact of Recent Court Decisions," *Social Service Review*, vol. 47, no. 1 (1973): 1–15.

36. Kay, p. 75.

37. Ibid.

38. Ibid., p. 65.

39. Ibid., citing 48 Cal. App. 2d 848, 120 P. 2d 690 (1942); id., at 852, 120 P. 2d at 692.

40. Sanford N. Katz, *When Parents Fail* (Boston: Beacon Press, 1971), p. 169.

41. Ibid., p. 169.

42. Ibid., p. 70.

43. Ibid., p. 72.

44. Ibid., p. 73.

45. H. David Kirk, *Shared Fate* (N.Y.: The Free Press, 1964), p. 129.

46. Ibid., p. 2.

47. Ibid., p. 3.

48. Ibid.

49. Ibid., p. 135.

50. International adoption agencies have been importing Asian babies, especially Korean babies, for American adoptive couples for some time. More

recently these adoption agencies have also imported babies from Viet Nam, Bangla Desh, and Colombia, South America. Thus poor Third World countries are exporting their babies for affluent Americans to adopt. A caseworker at a Massachusetts adoption agency told me recently that couples rush to the agency eagerly when immigration restrictions are periodically lifted, allowing importation of babies.

51. Kornitzer, p. 24.

52. Kirk, p. 137.

53. Jaffee and Fanshel, p. 71.

54. Eugene A. Weinstein and Paul Geisel, "An Analysis of Sex Differences in Adjustment," *Child Development*, 31, 721–728.

55. Edgar Borgatta and David Fanshel, "Behavioral Characteristics of Children Known to Outpatient Clinics with Special Attention to Adoption Status, Sex, and Age Groupings" (N.Y.: Child Welfare League of America, 1965).

56. Jaffee and Fanshel, p. 64.

57. Margaret Kornitzer, *Adoption and Family Life* (N.Y.: Humanities Press, 1968).

58. M. E. Edwards, *Proceedings of the Royal Society of Medicine*, vol. 47, no. 12 (1954): 1044.

59. Margaret Kornitzer, *Child Adoption in the Modern World*, p. 162.

60. California Civil Code section 215. Cited by Kay, p. 60.

61. Legitimacy Act, 1926. Cited by Kay, p. 60.

62. Kay, pp. 60–61.

63. Kay, p. 61.

64. Kirk believes that adoptive parents' adjustment to their role is influenced by their ability to resolve their own feelings about the natural mother's sexual behavior. Drawing upon the insights of Jean Paton (*The Adopted Break Silence*), he argues for encouraging open communication between adoptive parents and natural parents before the child is placed, in order to help the child cope with questions about his background.

65. V. George, *Foster Care* (London: Routledge & Kegan Paul, 1970), p. 37.

66. H. B. M. Murphy, "Foster Home Variables and Adult Outcomes," *Mental Hygiene*, vol. 48, July, 1964, pp. 587–99. Cited by Rosemary Dinnage and M. L. Kellmer Pringle, *Foster Home Care* (N.Y.: Humanities Press, 1967), p. 167.

67. I do not mean to suggest that adequate pay alone will guarantee competence in foster parenting. As with any work, good pay is not the only variable in attracting competent people. Employers know, however, that their salaries have to be competitive with other salaries in order to attract workers.

68. Dinnage and Kellmer Pringle, Ibid., p. 38.

69. Maas and Engler, Ibid., p. 209.

70. Ibid., p. 67.

71. Ibid., p. 283.

72. Ibid., p. 138.

73. Gloria Etri, "A Motivational Study of Successful and Unsuccessful Foster Parents" (MSW thesis, Fordham University, 1959).

74. Elizabeth G. Meier, "Current Circumstances of Former Foster Children," *Child Welfare*, vol. 44, no. 4 (1965), 196–206; "Adults Who Were Foster Children," *Children*, vol. 13, no. 1, (1966), pp. 16–22.

75. George, pp. 10–11. Quotes within citation are from Fawcett, *Pauperism: Its Causes and Remedies.* On the other hand, some people feared leaving children

with "immoral" parents. They also feared placing children close to their parents, because parents would continue to exert an undesirable influence upon the children. "No real evidence was produced about this but the fact that children became dependent upon the state because of their parents' misfortune or misconduct was proof enough of the parents' inadequacy." (George, p. 14). These early debates shed a great deal of light on current foster care practices.

76. Ibid., p. 179.

77. George's study in England showed that only one-quarter of legitimate children had parents living together; Parker's study in England showed 20% of natural parents living together. [R. Parker, *Decision in Child Care* (London: Allen & Unwin, 1966).] Jenkins and Sauber found only 24% of foster children in their New York City study living with both parents. [Shirley Jenkins and Mignon Sauber, *Paths to Child Placement: Family Situations Prior to Foster Care* (N.Y.: Community Council of Greater New York, 1966).] Jeter's study in the United States showed 19% of parents living together. [H. Jeter, *Children, Problems and Services in Child Welfare Programs* (Washington, D.C.: U.S. Government Printing Office, 1963).]

78. H. R. Schaffer and Evelyn B. Schaffer, *Child Care and the Family*, Occasional Papers on Social Administration, no. 25 (London: G. Bell & Sons, 1968).

79. Shirley Jenkins, "Separation Experience of Parents Whose Children Are in Foster Care," *Child Welfare*, vol. 48, no. 6 (June 1969): 334–341.

80. Jenkins and Sauber.

81. George, p. 9.

82. Ibid., pp. 9–10. Quotes within citation are from "Women and Charitable Work," *Cornhill Magazine*, October 1874.

83. Ibid., p. 6.

84. Ibid., p. 7.

85. Ibid., p. 28.

86. Ibid., p. 36.

87. Ibid., p. 37, Citing Mr. W. Crooks, Guardian of Popular Union, evidence to Mundella Committee.

88. Ibid., Citing Col. C.W. Grant, *A Practical Guide to the Boarding Out System*, p. 34.

CHAPTER SIX
TOWARD AN "IDEAL" CHILD
CARE SYSTEM

It is risky to talk of an ideal system. Ideals can harden into ideologies, and ideologists can subvert reason by their insistence on realization regardless of objective conditions. When people discover that they cannot conform to an ideal, they may become cynical, disillusioned, apathetic, or guilty, or they may compensate and turn to reaction formations which retain the shell of an ideal but lack the substance. Then their guilt or cynicism makes them less able to analyze what went wrong and to try new forms. The form of adoption in Tahiti seems to be a case in point. The original ideal was probably to use adoption to strengthen social solidarity and to enhance psychological security. In its present form, the system retains the ideal goal as an abstract ideal but achieves the opposite. It serves now as a system to make all relationships insecure in an alienated society. Stanley Diamond believes that the same gap between the real and the ideal has occurred in the Israeli kibbutzim.[1]

Karl Marx, a materialist, was wise enough to avoid utopian description of the ideal (classless) society, because, as Paul Tillich says,

> it would be merely an ideological attempt to describe a social situation for which not all the material foundations are in existence.[2]

The content of the ideal society "must be derived more or less from the meaning of the negative aim of history: liberation of man from self-estrangement,"[3] which Marx believed was rooted in the division of labor.

"You cannot 'abolish' the family. You have to replace it,"[4] said Leon Trotsky. Speaking of the aftermath of the October 1917 Russian Revolution, when efforts were made to collectivize some family functions, Trotsky summed up the results:

> It proved impossible to take the old family by storm—not because the will was lacking, and not because the family was so firmly rooted in men's hearts. On the contrary, after a short period of distrust of the government and its crèches, kindergartens and like institutions, the working women, and after them the more advanced peasants, appreciated the immeasurable advantages of the collective care of children as well as the socialization of the whole family economy. Unfortunately society proved too poor and little cultured. The real resources of the state did not correspond to the plans and intentions of the Communist Party. . . . The actual liberation of women is unrealizable on a basis of "generalized want." Experience soon proved this austere truth which Marx had formulated eighty years before.[5]

The retreat from the "social feeding" and socialized child care was not, Trotsky pointed out, a condemnation of the socialist system, "which in general was never tried out." It was, rather, a condemnation of a system unable to function because of the lack of social resources to support the ideal. The social laundries "tear and steal linen more than they wash it";[6] the number of crèches were inadequate to the need, and the quality of care in the Moscow and Leningrad crèches was

> not satisfactory as a general rule to the least fastidious demands. "A crèche in which the child feels worse then he does at home is not a crèche but a bad orphan asylum," complains a leading Soviet newspaper.[7]

The Stalinist bureaucracy was unable to provide for the thousands of homeless and uncared-for children, the

> more than a thousand children (in Moscow alone) living in "extraordinarily difficult family conditions."
>
> A vast amount of the homelessness of children . . . is a direct result of the great social crisis in the course of which the old family continues to dissolve far faster than the new institutions are capable of replacing it.[8]
>
> The triumphal rehabilitation of the family, taking place simultaneously—what a providential coincidence!—with the rehabilitation of the ruble, is caused by the material and cultural bankruptcy of the state. Instead of openly saying, "We have proven still too poor and ignorant for the creation of socialist relations among men, our children and grandchildren will realize this aim," the leaders are forcing people to glue together again the shell of the broken family, and not only that, but to consider it, under threat of extreme penalties, the sacred nucleus of triumphant socialism. It is hard to measure with the eye the scope of this retreat.[9]

In an Israeli kibbutz, Spiro documents the same kind of gap occurring between ideals and reality. Because of the manpower shortage, it was impossible to provide enough staff to provide the individualized attention and to ensure the continuity of care which the Israelis desired for their children.[10] In allocating the proportion of service workers to productive workers, the community found it necessary to give a high priority to productive workers. The desired liberation of women from "domestic slavery" was not achieved. In fact, the women lost some of the creative potential they had previously been able to find in diversified and self-scheduled homemaking, since they were assigned specialized domestic jobs in the kibbutz. Perhaps again Marx's dictum about the impossibility of liberating women under conditions of "generalized want" was demonstrated.[11]

Similarly, when one considers changes in the child care system, one must analyze the objective conditions of a society before deciding how to attempt change or what change to attempt. An analysis of objective conditions does not, however, necessarily point the direction for change. One's values and political orientation also determine the kind of change one seeks. Thus Edward Banfield and Roger Freeman, conservatives who seek to keep the poor in their place, propose taking children away from some mothers on welfare as part of their "poverty program." Roger Freeman reveals his assumptions about the poor when he says,

> Maybe we should consider whether a child is always best off with his mother or whether growing up in a well-run institution may not give it a better chance in life than living under inferior parental care or in a detrimental environment.[12]

This, plus a proposal for giving cash bonuses to poor women to have themselves sterilized, constitutes Mr. Freeman's alternatives to the proposed welfare reform of the Family Assistance Plan! The FAP will promote illegitimate births, disrupt labor markets, and lead to "steadily worsening social ills and civil unrest," says Mr. Freeman.[13] Mr. Freeman is not simply indulging in idle chatter, he was signaling the direction that the Nixon administration planned to take. The Family Assistance Plan, originally proposed by Mr. Nixon, was defeated in Congress with the help of Nixon's indifference to it. The only welfare "reform" passed by the 1972 Congress was the Talmadge Amendment, which required all AFDC recipients to register for employment and to work if their children were over 6 years old. The administration's national budget for fiscal year 1974 proposed more "efficiency" in welfare administration (no more money, just more fraud squads). The budget included funds for foster care and "family planning" ("birth prevention," says Mr. Freeman, in an appeal to do away with euphemisms); but reduced funds for day care, jobs and job training, health services and research, education, low-income housing, and social services. Some funds for defense and some subsidies to corporations were not cut; others were increased. This is a clear political statement that the state supports the military, certain corporations, and those employed by war industry, at the expense of the poor. The administration's response to poverty is to eliminate the poor through "birth prevention" or by taking their children away.

We do not lack a good child care system because of "generalized want"; this is the wealthiest and most technologically advanced country in history. We have decadent institutions because of both the state's cultural bankruptcy and a profit-making economic system in which the few exploit the many. I do not believe that there is any way to make the radical changes that the child care system demands without making radical changes in the distribution of wealth. Perhaps such a change will not come for a long time, if at all. I do not see a socialist revolution looming on the horizon in America. Barbarism, as Marx said, is the alternative to socialism. Yet there are strong democratic forces countering it, and it is not yet clear which will win.

I do not know exactly what an "ideal" child care system would look like, but in moving toward such a system we must aim for the liberation of people from alienation from themselves and each other. If that is our guideline for everything we do, the specific structures we build will flow organically from the liberating process, since the people the system is designed to serve are best qualified to determine for themselves what helps them to feel whole.

The Future of the Family

The forms that the child care system takes will be determined by the forms the family takes, and no one can predict at this point what those forms will be. We know that sexual repression has lifted considerably in the past decade. The double standard of sexuality has loosened; young people no longer view premarital intercourse as deviant behavior; sex can be discussed openly without embarrassment; homosexuals are coming out of the closet; and everyone is trying to understand the nature of sexuality. Says one sociologist,

> We've opened a great many doors and a great many options. We really have a much more open premarital, marital and extramarital system than we've ever had. We're more aware that some people can enjoy life styles in any of these ways that other people cannot.[14]

The advantage of the new sexual permissiveness, according to Reiss, lies in the increased options for people, which can give more psychological freedom; the disadvantage is the risk of experimenting in a way that might destroy something more meaningful to an individual.

Margaret Mead looks forward to the time when

> parenthood will be a vocation and not a necessary condition of every man and woman regardless of their fitness for it.[15]

She does not advocate passing laws about this, but rather creating

> a climate of opinion which instead of hustling everybody into marriage and parenthood will say instead: What are you getting married for? Why are you having children? What makes you think you will be good parents?
>
> We will be moving toward a world that not only does not demand that everybody have children and that wants all children to be well born, but which can be organized so that all the other people who don't have children will have some access to children.
>
> We don't know any society that has remained a good society in which there was not a genuine concern for the next generation.
>
> It is through particular children that one is led into some concern for the future and today we are extraordinarily in need of some concern for the future.[16]

Mead says that World War II marked a dividing line in the structure of the family in the United States. The nuclear family (husband, wife, and young children living by themselves in their own house) was a postwar development against which many young people are rebelling. Mead does not advocate eliminating the family, but advocates giving the family more protection and more support.

She believes that "you can't have a viable community without three generations."[17] Towns should be planned to break down age and class segregation:

> What we want to do is surround the family, each young couple with
> children, with enough people to help them, with many pairs of hands,
> with aunts and uncles—not necessarily biological ones but people who
> will play the roles of aunts and uncles and grandparents and older brothers
> and sisters—with a whole group of people such as we had in the small
> neighborhoods and small towns in this country 75 and 100 years ago.[18]

In a similar vein, Urie Bronfenbrenner believes that age segregation poses
a critical problem for human development

> of the greatest magnitude for the Western world in general and for
> American society in particular.[19]

Bronfenbrenner suggests placing day-care centers in junior and senior high schools
so that older children can work in the centers. This would be good for both groups,
since "older children are more powerful models than adults, and older children
would learn to take responsibility for young children."[20] Bronfenbrenner also
urges us to find ways of breaking down the segregation of old people stranded in
their housing projects and communities. Both the young and the old need contact
with each other.

How does the structure of the family relate to the structure of foster care?
Most families live in cities or the suburbs, and do not have room for relatives in their
homes. The extended family belongs to the rural and smalltown past. Viewing the
realities of urban family life, Carol Meyer argues that foster care is based on the
rural model of family life that no longer exists.

> It is a rural myth to believe that we can always substitute a better family
> life for children than the one in which they presently live. Where is the
> better family? . . . Is it not an aspect of the urban reality that all families
> have urban-conditioned problems . . . ?[21]

Meyer suggests that small-group care, based in neighborhoods, is a "modern
kind of program, meeting a need that has been specifically created by urbanization."[22] Group care diffuses the conflict of loyalties a child has between foster
parents and natural parents; it avoids role confusion for foster parents; and it does
not exclude natural parents as does foster care. Basing the group in the neighborhood would mitigate the depersonalization of urban life. Social insurance functions
that were once provided by the extended family must now be provided by the
larger society. These functions, suggested Meyer, would include a complex of
family and child welfare services: income insurance, day care, family day care,
homemaker service, group homes, protective service dealing with child abuse,
adoptive services, therapeutic group and foster family services, and "a host of
newly devised services for youth."[23]

In a similar vein, Reid urges scattered small institutions close to parents,
since studies show that children who are placed close to their parents are more

likely to return home.[24] Dinnage and Pringle argue for educating the community to accept "problem" families, and to accept the need for long-term support for such families ("semi-permanent 'mental crutches' as it were"). With such close, long-term support, Dinnage and Pringle believe that such families

> may in many if not most cases, be able to give their children a sense of security and belonging, for which there is no wholly effective substitute. . . .[25]

Jenkins suggests "neighborhood parenting," i.e., the use of stable families in the community to care for the children of unstable families. She also suggests stand-by foster homes, subsidized apartments or group homes supervised by locally based agencies, small-group homes attached to the public school for short-term or emergency needs. Children having trouble at home who need a cooling off period for overnight or a weekend could stay at a group home. Jenkins advises setting up panels of neighborhood lay guardians who would act as family advocates to help families negotiate with bureaucratic agency structures.[26]

The weight of expert opinion is against foster care, especially for older children. Studies of foster home placements show that breakdowns in placements rise sharply after the age of 5 (V. George [27]) or 7 (Trasler [28]). In George's study, only one of ten placements of adolescents succeeded. His figures on adolescent placements square with my own practice experience—one in ten is about the odds I always assumed for the success of an adolescent foster home placement, except when the adolescent had grown up in the home. Social workers may be working against a cultural universal in placing adolescent boys in foster homes, since most of these boys have been raised by their mothers. (Stephens, an anthropologist, shows that one of the few near-universal findings about the family is that adolescent boys raised in female-headed families almost always leave their home.)[29]

In my experience, placements of girls in foster homes worked out only slightly better than placements of boys. Even if the girl stayed, she usually had a stormy relationship with the foster parents. On the other hand, small-group homes usually worked out much better for both boys and girls.

Even if older children were no longer cared for by foster parents in a nuclear family but in small groups, there would still be a need for child care workers in small-group homes. There would also be a need for foster parents (or child care workers, the term I prefer) for very young children and babies awaiting placement in adoptive homes.

Agencies have always had trouble finding enough good foster parents—especially the "earth-mother" kind of farm woman who thrives on having lots of children around her. (Mrs. E. in the foster parent discussions of 11-26-68, 3-18-69, and 5-13-69, App. A, B, and F, is a good example of that kind of woman.) Part of the problem in recruitment lies in agencies not offering a decent salary. I recall receiving a telephone inquiry from a man in Ontario about being a foster parent. When I told him the pay he said indignantly, "My dear, how do you expect to get people to work for that kind of money?" I replied that people's willingness to be exploited never ceased to amaze me.

Yet the recruitment problem is not only related to money. People do not come forward in droves even to the few agencies that pay foster parents a decent salary. I suggest that agencies are looking in the wrong place: they should look to the youth for their staff. I believe that the youth who are questioning society's "rat race" philosophy are the potential replacements for the old farm earth-mothers, who are going out of style. The youth have some of the same values that have made it possible for the earth-mothers to love so many hurt children. I have known many of these youth in colleges. They are searching for worthwhile work; they want to serve; they have enormous reserves of energy and creativity. They are fun to be with, and they love children. Their identity is not intimately connected with being parents at this stage of their lives, but they do need to prove their competence in work. Therefore, they would probably be less likely than foster mothers to compete with the natural parents for a child's affections. They either already identify with natural parents, or easily can be encouraged to do so. I know this to be true, because I have worked with many of them.

Most of these youth, however, will not allow themselves to be exploited as willingly as have most foster parents. They want a *good* job that is recognized as socially valuable. That recognition will have to come in the form of decent pay, decent working conditions, and equal occupational status within the agency. Young child care workers in institutions move on to other jobs partly because they are on the bottom of the status ladder and treated accordingly. They regard many professional social workers as snobbish and removed from the reality of a child's day-to-day life. Although the child care workers seek help and training in their jobs, they resent a good deal of what they see as "ivory tower" advice given by social workers and psychiatrists. Many foster parents share the same feelings about social workers, but don't dare say so to the social workers. That is one reason they need their own organization—so they can air their gripes without fear of recrimination, and so they can set up organizational structures to deal with these gripes.

Working Women and Communal Child Care

The growing numbers of mothers in the work force is perhaps the most significant phenomenon for the future of the family and child-rearing. Most of these women have had to work in order to supplement their husbands' income or, in the case of women who are the sole wage earners, to support their family. Recently, however, increasing numbers of affluent mothers who feel isolated want to work outside their homes. They want day care for their children. During World War II, when the state needed women to work, the state subsidized day care facilities. When the men came home after the war, many women lost their wartime jobs, and the state withdrew its day care subsidies, except for New York and California, which continued some support. Women were encouraged to stay home and raise children. Despite this, many of them stayed on in the work force and many more continued to enter it. Poor women always needed day care, but did not get much of it from the government until the Head Start program in the late 1960s. Affluent women have recently begun demanding day care, and a comprehensive day care bill extending the Head Start program to all income levels in cities with populations over 5,000 was passed by Congress in 1971, but vetoed by Mr. Nixon. The bill was backed strongly by organized labor, civil rights groups, women's and church organizations. It would have set up "child development centers" around the country, operated primarily by local communities with 80% federal funding. Mr Nixon and other conservatives, however, "saw the spectre of the commune"[30] in the bill. They feared that the bill would weaken the family and

> would commit the vast moral authority of the national government to the side of communal approaches to child rearing over against (*sic*) the family-centered approach.[31]

James Buckley, Conservative party senator from New York, said that

> it was okay to provide day care for "the children of irresponsible or derelict parents, or for working mothers who are otherwise unable to make adequate arrangements for their children,"[32]

but he was opposed to universal day care. David Deitch believes that the conservatives' fear of a "communal approach" to child-rearing stems from the fear that such child-rearing would break down the authoritarian hierarchical family structure, which socializes children to be obedient workers for corporations. Deitch does not believe that day care centers in America would

> be permitted to go so far as to interfere with corporation production requirements, but capitalist ideologues like the Buckley brothers are afraid.[33]

Deitch argues from the assumption that, since the nuclear family has perpetrated authoritarian character structures, the communal child-rearing will break down hierarchical authoritarianism. While I agree that the authoritarian nuclear family often does socialize children into authoritarian patterns of behavior, I do not think that communal child-rearing is necessarily less authoritarian. It depends upon who controls the child-rearing institutions, and for what purposes. Bronfenbrenner's study of the Russian school system [34] and Kassof's study of the Russian communist youth organizations [35] show that communal methods used by a totalitarian state socialize the child for unquestioning obedience to the bureaucrats in power at school and at the work place. Their methods are not fully effective, as Kassof documents, not because the bureaucrats don't bend all their efforts toward obtaining obedience, but simply because children have a vital spirit that slips out in devious ways under even the most watchful eyes. My own heretical spirit joins with the youthful Russian *nibonicho* ("neither God nor the Devil") who sit inconspicuously in the rear of boring Komsomol meetings and jeer,

"Stormy ovation, all rise!" ("This is a sarcastic imitation of stenographic reports of official Soviet meetings, which include a graded series of applause ratings."[36]) The *nibonicho* are the courageous ones who refuse to sit quietly through the boredom of endless bureaucratic debates about production quotas and how to collect scrap metal. The *nibonicho* and the "idlers," who have rejected the work ethic altogether,[37] are driving the Soviet authorities up the wall, even more than the hippies are bringing down the wrath of the United States authorities.

Kassof describes the Russian plan, first announced at the 1956 Twentieth Party Congress, to create boarding schools for virtually the entire school-age population "in order to reinvigorate the indoctrination of Soviet youth."

> The existing system of primary and secondary education is to be replaced with boarding schools where children will be subjected to a round-the-clock program away from the influences of the family and the street. Although the plan is also concerned with improvements in curriculum and instruction, its ultimate purpose is to effect total control over the early formation of basic attitudes and values.[38]

I am sure the *nibonicho* will join me in saying, "Stormy ovation, all rise!"

Martin Wolins, Albert Rabin, and Bruno Bettelheim argue for group care for the children of the poor, especially AFDC mothers.[39] In analyzing their proposal, I should first like to make it clear that a proposal for group care of *all* children is quite a different matter than a proposal for only *poor* children. Communal living does seem to have a great appeal to many adolescents and young adults, and I believe society should respond to what seems to be a felt need of some youth by helping these young people to "get it together" in ways that are comfortable for them. In the absence of established facilities where they can feel understood, counterculture youth have been devising their own institutions: crash pads and group residences, communes, drug centers, "rap" centers, "Hot Lines," peer-group counseling. I do not believe, however, that such institutions can be planned and controlled primarily by state officials, since it is the state officials who have alienated the youth from institutions. The youth themselves should have majority control over the kinds of living arrangements they want. In contrast to totalitarian states, this country, in my opinion, still has enough tolerance for diversity for many kinds of experimental institutions. As Paul Goodman suggests, the communes are a large demonstration project in new forms of family living.

Any program designed only for the poor is probably doomed to be a poor program—that is the iron law of welfare. Judging from the history of programs for the poor (with the possible exception of some of the OEO programs), there is no reason to believe that institutions for the poor will be well run. Chances are very good that they will be inadequately staffed, the staff will be underpaid, and both residents and staff will be stigmatized. They will be, as low-income housing is, "low amenity" institutions.

But let us assume, for the sake of argument, that the institutions would be well run. What models do Bettelheim, Rabin, and Wolins suggest that we adopt? The Israeli kibbutzim, for one. Let's analyze that. First, it is naïve to assume that social institutions can be imported like new cars. Institutions evolve in a country in ways peculiar to that country's perception of its needs. The kibbutzim were created in an explicitly Jewish nation [40] to defend the border against neighboring countries and to develop agricultural land. Those are not the needs of the United States today, which is an urbanized country that insists on the separation of church and state. The descriptions I have read of the people raised by the kibbutzim remind me somewhat of my own family and neighbors in Northeastern Colorado, where my father homesteaded at the turn of the century. The kibbutz-raised people and my neighbors were friendly but emotionally reserved, conformist, practical, pragmatic, energetic, work-oriented, rather uncreative in artistic fields, and not, by and large, intellectuals. The men were good mechanics and could fix almost anything, but they did not become poets or philosophers. There are two big differences between the two groups: the kibbutz-raised people are used to cooperative work and make good team workers; my family and neighbors were more individualistic, although they did form cooperatives and helped each other out quite a bit. Also, the kibbutz-raised people are more aggressive than were my family and neighbors. But we did not have borders to defend, nor did we as children have such stiff competition for adult attention as the young Israelis do.[41] I left the country because I found life there rather dull. The people were honest and decent, but the big city beckoned, as it beckons to many of the young Israelis.

Wolins argues that the kibbutzim ideology is especially appealing to adolescents; that adolescents need ideology; and that the failure of United States child-caring institutions stems in part from the lack of an ideology.[42] The Jewish nation-building ideology has inspired a good many, but the United States has been built, and the only new frontier is in outer space. Agribusiness has taken over farming, and the corporations do not need youth. That is a large part of the reason for the malaise that all youth are suffering from now, as Paul Goodman argued so persuasively in *Growing Up Absurd*.[43] The youth need to be incorporated into society in socially valued work, but the unemployment rate is higher for youth than for any segment of the population. Higher education can keep youth busy for awhile, but the economy will not now absorb all those who graduate from graduate school, let alone college. Poor children are needed least of all in a post-industrial technological society. The only ideology I can imagine that might capture the imagination of poor youth is the ideology of revolution, and that surely will not be sponsored by the state in "well-run institutions."

The other model of group care put forward by Wolins is the Austrian *kinderdorf*, which uses the Catholic religion for its ideology. The *kinderdorf* is the very model of the model suburban middle-class Austrian family minus the father. The natural parents are excluded, with no nonsense about it:

> Having begun with an evaluation of parental deficiency in each case, they make no claim about modifying it or even living with it. Then, free of the encumbrance, they plan a long-range program for the child in their setting.[44]

Surely this is the triumph of the middle class in substitute child care!

The main problem with group care, it seems to me, is the problem of how to preserve privacy and individuality within the group setting while providing children the enjoyment of each other's company. Another problem, especially with young children, is the problem of providing enough adult staff to give the children the individual attention that they need. The main problem with the nuclear family, it seems to me, is the compulsive nature of continual intense interaction between a very few people, an interaction that can burden family members with inescapable emotional requirements. Can the family be retained as an individualizing agent, adaptable to the individual rhythms of each child, while avoiding compulsive neurotic relationships? Perhaps the children of Samoa whom Margaret Mead studied had the best of both worlds. There, "few children live continuously in one household, but are always testing out other possible residences."[45] This is done under the guise of visits, with no suggestion of truancy.

> No Samoan child, except the taupo (like a princess), or the thoroughly delinquent, ever has to deal with a feeling of being trapped. There are always relatives to whom one can flee.[46]

All boys and girls call each other brother and sister regardless of the kinship relationship. Perhaps Mead has this society in mind when she suggests that America build communities where many "relatives" will help each other out—even if they are not biological relatives.

Diamond argues that the family is a necessary protective buffer between the individual and the state, and believes—contrary to Spiro—that the kibbutz is not an extended family or a folk society—but *is* the state. The demands of the state impinge directly upon the individual without the intermediate emotional escape of the family. The family is no longer the mediator between society and the child,

> diffusing, individualizing and synthesizing social imperatives, and affording the possibility of idiosyncratic response.[47]

Diamond does not believe, however, that nurseries necessarily depersonalize children, as he thinks the kibbutz group care has done. The key factor in whether depersonalization in group care occurs, Diamond feels, is the quality and depth of the relationships between generations.

Whether communal child-rearing creates conformists or creative individualists depends upon the goals of the total society and upon the economic structure of society. It also depends upon who controls the child-rearing institutions. That is why radicals who agitate for day care insist that the local community and the parents control the day care centers. When radicals begin to pay attention to the substitute child care system, they should make the same demand.[48]

State Control, Bureaucracy, and Accountability

Since the end of World War I, states all over the world have been increasing their control of child welfare. Social workers in the United States tend to favor increasing state regulation of adoption (both relative and nonrelative, but especially nonrelative). States which require official approval of adoptions designate approved social agencies to investigate all adoptive applications. This is happening in the absence of any hard proof that agency adoptions are superior to nonagency adoptions.[49] States in the United States are gradually taking over foster care placement of children, either directly through public agencies or indirectly through subsidizing private agencies. Sectarian child care is on the wane, and public child care is on the rise. This is potentially more democratic, since state agencies are required to serve everyone with equal justice. Private agencies may be more responsive to special groups, however, since they receive their funding from and are controlled by these groups. Special needs can get overlooked in large bureaucratic public agencies, as Maas and Engler show in their study. On the other hand, private agencies can be just as unresponsive and as bureaucratic. State agencies are democratic if the state is democratic: it depends on whose needs the state serves. The dominant class of a state defines the needs of the state, and the nature of child care flows from those definitions.

Most public child welfare institutions are grossly underfinanced, understaffed, and overbureaucratized. They lack mechanisms of accountability to the community. Communities are generally unaware of children in foster care because agencies are not accountable, and because agencies have not considered it their responsibility to publicize their work or to educate the public. The nature of bureaucracies is for bureaucrats to work in secret. Joseph Reid, commenting on the findings of Maas and Engler, says that the community should be even more concerned about children in foster care than it is about cases of communicable disease, which must be reported.[50] Katz speaks of the dangers inherent in courts delegating total child welfare responsibility to public welfare agencies:

> Frequently understaffed by inadequately trained personnel, applying outmoded concepts of child development and often rejecting social values dominant in the community, these agencies operate almost totally independent of the courts in providing protective service for parents and in choosing an appropriate placement—institutional, foster, or adoptive— for the child. Because courts often have no other source of relevant information about the child, the parents, or community resources, they tend to accept agency judgments with little question. As a consequence, these agencies exercise almost unbridled discretion, and their decisions may or may not take into consideration those factors that should be relevant in child placement decisions. Thus, custody decisions, which raise the most important questions to come before a court in this area, and about which a judge agonizes more . . . than about any other type of decision he renders, are often made in a vacuum without adequate consideration of the competing values which should be balanced.[51]

Professionalism

One frequently encounters the assertion in child welfare literature that the system would be improved in adding more trained workers to it. I should like to question this assumption, and suggest that a social worker is generally more influenced by the agency culture, community facilities, and class background than by her training. George's study of social workers in England showed that

> trained child care staff performed their duties in much the same ways as their untrained colleagues.[52]

Most of the differences that emerged were departmental rather than between trained and untrained staff.

> It seemed as if each department had a tradition and culture which influenced the work of child care officers much more than it was influenced by the individual attitudes of officers.[53]

Untrained officers, however, were more likely to rate free use of house for play important while trained officers considered it unimportant.[54] There was also a greater tendency for untrained than trained staff to refer to the neighborhood, and for untrained workers to consider the fact that foster parents were locally born as important. Most trained workers considered a foster mother's involvement in local organizations as unimportant, while an untrained worker rated this as very important.[55] Only one-eighth of the workers, mostly trained, reported on the foster father's work history or his present role at work. There was even less interest in the family economy—only two out of twenty-eight workers asked foster parents about it. Both trained and untrained workers gave minus ratings to foster mothers who were employed outside the home.[56] In one department with a majority of trained staff, untrained staff interviewed applicants more times than did trained staff before approving them as foster parents. The same untrained workers were also more likely to interview foster fathers alone than were the trained staff. George suggests that these few untrained staff were anxious to "make up for their inferior status as untrained."[57]

Perhaps the most damaging indictment of training that George makes is his statement that all workers' personality assessments of applicants were

> in such simple language and of such uncomplicated nature that it was very easy to classify applicants in these categories: pleasant, forthright, eager to please, easy-going, tolerant, intelligent, self-assured, common-sense, reserved and nervous.[58]

Anyone's next-door neighbor could have done as well! If I had to choose between the trained and untrained, as George describes them, I probably would choose the untrained. They were at least more attuned to the local community and more aware of children's need for unrestricted play.

Maybe some day social work education will eschew pseudoscience with its jargon in favor of a genuinely intellectual humanism, an equal partner with the other arts and sciences rather than an unwanted bastard. Maybe some day it also will eschew top-down élitism in favor of bottom-up democracy. On that day, maybe professionals will make a difference.[59]

Maas and Engler show a similar picture of bland and unimaginative assessments of adoptive parents by caseworkers. The adoptive parents chosen by the workers in all nine communities were "shockingly similar."[60] The typical man and wife were white and Protestant, had strong inner controls and little personal flexibility, placed a heavy emphasis on education and ambition, were rational and task-oriented, lived in a single-family dwelling, earned "much more than the average annual income in their communities,"[61] had a median education of high school graduation. Both were members of the same church. Parents who adopted children other than white infants, however, were more accepting of imperfections, were less anxious about achievement, and placed a high value on loving a child.[62]

A decade after Maas and Engler's study, Bradley said essentially the same thing about adoption workers. She viewed

> adoption agencies as a product of our middle class culture, responding to pressures within a community in order to gain its support, and also incorporating some aspects of the value system of that environment, which includes values that are not wholly accepting of the deviant child.[63]

Bradley said that all agencies, and particularly public agencies, did not encourage "individual initiative and exploration of new methods by individual workers."[64]

These findings show that adoption workers are more influenced by their own middle-class background than by their training, since the parents they choose for the "perfect" white babies are like the workers: white, middle-class, upwardly mobile. Further evidence that class is more important than training is provided by Maas and Engler's finding that more professionalized communities allowed children to stay in foster care longer and sent them home less frequently. That probably reflects the case workers' middle-class bias against poor parents. Case workers also tended to downgrade parents, especially mothers, in their estimation of parents' intelligence.[65]

Winifred Bell documents the class bias of social workers of the pre-Depression period. Some leaders of the social welfare profession opposed proposals for a national ADC program because of the possibility that "unsuitable women" might get benefits.[66] Piven and Cloward point out that similar class biases still operate in the welfare program. A recent HEW study found that

> the more professionally oriented the welfare staff, the lower the proportion of poor who got relief.[67]

Professional social workers in welfare departments prefer to give counseling, diagnosis, literacy training, and vocational training, rather than money.[68] Similarly, in child welfare, professional social workers prefer to give foster care, adoption, and casework treatment rather than money or extended homemaking services to families.

From his review of the research on trained versus untrained, Kadushin concludes that despite the supposed clear differentiation between professional and non-professional workers, once they are hired by an agency it is difficult to tell them apart in terms of job content, agency policy, in-service training, or supervisory procedure.[69]

A study of trained and untrained social workers in a psychiatric hospital arrived at the same conclusion.[70] Scott Briar shows that workers base their placement decisions more on the availability of facilities, particularly within their own agencies, than on any theory about what the child needs.[71]

Political vs. Technical Decisions

Expert opinion on the child care system is generally ignored by state officials unless it supports what the officials want to do anyway. Most people do not pay much attention to experts until political battle lines are drawn; then the public begins to get information. Child welfare has not changed in decades because it has not yet become an important political issue. It has become a political issue in the black community; I look forward to the day when poor white people and their allies join with black people around the same issues.

Foster parents have been organizing in the past decade to protect their interests in the system. That could lead to a much needed increase in their status, and it is certainly a welcome development. Foster parent organizations are too weak at this point to make much of a dent on the system or even to show the direction that they are likely to go. The big question is will they see their interests as opposed to the interests of the natural parents, or will they understand that the welfare of the children dictates solidarity between parents and foster parents? Judging from my own experience with foster parents, I believe that they may some day ally themselves with oppressed groups, since they have experienced a good deal of oppression themselves. Needless to say, it does not always work that way. But if their organization helps them to see themselves as professional child care workers, they may have less need to compete with parents for the children's affection, since they can get their satisfaction from competence in a socially valued career.

Social policy planners—the "technocrats" in the field—generally accept the present two party political system as a "given" and are not likely to join any major grass roots' challenges to the system. When social planners do political work, they align themselves either with the officials in power or with the other major party candidates who are challenging the party in power. Social planners are more likely to use consensus tactics than confrontation tactics, since they prefer to avoid conflict.[72] Those who align themselves with the party in power, such as Daniel Patrick Moynihan and Edward Banfield, construct the ideological system that the administration uses to maintain power. The needs of the state exert a powerful influence on the kind of ideology the "planners" put forth, even though behavioral scientists claim to be "objective," "neutral," and "value-free." There simply is no such thing as a "value-free" behavioral science. Nor is there any such thing as a "value-free" therapy. All treatment issues are, in some sense, political issues.

Some social welfare specialists, psychiatrists, and psychologists put forth suggestions supposedly based on objective scientific evidence, free from political considerations. Many of these specialists consider themselves politically liberal, and would be offended if they were accused of furthering the goals of a conservative administration. Yet their "scientific" recommendations can be used in politically reactionary ways. I think that Martin Wolins and Bruno Bettelheim are two such liberals whose proposal for institutionalization of poor children may be adopted eagerly by the present administration for reactionary purposes. H. Skeels' proposal to put poor children in adoptive homes can also be used in a reactionary way. Skeels makes the ambitious claim that adoption for children of poor parents can be a large-scale solution to poverty:

> We have adequate knowledge from designing programs of intervention to counteract the devastating effects of poverty, socio-cultural deprivation, maternal deprivation, or a combination of these ills.[73]

It is naive to assume that adoption could even begin to eliminate poverty.

American Values and Kinship Structure

> The dominant values of the total culture must find expression in the kinship system. . . . Kinship must teach (the child) the fundamentals of his whole culture.[74]

American kinship terminology reflects the dominant American values of individualism in the nuclear family:

> Only those who truly occupy the particular genealogical positions are seen as the proper persons to play the roles and receive the designations associated with those positions. Americans distinguish "father" from "stepfather," "mother" from "stepmother," "real sibling" from "half-sibling," and so on. . . . The occupation of a structurally identical position and the playing of an identical role is not enough to warrant the use of the kinship term appropriate to that position and role. . . . This practice is very different from, for instance, the Zuni one, where a term is applied when it designates the role-relationship regardless of the appropriateness of the genealogical positions occupied by the persons concerned.[75]

This individualism and possessiveness of American kinship structure makes foster care and adoption particularly confusing to a child in developing his identity. The bilaterally organized kinship system, in which there is no enduring kinship-group structure available, adds to the genealogical insecurity. In a bilateral kinship structure,

> economic support for women and children is located in a series of statuses, the principal ones being those of son, husband, or lover.[76]

A bilateral kinship structure is ideally suited for very mobile societies, but it does not give long-term security for poor women and their children. Rich children inherit wealth from their fathers; poor children inherit poverty from their mothers.

The individualistic orientation of American parents toward their children makes it hard for foster parents to share children with natural parents, and makes it practically impossible for adoptive parents to share their children with natural parents. Leon Yarrow, discussing the possible consequences of radically severing an adopted child's ties from his natural parents, said,

> Part of one's sense of identity undoubtedly derives from feelings of belonging within a family framework and having historical continuity within this framework. The lack of knowledge among adopted children of their natural background may adversely influence the development of their sense of continuity. . . . The probability of conflicts in identification is likely to be enhanced in adopted children by the existence of more than one role model. For the adopted child, the unknown parental figure may exist as a possible fantasy identification model. The existence of a model whose values may be perceived as different from his adoptive parents and whose behavior may be judged as deviant from the norms of his adoptive parents' social group may create further conflicts in identification for the adopted child.[77]

The ideology of adoption agencies which encourages discontinuity in genealogy and chooses adoptive parents who are geared to achievement and upward mobility seems particularly in keeping with the American character structure. The historian Christopher Lasch discusses the progressive political ideology in American history:

> Not only the superficiality of progressivism but the radical discontinuity of American culture . . . derived from the ceaseless search for beginnings of which the frontier had provided the most durable set of images—the flight from complexity, the flight from the past, the belief that the past is an encumbrance that can painlessly be discarded in the restless search for a better future.[78]

Some adult adopted children do not believe that the past "is an encumbrance that can painlessly be discarded." An organization of adult adoptees has formed in Massachusetts, and perhaps in some other states, to press for the right to search into their past. An adult adoptee told Jean Paton:

> . . . I would like to know my natural parents, but I am far from sure this would lay the old ghosts. Couldn't an adopted child know he has two sets of parents, equally indispensible, the natural and circumstantial, without the latter going into a tailspin at the mention of the former?[79]

A few adopted children in Paton's study had "noteworthy success" in incorporating two sets of parents.[80] One adoptee wanted to search for natural parents but did not dare:

> I feel I owe her (adopted mother) some gratitude and she has not worked out her feelings about adoption by any means, even less so than I! . . . So far my dread of her hysterics has been greater than my curiosity. . . .[81]

113   TOWARD AN "IDEAL" CHILD CARE SYSTEM

Paton concludes,

> It seem to us . . . that until biology becomes unimportant culturally, some curiosity toward the natural situation will be bound to appear to a greater or lesser extent in any adoptive life.[82]

The British National Council for Civil Liberties says that a child's new parents should be required by the court legalizing the adoption to tell the child that he is adopted. Their report, *Children Have Rights*, states,

> This not only puts the relationship between the child and the parents on an honest basis, but indicates the parents are being honest with themselves about the fact that the child is adopted. . . . At this moment it is virtually impossible for an adopted child to find out who his natural parents were, unless his adopted parents are prepared to disclose the child's original name.[83]

I should like to make an even more heretical suggestion to some courageous adoption agency and some courageous adoptive parents: Why not try an experimental demonstration project in which adoptive parents and natural parents share responsibility for a child, as long as the child wants two sets of parents? There are some mature and stable unmarried mothers who could handle this responsibly; there must be a few adoptive parents who would see it as a challenge in parenting. Is there an agency that would dare to make such a break with tradition?

But What about the Abused and Neglected Child?

I suspect that some readers who have got this far have been protesting angrily about the children who are cruelly abused and neglected by their parents. Those readers may think that I am romanticizing parents in arguing for their rights to their children.

I know about those battered and neglected children. I have worked with some of them, and I have had my moments of fury at parents who abuse their children. Even for someone who believes as strongly in causation as I do, it is sometimes hard to take a dispassionate view of abusive parents. In fact, I get angry when any adult strikes a child, since it seems such an unfair power struggle for adults to use their power in that way. Of course children must sometimes be protected from their parents; probably *all* children at some moments in their lives need such protection. That is why I argue for some institutionalized method of temporary escape from the family—if not kindly relatives or friends, then perhaps an officially appointed neighborhood parent, a neighborhood- or school-based social worker, a peer group, a settlement house, a children's ombudsman. We should, as Margaret Mead says, create a climate of opinion among all classes of people that having children is a highly valued vocation, not a duty, and that children have a right to their parents' respect and love. I say this knowing, of course, that love cannot be legislated.

We probably should also create a climate of opinion in which parents are not stigmatized for wanting to give up children whom they never wanted in the first place and for whom they are simply incapable of caring. Chestang and Heymann [84] make a convincing case for helping some ambivalent parents release their children for adoption by casework counseling early in the placement experience. The parents they describe—and all of us who have worked in the child welfare system have known some of them—probably could not love their children wholeheartedly even with all the social supports in the world. Social workers may serve some parents and children best by relieving the parents' guilt about giving up their children for adoption. Even in those cases, however, we must be sure that we can, in fact, place the children in adoptive homes, and we must be very cautious about misreading the ambivalence. We must also be accountable to the community and the children for what we do. Removing a child from his parents is as serious as radical surgery, and as with radical surgery we should have more than one person's opinion on the necessity for it. Perhaps a neighborhood-based advisory board could help on such decisions. We should also remember that at some future date, the child may want to meet his natural parents, at least once, simply to bring his fantasies in line with reality. I believe a child should have this right.

We do not know how many placements are unavoidable, because we have never been in a position to give the kinds of social supports necessary to avoid them. Several studies show that a large number of placements could have been avoided by the use of adequate income maintenance, extended homemaker service and day care, adequate health care, and adequate housing.

What Is to Be Done?

Our objectives for change in the child welfare system should be to reduce alienation, increase self-confidence, and increase the decision-making power of those served by the system. Anyone who feels alienated because of her special status in the child welfare system should organize with others who feel similarly alienated. This might include foster parents, foster children, adoptive parents, adopted children, parents of children in foster care and institutions, children in institutions. Agency professionals who feel alienated from clients because of professional status should join these movements to help to organize them—not only to help change the system, but to help overcome their own alienation. If children are to be organized in groups of their peers, they will probably need the professional's help, although foster parents could also give the necessary help. The youth I worked with in Colorado required very little help from me, since their foster parents did most of the organizing work. Parents will also need the help of sympathetic professionals.

I believe that parents' groups should be more task oriented than therapy oriented, i.e., focused on the task of parenting and dealing with the agency and their living environment. These parents have had enough guilt and shame laid on them. Therapy that stresses intrapsychic speculation is more likely to increase the guilt, while an organization focused on the problems involved in getting their children back could lead them into struggling around environmental and inter-personal problems and could force the agency to deal with parents' problems sociologically and politically as well as psychologically. Relatively few child welfare social workers are battling with landlords to get repairs done, with welfare departments to get higher grants, with health clinics to get better health care, or with their own agency to get more money for foster parents or a homemaker service for parents. It is safer to do therapy.

I envision the new breed of child welfare professional as a politically sophisticated, intellectual activist who can help parents, foster parents, adoptive parents, and children negotiate with the system; an activist whose power lies in her knowledge of the child welfare system and society; an activist who knows how to use that knowledge to help the powerless get power.

Notes to Chapter Six

1. Stanley Diamond, "Kibbutz and Shtetl: The History of an Idea," *Social Problems*, vol. 5, no. 2 (Fall 1957).

2. Paul Tillich, "Marx's View of History," *Culture in History*, ed. by Stanley Diamond (N.Y.: Columbia University Press, 1960), pp. 636–637.

3. Ibid.

4. Leon Trotsky, *The Revolution Betrayed* (1937) (N.Y.: Pathfinder Press, 1972), p. 145.

5. Ibid.

6. Ibid., p. 146.

7. Ibid., p. 147.

8. Ibid., p. 148.

9. Ibid., pp. 151–152.

10. Melford Spiro, *Children of the Kibbutz* (N.Y.: Schocken Books, 1966), pp. 36, 78.

11. Melford E. Spiro, *Kibbutz, Venture in Utopia* (N.Y.: Schocken Books, 1964), pp. xiv–xv. Commenting on a subsequent visit to the kibbutz he studied, Spiro notes that the community had become more prosperous. Although he did not do a follow-up study on the condition of women, which had been the most vexing problem of the community when he studied it, he speculated that this problem might have been alleviated under conditions of greater prosperity.

12. Courtesy of the *Boston Globe*, 28 January 1972.

13. Ibid.

14. "Reiss: Rapid Changes in Sexual Behavior," *The University of Iowa Spectator*, vol. 5, no. 5 (April 1972): 4–5. (Report of a speech by Ira Reiss at an Iowa workshop on "The Changing Family Structure.")

15. "Margaret Mead: New Generation Coming of Age," Ibid. Report of a speech by Margaret Mead.

16. Ibid.

17. Ibid.

18. Ibid.

19. Urie Bronfenbrenner, *Two Worlds of Childhood: U.S. and U.S.S.R.* (Schenectady, N.Y.: Russell Sage Foundation, 1970), p. 118.

20. James F. Clarity, "Demands for Day Care Rising among the Affluent," *New York Times*, 28 March 1971.

21. Carol Meyer, "The Impact of Urbanization on Child Welfare," *Child Welfare*, vol. 46, no. 8 (October 1967): 438.

22. Ibid., p. 439.

23. Ibid., p. 442.

24. Joseph H. Reid, "Action Called For—Recommendations," Chap. 24, in Maas and Engler, *Children in Need of Parents* (N.Y.: Columbia University Press, 1959), p. 393.

25. Rosemary Dinnage and M. L. Kellmer Pringle, *Foster Home Care* (N.Y.: Humanities Press, 1967), p. 47.

26. Shirley Jenkins, *Priorities in Social Services: A Guide for Philanthropic Funding*, vol. 1, Child Welfare in New York City, Praeger Special Studies in U.S. Economic and Social Development (N.Y.: Praeger Publishers, 1971).

27. V. George, *Foster Care* (London: Routledge & Kegan Paul, 1970), p. 190.

28. *In Place of Parents*, Gordon Trasler (London: Routledge & Kegan Paul, 1960), p. 215.

29. William N. Stephens, *The Family in Cross-Cultural Perspective* (N.Y.: Holt, Rinehart and Winston, 1963), p. 17. Stephen says:

> It seems to be almost universally true that in societies with a high proportion of mother-child households, boys move away from home at or before puberty. . . . Since Murdock designated one-fourth of the societies in his *World Ethnographic Sample* as "mother-child-household societies," and since this condition is—at least—almost universal for all mother-child-household societies, it is clear that the adolescent boy's "living out" (or at least "sleeping out") is a very common condition the world over. In a good many of these cases, apparently, the separation is not complete. The boy does not sleep at home (he has his own sleeping hut, or sleeps in a bachelors' house); but he may eat at home, he may do some work for his parents, and he may spend some time around home. However, in a few societies the separation between a boy and his family does appear to be pretty drastic. Among the Murngin and the Nyakusa, for example, adolescent boys have their own villages. . . . In some avunculocal societies, such as the Trobriands, the boy moves to the village of another relative. . . .

30. David Deitch, "In the 'day care bill' conservatives saw the spectre of the commune," Courtesy of the *Boston Sunday Globe,* 19 December 1971.

31. "Nixon vetoes extension of poverty war," Courtesy of the *Boston Globe,* 10 December 1971.

32. Deitch, "In the 'day care bill.' "

33. Ibid.

34. Bronfenbrenner, *Two Worlds of Childhood*, p. 118.

35. Allen Kassof, The Soviet Youth Program, *Regimentation and Rebellion* (Cambridge, Mass.: Harvard University Press, 1965).

36. Ibid., p. 141.

37. Ibid., Chap. 7, "The Case of the Idlers," pp. 144–170.

38. Ibid., p. 165.

39. Albert I. Rabin, "Kibbutz Children," *Children*, vol. 16, no. 4, July–

August 1969, pp. 160–162; Martin Wolins, "Another View of Group Care," *Child Welfare*, vol. 44, no. 1 (January 1965): 14; Bruno Bettelheim, *Children of the Dream* (N.Y.: Macmillan, 1969).

40. Uriel Tal relates an anecdote about two priests on a pilgrimage to the Holy Land who observed a Bible class at a kibbutz.

> Later, when the two pilgrims continued their journey, they exchanged impressions. "The one thing I did not like about that lecture," said one, "was the political indoctrination the children underwent." "What do you mean?" asked his companion. "Well," he replied, "don't you remember how often they were told that the day will come and 'Israel will be third with Egypt and Assyria, a blessing in the midst of the earth'?" "My dear friend," exclaimed the other priest, "that was not politics! It happened to be one of the most beautiful prophecies of Isaiah—chapter 19, verse 24."

Tal gives that as an example of the fact that Israel is a religious state. ("Jewish Self-Understanding and the Land and State of Israel," *Union Seminary Quarterly Review*, vol. 26, no. 4 (Summer 1971): 351.)

41. Spiro, *Children of the Kibbutz*, pp. 432–433.

42. Martin Wolins, "Political Orientation, Social Reality, and Child Welfare," *Social Service Review*, 38 (December 1964): 429–442.

43. Vintage Books, N.Y., 1960.

44. Wolins, "Group Care: Friend or Foe?," p. 52.

45. Margaret Mead, *Coming of Age in Samoa* (N.Y.: Mentor Book, New American Library, 1949), p. 34.

46. Ibid.

47. Diamond, "Kibbutz and Shtetl: The History of an Idea," p. 89.

48. The black community is already demanding community control over foster care and adoption. I am not sure whether they are making this demand for all segments of the community. If it is mostly black professionals who are represented, lower-class parents might still be excluded from decision-making power. Thus class divisions could still be perpetuated in the name of community control. This must be avoided.

49. Dinnage and Pringle, p. 45.

50. Maas and Engler, p. 391.

51. Sanford N. Katz, *When Parents Fail* (Boston: Beacon Press, 1971), pp. 145–146.

52. George, *Foster Care*, p. 226.

53. Ibid., p. 141.

54. Ibid., p. 106.

55. Ibid., p. 106–107.

56. Ibid., p. 108

57. Ibid., p. 97.

58. Ibid., p. 114.

59. See my articles "Social Work As A Liberal Art," *Social Work* (July 1967), pp. 102–105, with regard to the former and "Welfare and Totalitarianism, Parts I and II," *Social Work* (January and April 1971), with regard to the latter.

60. Maas and Engler, p. 374.

61. Ibid., p. 371.

62. Ibid., p. 377.

63. Trudy Bradley, *An Exploration of Caseworkers' Perceptions of Adoptive Applicants* (N.Y.: Child Welfare League of America, 1967), p. 190.

64. Ibid., p. 193.

65. Workers in Centralia perceived the children's fathers and mothers as having below-average intelligence, despite the fathers' average attainment of 11th grade education and the mothers' education of 9th or 10th grade (p. 205). In Jamestown, workers saw mothers as less intelligent than fathers, although the mothers were in fact better educated (p. 203).

66. Winifred Bell, *Aid to Dependent Children* (N.Y.: Columbia University Press, 1965), pp. 118–119.

67. *The Administration of Aid to Families with Dependent Children New York City, November 1968–February 1969*, New York State Department of Social Services. Cited by Frances Fox Piven and Richard Cloward, *Regulating the Poor* (N.Y.: Vintage Books, 1971), p. 176.

68. Piven and Cloward, p. 177.

69. Alfred Kadushin, "Child Welfare," *Research in the Social Services: A Five-Year Review*, ed. by Henry Maas (N.Y.: National Association of Social Workers, 1971), p. 45.

70. Robert L. Barker and Thomas L. Briggs, *Differential Use of Social Work Manpower* (N.Y.: National Association of Social Workers, 1968).

71. Scott Briar, "Clinical Judgment in Foster Care Placement," *Child Welfare*, vol. 42, no. 4 (1963): 161–168.

72. For a discussion of both the creative and destructive aspects of conflict, see Lewis A. Coser, *Functions of Social Conflict*. (N.Y.: Free Press, 1956).

73. H. Skeels, "Effects of Adoption on Children from Institutions," *Children*, vol. 12, no. 1 (1965): 33–34. Cited by M. L. Kellmer Pringle, *Adoption: Facts and Fallacies* (N.Y.: Humanities Press, 1966).

74. David M. Schneider and George C. Homans, "Kinship Terminology and the American Kinship System," in *The Family*, ed. by Norman W. Bell and Ezra F. Vogel (N.Y.: The Free Press, 1968), p. 524.

75. Ibid., p. 519.

76. Raymond T. Smith, "Community Status and Family Structure in British Guiana," in *The Family*, p. 286.

77. Leon J. Yarrow, "Theoretical Implications of Adoption Research," *Child Welfare*, vol. 44, no. 2 (February 1965): 70–71.

78. Christopher Lasch, "On Richard Hofstadter," *New York Review of Books*, 8 March 1973, p. 8.

79. Jean Paton, *The Adopted Break Silence* (Acton, Calif.: Life History Study Center, 1954), p. 162.

80. Ibid., p. 126.

81. Ibid., p. 136

82. Ibid.

83. "A Child's Rights," Courtesy of the *Boston Sunday Globe*, Parade sec., 13 June 1971, p. 7.

84. Leon W. Chestang and Irmgard Heymann, "Reducing the Length of Foster Care," *Social Work*, vol. 18, no. 1 (January 1973): 88–92.

APPENDIXES
Where Are the Children?

I present here verbatim taped transcriptions of six separate group discussions that took place in 1968–1969 as part of the Foster Care Research Project of Child and Family Services, Inc., Hartford, Conn. The idea for the project originated with James Black, staff psychiatrist. Jim believed that foster parents would function better in their jobs if they were treated as colleagues of equal importance to other staff members, and this is what the project was all about. We tried to examine authority relationships throughout the foster care system, and hoped thereby to free people to act with more initiative and independence. Foster parents who took part in the project were divided into three groups, of which two—structured and unstructured—met regularly at the agency; the third, used as a control, did not meet at all. Before the project was initiated, the agency formulated the following policies regarding foster care:

1. Foster care should be short-term rather than interminable.
2. Children should return to their parents if at all feasible.
3. Parents should be helped as much as possible to get their children back.
4. Parents should maintain close contact with their children in foster care.
5. Foster parents should be encouraged to take initiative in working with the children's natural parents and should, if at all possible, maintain friendly relationships with them.

The agency's program is specifically geared to handle emotionally disturbed children in both residential treatment and foster care, and its foster parents received $35 a week per child at the time of this project—about twice as much as did state foster parents. Most of the agency's foster children have already been committed to the state, have lived in state-supervised foster homes, and have been judged too difficult to handle in them by the time they are referred to Child and Family Services.

The foster care project is continuing in a more rigorous form, under the auspices of a National Institute of Mental Health grant.

APPENDIX A
FOSTER PARENTS DISCUSS THEIR
WORK WITH NATURAL PARENTS

After the research groups were ended, Kathleen Olmstead and I called together some foster parents to share their thoughts about working with natural parents. The foster parents involved in this discussion were:

Mr. and Mrs. M., who cared for an 8-year-old boy for about a year, then took the boy's brother who had stayed in the residential treatment facility called the "Village."

Mr. and Mrs. B., who cared for both a 2-year-old Puerto Rican child whose parents had been charged with neglect and another girl, 5 years old.

Mrs. E., an experienced, older foster mother who had cared for many of the agency's children. At the time of this discussion, the author was working with Mrs. E. to reunite a 6-year-old foster child with his mother. This boy had been taken from his mother on a neglect charge when he was 2 years old, had lived with other foster parents prior to the present placement, and had had infrequent contact with his mother because of the reluctance of the previous foster parents and the state child welfare agency to encourage such contact. The mother had subsequently divorced the child's father, and was living in a stable relationship with a man by whom she had had two children. She planned to marry him and wanted her child, whom I shall call Billy, home. Despite a consistent and determined desire to get her child back, the mother was understandably anxious about her ability to care for a child with whom she had little continuous contact, and who was now defined as "emotionally disturbed." The author talked with the foster mother about inviting the mother to her home for a weekend so the mother and child could get to know each other better with the support of the foster mother.

5-13-69

MRS. E.: Billy's mother, she stayed with us for two nights. . . .

B.M.:[a] And it was so unprecedented, you know, for a foster mother to do this. . . .

MRS. E.: It was unprecedented for us, too.

B.M.: It was unprecedented for you, and I think it's unprecedented for agencies, because kind of traditionally agencies have kept foster parents and parents kind of separated, you know. I mean they haven't encouraged foster parents to really work very much with parents.

MRS. E.: I don't think I'll ever forget—she came to the door and she said, "You know, I spent a month in jail. Do you still want me in your home?" I said, "What were you in jail for?"

---

a. Betty Mandell

K.O.:[a] . . . traditionally foster parents and parents are kept apart.

MRS. E.: Well, I really like it *[working with parents]*. I think I get along-- Take George *[another foster child]*, for instance. I think that if his mother hadn't accepted me so readily I might have found it difficult reaching George. George treats me like a family. You know, he really had no difficulty in responding to me. In fact, his mother rather likes the situation. It helps. I think Billy and I get along well because his mother doesn't resent me as much as she resents most people.

B.M.: You think you got along better with Billy after his mother got involved?

MRS. E.: Yes, I think so because he wasn't—well, I wouldn't say after his mother got involved, because before that time I was getting very close to Billy. This was before he knew he had another mother to go to, and he was perfectly happy to accept me as another mother. As long as somebody would be good to him and teach him. He liked to have you do things for him. But, when she got into the picture, when he knew there was a possibility of him going back to her—— Billy is bright enough to try to play one against the other. And when he found out that we were, well, friends in his way of looking at it, he didn't try so hard.

K.O.: You know, I wonder if kids don't always play one against the other.

MRS. E.: Well, your own children do.

K.O.: Yeah, but you were commenting when Shirley *[Mr. and Mrs. B.'s foster child]* tries to call you Mrs. B. when her mother's there——

MRS. B.: Yeah, she makes a mistake and calls me "Mommy—Mrs. B."

B.M.: And she calls you Mommy other times?

MRS. B.: Other times, I'm always Mommy.

MRS. E.: Sure, 'cause Fred *[a foster child]* calls me Grandma when his mother's there, but now I notice Mom slips out all the time and she just gives him a little smile and she's very good about it, and I'm sure it must hurt. I think that of all the mothers I've met in this thing—I haven't met too many, but those I've met— I honestly think she finds it the hardest of any of them to part with her angel, even though she freely admits she can't get along with him.

B.M.: How does she feel about you? Does she feel competitive?

MRS. E.: Oh, she's very nice to me. And once or twice she said something that made me feel she was a little bit hurt perhaps, and I said, "Yeah, I can understand how you feel." She said, "No, that was selfish on my part." She said, "Sometimes I can't help thinking about it, but I should maybe, should have tried harder, or maybe I didn't try hard enough."

B.M.: What about competition between natural parents and foster parents? I think natural parents would generally feel hurt that somebody else can do a better job, or at least that's how they would see it, wouldn't they? Have you sensed it in your parents?

MRS. B.: Oh, yeah.

MRS. E.: Well, Billy's mother has it made. She won't concede that anybody could have done a better job. You know that.

---

a. Kathleen Olmstead

B.M.: Yeah.

MRS. E.: She's dying to get him home so he won't——

B.M.: Well, that's the way she deals with it, because she was very insecure about her ability to——

MRS. E.: And I laugh, I get a kick out of it because I think she's got to do this to make herself feel that's she's not so bad. She's got to make Billy want to come home to be better, you know.

MRS. B.: I'm just beginning to work with Shirley's mother, so—I mean, I've only had Shirley since March 11 and we haven't had that many meetings really. So I'm just beginning to get to know Shirley's mother, but I think that she really appreciates what I'm doing because I can find myself now reprimanding Shirley in front of her, and she sticks up for me, where she doesn't want to discipline Shirley in front of me I don't think. But yet what I say goes. And she likes it this way.

B.M.: So she takes the background when she's at your house?

MRS. B.: Yeah, and this is——

K.O.: But she does this, she's the kind of person who'd take the background anyway. She's so, she doesn't feel very important.

MRS. E.: But that isn't, I mean isn't that generally the kind that the children are placed, I mean that the parents of most of these children are like that anyway, aren't they? I mean, in front of you they take a back seat but after that—— You know, they aren't all blunt like Cooky [*Billy's mother*] . Cooky will come out and say—she'll swear every other word—she'll say, "I don't know where in hell he gets all his damn swearing." I haven't heard Billy swear, not once.

B.M.: I've gotta get him home because he's picking up bad habits!

MRS. E.: And, you know, and I haven't heard Billy swear. I don't go following Billy around to listen to what he's saying to other little boys.

K.O.: But I wonder if, traditionally, if we keep parents—own parents—and foster parents apart and never mix them together—it's taboo to put them together—if this doesn't just worsen it for kids. I believe it does. It makes them feel the competition more keenly. Where they can see an own parent and a foster parent together—comfortable together—then it's not such a frightening thing.

MRS. B.: This is good. With Shirley, this is really great. Because I know, last week I was here. We were playing on the swings and she saw that her mother and I were getting along very well. In fact, I think she saw that we were getting along too well because I was paying more, a lot of attention to her little sister as well as [to] Shirley and she didn't like that very well. But she did say something, she said, "I've got two mommies," you know, and she was very happy about it and the mother was very happy about it. We seem to be able to get along fine.

B.M.: That's the ideal state, isn't it, for a kid to be able to say, "I've got two mommies," with pleasure?

K.O.: Yeah, and it's almost as though—— Earlier she had said, "Mommy, I mean Mrs. B."

* * *

MRS. E.: Well, they sense the tension, I know. With one of the other boys I have now, the mother is very antagonistic. I don't know what she'd be like if she were cold stone sober. Generally speaking when she calls she's had a beer or two or more and when she brought him back Sunday night, she'd had several. I wasn't home but she gave [*undecipherable*] hard times. And being very, very critical—not of the home, which might well have been Sunday night and I wouldn't have cared, but of whether [her son] was favored or treated fair and square, you know that sort of thing, where she didn't even know the facts in the case.

B.M.: In other words, she's always attacking you, huh?

MRS. E.: Yeah, but I mean it rolls off me like water off a duck's back.

B.M.: Well, it wouldn't off some foster parents, would it? This wouldn't work with all foster parents.

MR. B., MRS. B.: No, huh-uh.

MRS. E.: She talked to me for an hour on the phone the other morning. She'd given him a jack knife for his birthday. She apologized many times for not asking my permission and I said, "Well, I don't know why you feel you should ask my permission if you wanted to buy him something. I just wanted to tell you that—I am very frank with you and all the parents—that if I didn't approve of it, I would just take it away and save it for him when he goes home and he brings it back." Just like the guns—we just don't allow guns, it's one of those things—our own children had them, but they could use them in moderation, but we've had cases where some of the kiddos take them to bed. Rather than say, "This child can have a gun, but this one can't 'cause he overdoes it," you know, that sort of thing, we just don't allow them. It's easier that way, easier for everyone concerned. And so she mentioned the knife, and I said, "No, I'm perfectly happy to have [her son] have a knife." So then she called me up again today and she said, "[My son] still got the knife?" I said, "Yes, as a matter of fact, he has it. It's put up for a week." And she was sort of annoyed and asked me to explain it, so I explained it to her. She said, "Do you think that was quite fair?" I said, "Gee, I try to be fair. I probably don't hit it 100% perfect, but I do try." And I had the feeling that she was very dissatisfied.

B.M.: Well, you know, some foster parents would call us up and say, "Take this kid away" or "Get the mother off my back."

MRS. E.: But she doesn't want him back. She isn't about to have him back.

MRS. B.: Well, I have trouble with a grandmother calling me every week.

B.M.: What do you think, should be agency step in and help field these things, or where and when should the agency step in, or how much can a foster mother take?

MRS. E.: When a foster mother cries, "Help!"

K.O.: Well, like this grandmother business. I have said right along, "Tell her to call me if you get tired of hearing it."

MRS. B.: Yeah. I haven't, and she——

Mr. B.: Well, I don't know. It's really a problem if she actually comes down and tries to snatch the kid, you know.

MRS. B.: She threatens.

Mr. B.: She says a lot, but she never does anything.

B.M.: Well, some social workers say don't even talk to the parents unless the parents first talk to the social worker. The social worker is always fielding it.

K.O.: That's the way it used to be here.

MR. B.: I find that they call [my wife] quite often about one thing and another.

MRS. B.: I got a call yesterday.

B.M.: And you don't mind it? You don't resent it?

MRS. B.: No, I don't really mind it. I want to be friends with the parents. I can't see——

MRS. E.: I think it's much easier to take care of that child if you're friends with the mother.

B.M.: In other words, it makes your work easier?

MRS. B.: Oh, yes.

B.M.: But some foster parents would say it doesn't make their work easier, that they want the parents out and they want the kid to themselves.

K.O.: Yes, I have a situation where there have been many, many difficulties surrounding visits—with the foster family being against them, my being for them, and the own family being for them. And when somebody is really against something, they'll use many reasons why it isn't good. One of the reasons being, "Well, when the child comes to the Village [to visit the mother], it upsets the child," and I say, "Well, gee, why don't I have the mother come to your house?" And [she says] "Oh, no!" And that sort of thing, where it's definitely, "We want the child, but we don't want any part of his crazy family."

B.M.: Yeah, and those people are generally much more judgmental of parents, don't you think?

K.O.: Judgmental, or maybe scared. I think in this situation there's——

MR. B.: They don't want to be involved.

K.O.: Well, I think there's a fear, which I can understand.

MRS. E.: What sort of a fear do you mean?

K.O.: A fear of—— a—— mental illness. The mother's had problems, has been hospitalized. I think the foster mother is just afraid of what might happen.

B.M.: I think that's true in the case we share. I think originally there was a lot of fear of his—— Well, of course she'd been told stories about the father interfering with placements before, and she'd built up—— She'd never seen the father, and she'd built up all these fantasies about what he might do when he came. And then, he was really a meek little, sad looking guy. She was amazed to see him, because he doesn't look like he'd hurt a fly.

MRS. B.: We've been through this too. [Course] we haven't lived in the Hartford area very long. When we moved here we heard all about what's going on with the Puerto Ricans and Negroes and so forth, and Carlos' father is Puerto Rican. For awhile I was a little scared about what it was really going to be like if he came and he brought his friends and his brother, and, you know, everybody else.

MR. B.: You really don't know what they're going to do until they come to see you.

MRS. E.: That wouldn't bother me though.

MRS. B.: It did me, but now—— .

MR. B.: Well, they all come—there's three or four of them—they all come, they don't come alone any more. She relies on them, I suppose, to bring her back and forth—but Shirley's mother, you know, she isn't our problem. It's the grandmother that you gotta watch out for, you know. She doesn't go along with this at all. She wanted to take the kid out of there and bring her into her nest, and that's the way it should be as far as she's concerned. She doesn't see it any other way. But the grandfather, he doesn't have anything to say about it one way or the other. He's perfectly content with the way it is, I think.

MRS. B.: Oh he misses her.

MR. B.: Well I think so, but I'm not at all sure that he wants to tangle with her either. She's a ball of fire, there's no way around that.

[Mr. and Mrs. M. enter here, having been at an adoption meeting in another building by mistake. I explain the purpose of the discussion to them, suggesting among other things that foster parents' work with natural parents could help relieve the manpower shortage in social work.]

MR. B.: [*Speaking of the factory where he works.*] When they keep laying off over there, I'll be looking for a job. They laid off 5,500—2,000 in the paper, but it's really 5,500.

B.M.: Are they going to get you?

MR. B.: I hope not.

B.M.: That's all right. We'll give you a lot of foster kids.

MR. B.: . . . that will tide me over until I get back to work.

B.M.: Sure. You'll have to keep them, though. You can't get rid of them when you go back to work.

MRS. E.: It's amazing what it will do for you, though. It really keeps you busy.

MRS. B.: I've got four, two of my own and two foster, and they keep me going.

B.M.: Back to natural parents—I was wondering if we could tell about some of the specific things that you have helped parents with. I thought of you and Fred's father. [*Speaking to Mr. and Mrs. M.*] Remember when he came and visited and he would throw Fred up in the air and it would scare the kid, and the father didn't seem to sense that it was scaring him, and—— Tell us about that, would you? How you handled it.

MRS. M.: I've kind of forgotten——

B.M.: Well somehow you handled it very sensitively, and got it across to the father that this scared the kid even though he didn't realize it was scaring him. But it apparently didn't threaten the father, because he always liked you very much.

MR. M.: Well, I think we were honest and open with them and didn't make them feel that they were a burden coming to visit the child.

MRS. M.: I think part of it is to accept them.

B.M.: They felt so relieved to be accepted, too, because their kids had been in other foster homes where they hadn't been accepted.

MRS. M.: We treated them as our friends.

MRS. E.: Isn't that the answer to it right there?

MRS. M.: I always feel sorry for parents, really because they want——

MR. B.: Well, they're scared when they come there to begin with. They don't know what to expect. They think we're a bunch of wolves, or something, anyway. They think that by putting their children in a home like this they're just throwing them off to the winds, you know, to somebody that could care less about them. And I really believe they think this and when they come to your house, they don't know what to expect.

MRS. M.: I think they just feel that we might have a bad opinion of them, you know, that they haven't been too good a parent. I'd imagine I would feel that way.

K.O.: I think an interesting thing that happened with the B.'s when we placed Shirley is her mother really wanted to inspect them, and they literally came in here to be inspected. Literally, they came to be looked at, as people, not the home——

MRS. B.: But I can't help but admire them for it, admire the mother for it. I really feel that because she did this, she must have a lot of feeling for her child.

B.M.: I would do the same thing if I placed my kid some place.

MRS. B.: I felt this is the thing to do, no matter what. Whether I was accepted or not, she was doing the right thing. She was doing what she felt was right, because she loved the child.

K.O.: She would not sign the papers until she had inspected them.

MRS. B.: And then after we talked, and we got along very well, for about an hour—over an hour and a half, I think—she still wanted to get my husband out of work and have him come here.

MR. B.: I was supposed to be there at noon or something——

MRS. B.: Well, you didn't know for sure. We didn't know for sure when the meeting was going to be, and then you took off somewhere from the shop.

MR. B.: And then you called, and it was getting kind of late then——

K.O.: It was a whole afternoon as far as I was concerned, and then when he came and she looked him up and down—— The thing he said that I thought was so great was, "We sure hope you'll come visit her, because you know we want her to go back home." That was the thing that I think really made a lot of sense to her too—but how many foster parents would be willing to do that?

B.M.: That's the trouble.

K.O.: I can think of some that if I called them up and said, "The child's mother wants to inspect you, would you mind coming in?"

ALL: [*Laughter*]

B.M.: Well you know, as [another social worker] and I were trying to think of who was good with natural parents, I mean you three couples were the ones that first occurred to us, and there weren't too many more as we thought about it. No, there were more—I mean, there are others who are good with natural parents, but there are a lot who wouldn't be as warm and accepting and welcoming and, like, have cook-outs as you did with Fred's parents, and that kind of thing.

MR. M.: I think it's very important, especially for the child if he's going to go home, because if the real parents can't visit, the child may forget about them. This would be very damaging to the child.

B.M.: But a lot of foster parents would like the kid to forget about their natural parents.

MR. B.: I wonder if the foster parents realize what they're working to gain. I mean, you take that child in hopes that somebody can rebuild his family so that you can get it back together again, and possibly some of them don't understand that this is happening. They think that the family's gone and that's it and I have the child, I'll have him until something else happens, you know? It may be that they don't quite understand what the job is.

K.O.: You think that some of them may sort of see themselves as rescuing a child from something bad?

MR. B.: Yeah, that's exactly what I think.

MRS. B.: With my friends, and so forth, this is what they think I'm doing. No matter what I say, this is what I'm doing.

MR. B.: And they feel the child should never go back to his family. They think he'll go right back to the place he was before and be just as bad off.

MRS. B.: And we've talked about what if the chance came up for adoption for one that I have, which is Carlos. It's possible, we don't know what's going to happen. They think it would be absolutely terrible if I didn't adopt him because I rescued him from this terrible thing and I shouldn't try to get him back with his mother or anything of the sort. This is what—it's not just one person—many people feel this way, that I've rescued him from the big bad witch——

MRS. E.: I would think if you didn't make friends with the parents that a parent could make the job so much harder because I know with [one of my foster children], he's long since gone home, he had a very hard life with his mother and she had a very hard life—her own life was very hard. I think she was definitely a victim of circumstances. I suppose most of them are anyway. But I enjoyed [the boy], but was very, very happy when he went home and I still love to hear from him. He calls me up. She calls me up. Now [the boy] has been gone two years I guess, pretty close to two years. And every now and then she calls me up. She's invited me down to where she works. I haven't gone, but I intend to go just as soon as I—— I told her when I stopped having so many children, I'd be down. And she's very nice to me. She's a person I couldn't probably hob-nob with, but I think it made it easier for [the boy]. It made the change easier for [the boy]. He knew that if he went home and it didn't work, that she would willingly let him come back with me, because she was afraid she couldn't handle him too. And she kept asking me, "You sure it's going to be all right? Will you take him back if I couldn't manage? If something goes wrong? Because I wouldn't want to upset him again." And if we hadn't made it a point to be friends with her, I think [the boy] would have been much more frightened of making the change.

B.M.: Well, I think that's true of Billy, too. I think it's been very helpful for Billy to have this kind of transition and I'm sure that he'll want to continue contact with you.

MRS. E.: Yes, he said tonight, "All the boys are coming down, [to visit me when I go home.] Now when are you coming down, Joe?" Joe said, "Ah, I'm not going to come down and visit you." He said, "Well, Mom said you all are."

B.M.: And I'll bet the mother keeps calling you too.

MRS. E.: Well she calls me twice a day. She wants me to call her tomorrow the moment you leave.

B.M.: Well how about this? Doesn't it take a lot of time?

MRS. E.: It's very time-consuming, especially when you're making a complete wedding outfit and you have to stop and put it down——

B.M.: Yeah. Do you think you ought to get extra pay? I mean, do you think this should be included as part of your job. I'm not saying you will get extra pay.

MRS. B.: I don't. I like it.

B.M.: Not these days, anyhow. Not the way they're talking about money around here.

MR. B.: I think it's part of the job.

MRS. M.: I do, too.

MRS. B.: It's so much an easier feeling. It really is, because I know I would have liked to have done this with the agency I worked for before. This was state, in Massachusetts. And there was no contact, hardly any contact at all. And the mother would have liked it much more. She would ask me if, sneakily, she could call me. I guess they must have told her that she was not to call or bother me or anything, and she would sort of sneakily ask if she could call and I'd have to say no, I mean——

B.M.: You're working for the agency.

MRS. M.: Right.

MRS. E.: Well, it used to be that way here, you couldn't do it.

MRS. B.: This is a shame, because the children went back to their mother and if there had been closer contact from the time they were with me, there wouldn't have been such a hard time when they went back.

B.M.: That was really a wrench for you and the kids both, wasn't it?

MRS. B.: Both of us, it was really terrible. I'd had them for three years and I had maybe four visits.

MRS. E.: There are some you'd like to forget.

B.M.: Some kids or some parents?

MRS. E.: Both. I had one that I was very happy to forget, but the mother wouldn't let me. She called me up periodically for two or three years afterwards. The last time she called me was after his session in June in court. The judge said, "If I could place him back in your home for a summer, maybe they could stall off sending him to a reformatory."

K.O.: You said thanks but no?

MRS. E.: I said I couldn't do it to my own boy who was the same age. They started out together at 6 or 7 and at that time, it was last year, he was 16, and I just couldn't do it to him.

MR. B.: There was one thing gained there, though. She had enough confidence to think that you could actually do something for him.

MRS. E.: Well, I don't know. I had him for four years, four or five, and when he went back I thought he was pretty well in command of himself. I think he had lots of basic problems, but he wouldn't constantly need someone with him. But I thought maybe along about then, where she'd done all right with her other one, that maybe she'd do the same thing.

MR. B.: Yeah, but you working with her had a lot of effect on her in thinking of a foster home.

MRS. E.: I don't know. She was really a doozy.

B.M.: The way things were as you described it in Massachusetts, both you and the mother always felt you were sneaking around if you had any kind of natural spontaneous contact. I mean, the mother would feel sneaky if she called and you would feel sneaky, too.

MRS. E.: A child would be bound to sense that though.

B.M.: You'd think so.

K.O.: I wonder why this was devised as the way of working with foster families and own parents through the years. Somebody must have concluded— 'cause even in our own social work training, we were taught this.

MRS. M.: We were told that in the beginning, too. About any contact that was being made. Because a couple of times I made contact and I thought I'd better call.

B.M.: And having me for a social worker, I said, "Well, go ahead and use your own judgment."

K.O.: You were told by whoever was doing the home study?

MRS. M.: Yeah, this lady—— Whenever a contact was made with the real parents, it was done through the agency.

B.M.: That was two summers ago, wasn't it?

Mr. B.: We don't do that. We tell them to feel free to contact us. I don't think you ever called any of them, have you?

MRS. E.: I do. I call.

MRS. B.: I would like to, one of them, but mainly because the little boy we have, Carlos, he's petrified of his mother—really, really petrified—and she's called me, lately she's called me and given an inkling that somehow she would like to have him back. And he's literally emotionally upset when it comes to his mother, he's very very upset and he, well, he breaks out in hives. His eyes all swell up, he cries, and then he'll sit quietly like a statue all the time she's there, whether it's an hour and a half or two hours or however long it is. He just sits there with no response at all except fear. And she's taken him for a whole day and he's done this. Well, myself, she's only visited him once in the last six months, I'd say. And I think that if she could have periodic visits with him and just *be* there, I think that eventually he woul think her a friend at least. And maybe somehow they can get back together. Because actually he's had a lot of emotional problems. He's turning out great, I think. He still has these little quirks——

K.O.: You're saying that you'd like to be free to call her?

MRS. B.: I would like to be free to call her.

K.O.: You don't feel you are.

Mrs. B.: Well, she doesn't have a phone. I have no way to contact her, really.

K.O.: Yeah, well if you did——

MRS. B.: I don't know whether I would be free or not. Because this is such a deep situation. I mean, you'd have to know the whole story, really.

MRS. M.: You want somebody else to accept part of the responsibility.

MRS. B.: I would like to be able to contact her, and maybe go get her and bring her to my house even. Or go for a ride, or somehow get him to accept her, at least as a friend.

B.M.: You feel you have permission to do this if you took the initiative?

MRS. B.: I haven't really thought——

B.M.: I mean, is the agency killing some initiative that shouldn't be killed, is what I'm saying, in foster parents. I don't know.

MRS. M.: I think so.

B.M.: Do you?

MRS. M.: Yes——

MRS. E.: Maybe I'm dumb. I don't feel it.

MRS. M.: Well, in the case of the one we have now. You know, he just wasn't allowed to go home. We were told this. And when we got to know him. I mean, I think we're just lucky with the kids we got. There's no problem—little problems, I mean nothing big. And after we got to know the parents, I used to feel so bad for them every time they left, you know, went home. And I thought, gee, if only he could go home for a day, you know. So I finally said to—no, I said to them one day, "Well, gee, maybe he can go home for a day." I felt so bad for them. So then I knew I'd put my foot in it and [the social worker], you know? Well, she thought about it and she said, "Well, I'll contact someone down near his parents and work with them down there." She said, "Yes, he can go home for a day," and I said, "Oh gee, what a load off my mind." Just then I thought, "Well, if anything happens to him now, I'm terrible, doing all this." So I really wanted her to accept some of the responsibility, you know? But he did go home for one night.

B.M.: And yet you were afraid to suggest it. You were afraid to put your foot in it.

MRS. M.: Yes, yes. I said it without realizing.

K.O.: You say that you feel the agency stops——

MRS. M.: Well, because I think I was told in the beginning, and then I was told when we got this little boy, "He just can't go home, you know, he mustn't go home."

Mr. B.: I don't think they'd want to make the decision without contacting the agency. They know—you know—one side of the story, and we only know what we see. You really shouldn't make the decision alone because this is a group thing, trying to figure out a family. You shouldn't be on your own with it.

K.O.: It is complicated, too, because I think with [the foster boy] , if I'm remembering the situation correctly, the state had a lot to do with this decision.

MRS. M.: Yes, it was the state.

B.M.: I was thinking, probably the state was back there someplace.

MRS. M.: Yes, it was the state. And then the state worked it out. He was sent home for a weekend. And to me that child has—he's really himself now since he knows he can go home once in a while. 'Cause he loves his parents, I'm sure he does.

MRS. B.: And with little Carlos—they had asked to take him out for a ride and I called the agency to make sure it was all right, figuring it probably would be, but I'd let them know for sure. And when I called the agency, they said, "Definitely no. No. Not at this time." With him, the parents are lying about each other and—well, one takes dope, one came after another with a knife, and one's after him with a gun. And—you know, there's an awful lot of violence and so forth. So I don't feel free to do anything, really—how far I should go, or who is actually lying, you know.

K.O.: Were you glad that the agency was in a position to say no at a time like that, or would you have rather——

MRS. B.: Well I really questioned it, because I thought, I mean, what's a ride, I mean, you know, where the mother is really trying——

MRS. M.: I think—— [*Undecipherable*]

MRS. B.: Well, see, I didn't know anything about it, and she was supposed to be taking dope at this time, and so forth and so on. Well, I didn't know anything about this. Well, she came to me afterwards and she told me that she wasn't and she actually even cried. And this is the first time she even said more than two or three words to me. She's always been a very cold one, and this time we talked I think for two hours, and we really ended up friends. And she said what her husband had done to her, and so forth, what she had done in the past, and why she was, how she was sorry, and why the state has custody of Carlos, and so forth and so on. I mean, I really learned an awful lot. I really feel sorry for the mother. I feel almost like going to get her and bringing her to my home, or bringing Carlos there, or——

K.O.: What would stop you from doing that?

MRS. B.: Well, I don't know what—the father has periodic visits with the social worker. I don't know how the social worker feels, whether she [the mother] is responsible enough to have visits or-or, I have no idea really. I feel like I'm in the dark.

K.O.: What stops you from getting in the light. I mean, what stops you from talking with the social worker about it?

MR. B.: She doesn't get on the phone and do it, that's why.

K.O.: I just wondered, why, you know.

MRS. B.: I think it's Carlos, really, Because, I mean, I want these visits, but I see him all upset and a nervous wreck, and vomiting. He swells all up, he breaks out in hives, and he's a wreck, you know.

K.O.: You're saying two things.

MRS. B.: I know I am, 'cause I feel two things. I really want to do—— I feel that the mother should come, but I don't know, you know, whether—— I just wish there was some way she could get there herself. I think that I——

K.O.: I think I'm hearing that you feel the agency is sort of—— a-a stumbling block, a constraining influence, that something has made it hard for you to clear this with the social worker. You maybe don't feel free to call up and say, "This is what I'd like to do," or you don't feel free to go ahead and do it, or something.

MRS. B.: Yeah.

MRS. M.:——[undeciperhable] because of fear——

MRS. B.: Yeah.

K.O.: Fear of what?

MRS. M.: Fear of—— Well I remember the first time——

MR. M.: Well, if something goes wrong——

MRS. M.: —Fred—— I thought, "Gee, suppose they don't bring him back, what will I do?" They just took him out for a ride and I thought I had assumed the responsibility——

MR. B.: Yeah, well that's the thing, and all of a sudden you find out that he's in Cuba or something, you know? Or Puerto Rico.

MRS. B.: Yeah, 'cause this is what has happened with the brother. The father came and took him for a ride and the brother ended up in Puerto Rico. And there's nothing they can do about it.

MR. B.: This could conceivably happen to the child we're caring for, you know? We say, "O.K., you take him for a ride," and the first thing you know he's in another country somewhere. What are you going to do now?

MRS. B.: But I don't want to be completely responsible.

B.M.: Yeah, and you're afraid that if you took the responsibility, you'd be blamed. Is there also a fear that the agency might say that you haven't been a good foster parent if you took this responsibility?

MRS. B.: No.

MRS. M.: Not for me, because in a way I couldn't care less.

MRS. E.: That's the way I feel.

MRS. M.: I want to do this, and if they don't think I'm capable, well then I must not be. I feel they have experience and are able to size people up. But I want to do it, you know, what I'm doing. And if I'm not doing it right, then somebody should tell me. You know, I'm really not worried about what they think.

K.O.: But I think you are.

MRS. B.: Well, I think I am a little, too, but——

MR. M.: I think you should contact the social worker often, more often, and talk more. You're pretty well out on a limb, I think.

MRS. E.: (Undecipherable)——like this morning [a social worker] and I were talking, and I talked 'til I got it off my chest. I was very annoyed with this weekend situation.

K.O.: He told me who was on the phone. Did you hear me say, "You'll be a long time?"

MRS. E.: Yes I did—and I really had an axe to grind. When I call, I make it worth my while.

B.M.: You mean, worth the agency's while. You reverse the charges.

MRS. E.: Yeah, in one breath—you see, I think K.O.'s saying two things. In one breath she says, "Ah, you should feel free to call," and in another breath she says, "Well you can't talk two hours." But, however, some people you have to hammer and hammer at to put your point across. I hope I got my point across. If I didn't, there's going to be what's commonly called hell to pay. I was very much annoyed with this weekend situation. I think it set [the foster child] back—well, a good year. I hope he'll pick up sooner. We left a very weeping boy tonight when I came in. Nobody loves me, you know, and I really don't belong here. "My mother says I don't belong here." Yet mamma doesn't want him. I don't want him permanently, either. I mean I—well, I suppose, like the rest of you people, I like to see them grow up and be somebody and be able to hold their own, and go back to their family. But when you see somebody baiting somebody, "I want you, but I don't want you," it's rough to say—should you sit back and let the agency let this little boy go home for a visit? And I think they should tell her to put her money where her mouth is, either take him or leave him. It's sad, because he can't take it. He's torn apart every single time. He goes all to pieces. Of all my children, he's the one that if I had to pick, I would take the least to. I mean, he's a kind of a pathetic little boy. If I had to say I wanted to adopt one of these boys, he'd probably be the last one. But I'm sure he's the one that needs loving the most, and I try to give him more than the others because of that. You know, he's like a boy who likes to be unhappy. He likes to play he's unhappy. I'll tuck him in at night and I'll say, "What's the matter, . . . , aren't you happy?" "I ain't never been happy. I don't know what happiness is." I'll say, "Oh, come on, . . . ," and I have to really play with him for a long while before I get him reacting like the other children.

MR. B.: If you want to see what happiness is, you want to go down and take a look at Carlos.

MRS. B.: Oh, he really is. This is the problem. This is——

MR. B.: You let him take one look at his folks, boy, and he——psew! He's gone—he don't want anything to do with them, he'd rather——

MRS. E.: See, we run the gamut in that, too, I mean from one extreme to the other.

MRS. M.: It's sad, though.

MRS. B.: He's laughing all the time. When I got him, he was screaming all the time, constantly screaming. Now he's always laughing.

B.M.: It's a real dilemma, because here's a kid whose parents really had damaged him. And therefore the foster parents really would feel they're doing a better job because you are.

MRS. B.: Right.

B.M.: And yet, how can you avoid getting this across to the parents? And how can they avoid not feeling defensive with you?

MRS. B.: When we got Carlos, he was like a vegetable. He was 2 years old, he weighed 19 pounds—malnutrition—no coordination at all, he couldn't even stand or no muscles, you know. He was just——

B.M.: I mean, parents feel so crummy anyhow. You know, they really feel——

MRS. E.: So why do they antagonize everybody, or why do they make themselves suffer and the foster parents suffer by coming to see him at all because they couldn't have cared or he wouldn't have been in that state?

MRS. B.: Well, this is what bothers me too because, you know——

MRS. M.: They couldn't have cared then, but maybe, you know——

MRS. B.: Well, the father always said he did, and always professed that he did.

MRS. E.: And maybe they couldn't, rather than wouldn't.

MRS. B.: This is the thing.

MRS. E.: I didn't say they wouldn't. I said they didn't care. I don't know why they didn't care.

MRS. B.: But they have another one that's perfectly normal, you know, younger. This is what——

K.O.: So they're improving.

MR. B.: I don't know. This is the kind of a case where I don't know about. I don't think they'll ever get back together. Yet they both seem to want him, you know, in some way or another.

MRS. E.: I'm hard. I think it's spite.

MRS. B.: This is what bothers me too. Just how far should I go? Just what is right and just what is wrong? Because I think the mother wants him now more just for spite because she can't have the younger one, and she's going to show him she can get Carlos, that he's not going to get Carlos, in fact she's almost said the same thing.

B.M.: So you're caught with ambivalent parents, as we all are, I mean who do and don't want their kid, who love and don't love.

MRS. M.: I also think—I don't know how right or wrong I am about this—but I think foster parents find out much more about parents than social workers will. I think real parents draw a line with social workers.

MRS. E.: Yes, they represent authority.

B.M.: I think you're right. I think they feel much more comfortable with foster parents. I'm sure that Billy's mother did feel a lot more comfortable with you than with me, or with the state worker.

MRS. E.: Well, if you're criticized as she had been from the time she was just a kiddo. And you're bound to put up a resistance to that. I mean, she'd never—— Her parting words the day she left at the train station—she didn't say, "Will you take me to the train station." I said, "What time are you leaving, Cooky?"

She said, "Well, I have to be in Hartford at thus and so. If we leave here at 10, you'll get me there on time." She didn't say, "Will you take me in?"

MRS. M.: [The father of Fred] couldn't stand social workers. [*The rest of this statement is not distinct on the tape, but I think Mrs. M. was telling the story of how Fred's father chased the state social worker off his property by brandishing a shotgun at him, when the social worker was planning to take the children away.*]

MRS. E.: He sounds like my father. My father would have done that if someone would have suggested he couldn't take care of his.

MRS. M.: With us, no. We were fine. It was the social workers he couldn't stand.

MRS. E.: Well, he has a right to his opinion. I admire people who can stand up and be counted if they believe something.

K.O.: I think a lot of these people who have had a lot of contact with the state, where the children are wards of the state, have had contacts with authoritarian kinds of social workers, and it gets them off to a bad start, and they meet in an office, even here, and they immediately see the social worker as an authority person.

B.M.: And of course a lot of these people have been charged with neglect by the state. And if you've been charged with neglect, you're not likely to love some social worker, and you would expect all social workers to be as critical.

MRS. E.: And some of them really haven't had fair play. I don't think Billy's mother had complete fair play.

B.M.: No, I think she had a raw deal.

MRS. E.: I do, too. I think she was the victim of circumstances from poor handling. I think perhaps from the beginning it might have saved a whole lot of sorrow there if she had an understanding person. I imagine that a lot of it was not as bad as she stated because she was young at the time and maybe she didn't know any better and she let people tell her things that now she wouldn't. She would fight back now.

B.M.: Well, yeah, and sometimes social workers peg parents at the point where they are not able to function. They keep them there. You know, they say they're bad parents, let's keep them out. They've been bad for the kid. They will always be bad for the kid. And they don't believe that people change.

MRS. B.: Don't you think, though with the state that it's because there are so many that they can't look into the real personal aspect of all of this and they are treated as, well, as their record 'cause I know even when we get our children you hear a record and you think, "Oh, brother," you know, "what am I getting into?"—— The children aren't their records. I mean, the children are persons. They're people, and their mothers and fathers are people, too. But you read it on paper, and it's altogether different from what it is.

K.O.: You know, you're both suggesting that in some ways the agency is sort of an inhibiting factor as far as what foster parents might do with own parents. I'd be interested in knowing—what could the agency, the social workers here, us, do differently? That would not be so inhibiting? How?

MRS. M.: The only thing I feel—I think when you get a foster child, I know you can't tell everything about your parents, but I think a certain amount should be known—that the foster parents could make a decision then. You know, should the child go out for a trip, go home for a night, go home for a weekend. And just be able to let the agency know, "Well, I'm doing this [letting him go home this] weekend or whenever it might be." As it is, you don't really know so much and you wonder, "Gee, will they [the parents] kill him? Will they bring him back? Will they take him away, or what?" And it's a worry, you know.

K.O.: So you think you should be given more information?

B.M.: You should know more about the parents, so you'll have more information to base a decision on.

MRS. E.: I've never had that problem.

MRS. M.: Yes, if you know more about the parents, I think you can make the decision—you know, what type, or why the child was taken.

MRS. B.: With me, actually, I think I'm giving everybody the wrong impression. I think with Carlos' folks, I think that they are as much in the dark as I am about everything, because with the father, now, he was a real charmer and he led everybody to believe that he was very hen-pecked. The mother was the ruler, and this was it. Well, then we find out just recently, which has been over a year that I've had Carlos, that things aren't that way at all—that the father is a very violent man, which we never would have believed; that the father has a real wicked temper, which never would have showed up. All these things are beginning to show up—that's he's violently attacked and threatened the mother, which is something we never would have believed. And he's living with another woman, which is something we wouldn't believe. You know, I mean, all these things have come out that we wouldn't have believed.

MRS. M.: But if you had known about them, maybe——

MRS. B.: But the social worker didn't know either, 'cause she was taken in as much as we were. She thought of him the same as I thought of him—a very charming person, a poor, hen-pecked husband. You know, he really played the role.

B.M.: He had snowed people, huh?

MRS. B.: He really did. He'd come to the house and he'd hardly say two words. The wife would, "Well, let's go——Well, don't push him," you know, this was it. And he'd smile and try to make friends with the baby and, "Uh-huh, this is the wrong thing to do. Don't push him. Leave him alone, let him make his own way." But all the time she acts like she's saying, "No, don't go near him," you know, "You've had your fun. You came. O.K., let's go." And all the time it really wasn't this way. And then one day he came to the house and he poured his heart out to me, supposedly, with tears, and we sat there at the table, and we really talked and talked and talked. And he came without her, because she had taken off with another man at the time. It really was quite a heart-jerking story, you know? And then it turns out he's taken off with another woman and things have completely reversed, and all the time we thought, "Oh, this poor man," and now we feel sorry for this poor woman.

B.M.: It's hard to know who to feel sorry for.

MRS. B.: Right. Now the agency, I know, was as much in the dark about this as we were. We're all playing the same game, I think, you know?

K.O.: But you felt that there was information that you could have had that hasn't been given you?

MRS. M.: I don't know if there was or not. If there is, I feel it's important that foster parents know quite a bit as far as the parents. That way you could make a decision about going out for a couple of hours.

B.M.: I think you're suggesting that the thing be reversed, though. Traditionally, the social workers made the major decision about visiting and contacts. You're suggesting the foster parent is in a better position to make that decision?

MRS. M.: I think that the foster parents get to know the real parents much better. They get to know the true parent much better than social workers do. I find this, anyway.

MR. B.: Here again, you're talking about a limited number of people, too.

MRS. M.: Oh yes, yes, but even so——

MR. B.: Because they couldn't use that here as a general practice, I don't think.

B.M.: I don't know. Maybe we could, if we looked at things differently. I think everything's open to examination.

MR. B.: Well, weren't you saying earlier that there are a lot of foster parents that don't want to have anything to do with it?

B.M.: That's true, but maybe it's been partly our fault, too. I mean, this woman we work together with, for example. I think she was briefed in the wrong way when we first started. I think she would still maybe want to keep parents out, but on the other hand, she was given fear that she shouldn't have been given in the beginning, you know? At the time of the study, I mean.

MR. B.: Well, I think everyone has to be open to break new ground, you know, any way you can find it, if you're going to get ahead in this kind of thing.

K.O.: Yeah, and besides, Mrs. E. certainly must have had the same kind of orientation——

MRS. E.: Yeah, I know I did.

K.O.: And I think the same person did—was it Mrs. A. that you saw first?

MRS. M.: Yes.

K.O.: So she would have oriented them the same way.

B.M.: Yeah, that's true.

K.O.: And there's two different outlooks.

B.M.: Oh, there's no question that there are lots of foster parents who wouldn't even want this decision.

MRS. M.: Oh, I can imagine, but then, you know, it's left up to whichever way you want it.

MRS. E.: I wouldn't want the decision completely, I would like to be able to call up——

MRS. B.: I wouldn't either.

MRS. E.: To call up and say, "I think he should go home. Will you O.K. it?" Because I just feel that if you're working for someone they should know exactly what's going on in your job. I really feel they should.

MRS. M.: I agree with that, but——

MRS. E.: But I'd like to know that—if you're living with a child, you certainly know that child better than a social worker. You have to know them better.

MRS. M.: Well, in our case, I kind of said, well I put my foot in it anyway . . . by saying, "Gee, maybe he should go home." So Christmas time he went home, and I didn't really enjoy Christmas day thinking about him. Because I didn't know that much about the parents, except what I'd gotten to know, you know, myself. . . . What am I doing here? But anyway, it turned out O.K. and to me it was the best thing that ever happened to him. He was so quiet and reserved before that. Then he was more willing to talk. And he cried. He cried and cried, and sort of came out. And we were much more understanding——

MR. B.: Just the opposite of the way it was with us.

MRS. M.: ——of the whole situation. So he's been home for weekends since, and I think it's good. I think it makes the parents feel good—see, we can have him and we can——

K.O.: What other things could the social workers or the agency do differently, besides telling you more about the families? So that they wouldn't be inhibiting?

MRS. M.: For foster parents?

K.O.: Uh-huh.

MRS. E.: Come out and be a baby sitter once a week so you could——

K.O.: Forget it.

MRS. B.: So you can get to know the foster child.

B.M.: That's not a bad idea. I really have thought that foster parents need a lot more relief than they get.

MRS. E.: Don't you think that if you have more than one, you can hire a baby sitter occasionally? But I don't, I like my own to baby sit because then I don't worry about someone else not understanding their ups and downs.

MRS. M.: We leave ours with a baby sitter.

MR. B.: We were invited over here once to sit down with the—you remember—the social workers and the state girl to talk over Shirley's situation. And I think—my opinion of that was that I learned quite a lot about what I was getting into before we even had the child, or even knew for sure whether we would get her or not, you know. And, to me, this was a big thing. I really enjoyed that. In fact, I got out of work for that one too, you know.

K.O.: They came to the intake conference.

MR. B.: To me, this was a big step. I think that, from my experience, if this was used more often maybe it might help to break some of the ground for a better understanding of what the child's problems are and what's happened. Because you're getting it right straight off the shoulder here, you know—what actually happened, you know, and why the child is there and what the problems are. And there's no two ways about it. If you don't get it there, you're not going to get it at all. Anything from then on you are learning together, you see. Here's the problem— now you're all getting it and if you get the child, O.K. If you don't, well, that's because something happened and it didn't work out.

K.O.: You almost didn't.

MR. B.: That's beside the point. When you get started with her, at least you knew what it was all about. And then, what the social worker learns and what we learn from that point on, I don't think you're missing that much after that, if you keep any kind of a contact with the agency at all. It seems to me that nobody's trying to hide anything, and everything is confidential anyway between the two.

MRS. E.: Why aren't you invited more to these conferences? I was last week and I thought it was wonderful, I really did.

MR. B.: Well, I think what they're doing here is breaking a lot of ground here recently. I'm gathering that all this has happened just recently.

MRS. M.: What are the conferences?

B.M.: Intake conferences. Before we accept a kid, we have an intake conference. Traditionally, only the staff here has been in on them, but more and more we're inviting foster parents.

K.O.: The foster parent that might be taking the child.

MRS. E.: I thought it was wonderful. There are so many more things you understand.

MRS. M.: Maybe. . . . [*undecipherable*] was an emergency, you know, a last minute thing, or something——[*This is indistinct, but she is speculating about why they haven't been invited to one.*]

B.M.: Well, with Fred we hadn't been doing it, and that shows the force of tradition and habit. You know, you come to an agency and you say, "Well, how are things done around here? I'll do them the same way," and it takes you a while to get secure enough to say, "I think I'll do them differently."

MR. B.: Well, what made you make the decision to ask us to come over to this thing, anyway?

K.O.: Well, I made that decision.

MR. B.: What prompted you to do this anyway? If you hadn't been doing it, something must have——

MRS. E.: Didn't it start with Billy's mother? Is that what it was?

K.O.: I don't think I would have done it—I'm not sure I would have done it if it hadn't been for our meetings over there. [*She is speaking of the research meetings.*]

MR. B.: Well, I know. I know a lot of things have happened because of those meetings. I wish they were there now. I think they would have added a lot. I'm sorry you didn't go.

MRS. M.: We weren't picked.

K.O.: Well, they weren't supposed to.

B.M.: Sorry, they got picked for the control group. Many are called, but few are chosen.

K.O.: The four of us were in the unstructured group——

MR. B.: So we know a lot of things that happened that you don't know about.

[Discussion about the research questionnaires.]

K.O.: I don't know—you asked—I think that it might make some difference who the foster parent was. There are probably people that I would hesitate to invite to come to an intake conference.

B.M.: Yeah, I would too. I'm not sure I should feel that way.

K.O.: I'm not sure I should either, but I think I might feel that way.

B.M.: I have a feeling that if we're going to do it for one, we should do it for all.

K.O.: Yeah. Now people in this room, sitting here right now were invited to come to this meeting because they've worked with own parents, because they accept own parents, because they like them, because they look at them as people, because they don't think they're all bad. And yet, I'm not sure that represents——

B.M.: There are some who would come and if they hear bad things about natural parents, they would feel more prejudiced toward them, is that what you mean?

MR. B.: In my job we feel that if we get 80% of the problems, the other 20% is——

B.M.: There are some who are very critical of natural parents, and want to keep them out.

MRS. M.: Do you think they should be foster parents?

B.M.: That's a good question.

MRS. E.: I do. I think for certain children. I know a family that has foster children, and in a certain age bracket, she does absolutely a wonderful job.

B.M.: Do these children have parents that they have a lot of contact with?

MRS. E.: Some have, and some haven't. But I mean they resent the natural parents most generally.

B.M.: Well, when I do a foster home study, I wonder, if somebody says, "I don't want to have much contact with parents," should I just automatically say, "Then you're not for our agency?" Or words to that effect?

MRS. E.: Mightn't she be a very good person for some particular type child? Or someone who isn't apt to have a long-term——

MR. B.: Maybe they've lost the parents altogether, or something like that. Maybe you could select foster homes in this way, or something like that.

B.M.: That's what I've concluded, that there are some kids who really don't have contact with their parents.

K.O.: Is it that, or is there another way that we should orient foster parents?

MRS. M.: It's fear. It's fear on their part, though. I mean, if they had some type of training for it, to make them aware. When I called here first thing, I had no idea, but I finally got the nerve to do it—really. And then when Mrs. A. came and she told me all these different things I thought, "Gee, I wonder if I'm able to cope with that kind of thing?" I didn't feel that I might be able. I wanted to, but I didn't think I might be able.

K.O.: I think there's more than fear. I think there's a competition. I think that a lot of people who are foster parents really need to feel like they're good parents and that there's a need to be better than the own parent. I'm not saying this is true of all of them, but I think that sometimes this happens.

MRS. E.: Why, though? I mean, why would——

K.O.: You know—who's the better mother kind of thing?

MRS. M.: But let's be honest. You know that you are better than some of them, but you don't show this to them. I mean, let's face it, really.

MRS. E.: Most people evaluate themselves, and know what they can do and what they can't do.

B.M.: Well, social workers have this better mother syndrome, too, you know, that kids love them more than they love their own mothers, and they get a lot of satisfaction from it.

MRS. E.: Well there's a sure cure for it.

B.M.: What's that?

MRS. E.: You have seven, eight, nine, or ten, and you don't have time to worry about who loves you the most. You just know you're here and you do the best you can.

B.M.: You only have so much to parcel out for each one, huh?

K.O.: O.K., but do all people feel this way? Or are there some foster parents who are very threatened? Frightened?

MR. B.: Everybody feels different about things. When you hire somebody, some people go better in this job than the other one does, you know? You have a wide variety of problems, so it seems natural that some foster parents would be better suited for this type of a situation, and some for this type. When you hire somebody, you know you don't got out and hire a whole flock of people, and they all got the same kind of knowledge or feelings and everything else, or everybody would be the same. It just isn't that way, so you have to grade your people and select a job to suit them, as near as I can make out. It's the best way you can do it.

K.O.: I think the difference is like—it's probably a silly example, but cooking—the child who goes home for a visit and comes back and says to the foster parent, "You can't make spaghetti the way my mother can," and the one foster parent who might, say, get all upset, feel that the child likes his own mother better and she can't please him, versus the foster parent who says, "I'll probably never be as good a cook as your mother is, aren't you lucky that you can go home and have spaghetti?" or whatever——

MRS. M.: That's a big deal, it's the best I can do.

B.M.: Goody-Goody for you, as my kid says.

K.O.: But I think that there are people who get real upset about this type of thing. They just feel competition. Or the child who comes back and says, "I don't want to come back. I want to be home."

MRS. E.: I have that a little with Joe [*a foster child*]. I'm being continually compared to Mrs. Y. [*a child care worker at the Village, where the child was placed previously*]. He just absolutely worships Mrs. Y. And I like Joe, and I like Mrs. Y. So I thought, "Gee, this is really getting to be a problem." I know I have him more or less on long term, I think that was the understanding with Joe, and I think he's happy there. But he really idolized Mr. and Mrs. Y., the houseparents.

K.O.: They've left.

MRS. E.: Oh, no, I didn't know that. Because he has asked me if he could have them out, and I said, "Yes, it will have to wait until after [my daughter's] wedding because right now I've got all I can handle. But after [my daughter's] wedding, I'll have them out." And many things that we have for breakfast now are things that Mrs. Y. cooked for him. And he likes doing it, and I let him do it. And he'll say, "This is what Mom Y. did for me, isn't it, Mom?" And I'll say, "Yes it is," and the kids all seem to like it. And sometimes he does bug me a little, I'll admit, she's so young and so pretty. And he also brings that out. I think it's wonderful that he can say these things. Sometimes I want to slug him, you know, I think, "Boy, Joe——," you know, one of these deals. But he is a nice youngster and I think I can understand why he does this. I think Mrs. Y. must have been what he would always want his mother to really be.

K.O.: But do you think most, or many, foster parents can feel this way?

MRS. E.: Oh, I hope so. Because Joe needs that.

K.O.: Have you known some who feel differently?

MRS. E.: Yes I have. But I try not to think that. I know a mother who does it with her own children. When her youngster compares her to somebody else, she's very resentful or finds wanting, you know.

MRS. M.: The kids say to me, "You're not like a mother."

MRS. E.: I don't think you are either. That's a compliment.

MRS: B.: "You don't act like a mother," they tell me, too. I get this, even from 4- and 5-year-olds.

MRS. E.: I have that when I fish, or climb a tree, or something like that, believe it or not at 56. But I think maybe if I were younger, I would resent being compared or—compared unfavorably, I'd say—with Mrs. Y. because I think she's a lovely person and I think she had to have what it takes to reach these boys. We had it this weekend with our own children, who were more or less performing, you know. We were out to dinner and one played the guitar and the other one sang, and Joe all through, he said, "Oh, [Mrs. E.'s daughter] got such a pretty voice, but you should hear Mr. Y. play and Mrs. Y. sing." [My daughter] was nice about it, you know?

B.M.: Well, of course, you get these kids who have had a lot of foster home placements, too.

MRS. M.: They're testing. They want to see how far they can go.

B.M.: Well I think you're right, Mrs. M. I think a lot of this is testing, and some foster parents can take it and some can't so easily.

MRS. E.: Like Joe's parting shot was to me leaving the car for the bus was, "You're a big liar." And my own children would have ran real fast had they said that to me. And I don't think I would have taken it like I did from Joe. And I thought, "Gee, I don't know whether to upset him now or wait 'til tonight when I get home and we'll talk about it." On the way down from the bus I was kind of running over in my mind exactly what this was all over, because it sort of left a gap in me, and it dawned on me in a way it really was a lie. I didn't mean to be, but there was part of the situation I didn't know about that I found when I got home. I had lied to him, but not knowingly. And—which reminds me, I forgot to bring it up tonight. So he still owes me the apology.

B.M.: Or somebody owes somebody an apology.

MRS. M.: I think all kids want reassurance. I know my own son, Mike— "I don't love you." I say, "Gee, I love you." But [the foster child], he's quiet. He says, "He doesn't like you." I said, "I know, but I love him. Anyone who's in this house, I love them." And he knows he's included, you know, since he's in the house. So I think they're just—— You make a big deal of it——

MRS. E.: Wait 'til they grow up and then tell you those things. My daughter told me—well, she's 26—and she told me that when she was a teen-ager she wished that one of our neighbors—that you people know in here—was her mother. But she said, "Boy, I'm glad I got that out of my system."

B.M.: My kid is always comparing us to other mothers and fathers. There's a lot of comparison, you know—this mother does things this way——

K.O.: Maybe we need an entirely different approach to training of foster parents, or orienting foster parents.

MR. M.: Yeah, I think 'twould be good to have just more than a special group of foster parents come to a meeting like this, because I think maybe some of the foster parents that really only hear about the bad side of the real parents—this may be the reason why they don't want them to come and visit. Now if they heard the good side, from us, for example.

MRS. M.: What's the good side?

MR. M.: Well, we accept them for what they are. They have their problems, so have we, but maybe a lot of foster parents don't realize this. They may just build up an imagination about the real parent and maybe if they were to hear more about them from foster parents that do accept——

B.M.: I think that would be very helpful. As a matter of fact, I was thinking of having this kind of meeting at a staff meeting. I think it would be good for social workers too.

MR. M.: 'Course I think you—I think any foster parents should allow the real parent to come at least once and find out for themselves. I mean, you can't really prejudge a person without meeting him.

MRS. B.: It's hard even the first time.

MR. M.: Well, we've been lucky. We haven't really had too much problem, even the first time. No problem, in fact.

MRS. M.: Whenever problems develop, I know on my part it was just a fear of what might happen, and really didn't.

B.M.: Yeah, that's generally true with fears.

* * *

[*Discussion about what age children the M.'s care for, and whether they want another child.*]

B.M.: I was wondering if you could talk a little bit about, you know, actual techniques. I mean, how do you help natural parents like learn how to take care of their kid?

MRS. M.: How do we help the natural parents?

B.M.: Yeah, I mean in terms of specific techniques. That example, for example, I gave of the way Fred's father threw him up in the air—that sort of thing.

MRS. M.: I can't remember. I mean, I remember the incident, but I can't remember what I said.

B.M.: I remember it very well because I was impressed with—— Now if I had said that to that father, he would have gotten very defensive, I'm sure. But somehow he didn't with you.

MRS. M.: I'm kind of silly in my way. People think I'm kidding, but I'm really serious.

MRS. B.: I do the same thing. I say what's on my mind impulsively. And sometimes it sounds really stupid, you know.

MR. M.: I think the first reaction from the real parents when they come to your home, I think more or less breaks the ice, really. They see the surroundings, they see how their child is being treated or where he lives. I think you can really talk more freely to them, whereas a social worker—well, it's a different situation.

B.M.: They're on their guard with a social worker more?

MR. M.: Well, yes. They've seen the surroundings where the child lives and I think maybe they could take an insult a little easier than—like, for instance, with [my wife], when she said to him about throwing Fred up in the air.

B.M.: It was advice, yeah. And what—the kinds of things that you would tell Billy's mother, you know, about—oh, what were some of those incidents? Where—oh, caught in the bed with a little girl——

MRS. E.: Yeah. And she really was afraid of Billy. I brought him down there for a one day visit, and she was absolutely frustrated. She couldn't handle him, she said he ran out across the street. In fact, the social worker, Mr. A., said she was in tears. She knew she couldn't handle him. And that's how I fell into this.

B.M.: That was the first home visit?

MRS. E.: Yes. And I said, "Well, my word, he's easy to handle. I wish she could see him in our home. In fact, I'd even be willing to have her come there and see." He said, "I'm going to take you up on that. When can you have her?"

B.M.: The state worker said, "When?"?

MRS. E.: A young man, I'm sure he's fresh out of college. He's awfully nice.

B.M.: But he's very open-minded.

MRS. E.: Yeah. And he said, "When could you take her?" And I thought, "Well gee, that's really—I can't really back down—and I said, 'Oh, any time,' thinking he's just joking." And he said, "No, I'm serious." He said, "That might really work out. I'd like to give it a try." I said, "Well, if she can stand me, I'm sure I can stand her." So she came up, and I might add we have eleven rooms and an old house, and sometimes I get to cleaning it up and sometimes I don't. Depends on what I've got in the works. I do a lot of things. I mean, I enjoy life, and I wouldn't swap my life for——. But at any rate, I imagine Billy's mother might be a good housekeeper, is that right?

B.M.: That's the one thing she's very proud of herself about. I've never seen her house. I'll see it tomorrow.

MRS. E.: Yes, and she told me that. If she lived nearer, she'd help me. She'd show me some short-cuts. And I said, "Well, that's fine. I wish you did too, because I would be willing to have you do some of these jobs." I'm perfectly willing, because ignorance isn't my problem. But, and I think she felt good because she could show me something. She said, "Well, I don't know why you can't do better. You have all the help you need. A dishwasher, you have this. And you have a husband who dotes on you, which he does. And she was just proud that she could tell me something. I didn't tell her that I thought what she could tell me didn't matter at all to me, because I have a firm belief that the old house will be there when I'm dead and gone.

B.M.: But she had to feel in control of the situation. She couldn't feel that you were in charge of her.

MRS. E.: She said, "I know I can't handle him." I said, "Oh, yes you can, Cooky, because I'm going——" I had to go to court that particular day. My son had a court thing for speeding, and I said, "I'm going to leave you completely on your own. Won't that be fun?" And she said, "Oh, I can't do it." I said, "Oh, come on." I said, "You're here at the end of the earth," and we are at the end of the earth. I said, "You'll just have to do it, Cooky." And she had her other two children with her when they came into the door, and——

MRS. M.: This is the mother?

MRS. E.: This is the mother. I'd never——

MR. B.: Is that her name, Cooky, or is that what you called her?

MRS. E.: That's what she calls herself, and she insisted on being called Cooky. And it's much easier than calling her something else, because if I call her Mrs. C., Billy calls her Mrs. C. He does everything I do. He sort of does things that way. And so she stayed and when I came back—I was uneasy when I was at court, wondering, "Gee, I don't know this woman." First thing she told me was, "Look I spent a month in jail for assault and battery with an attempt to kill." Next day she said, "I want to get married to [my boy friend]" The boy friend happens to be—this is all on tape—the father of these two children, "but I can't because my blood test wasn't clear." And she's in my home!

B.M.: Using your toilet.

MRS. E.: It's a fact. And if you don't think I was thrown to the wolves, I really did.

B.M.: Well, she pulled out all the stops.

MRS. E.: She certainly did. She wanted to see if I was shocked, and I didn't even let it sink in. But, boy, my husband said, "If I'd known that first, she wouldn't have come here." She did get married.

B.M.: She did your house cleaning.

MRS. E.: It's amazing about things like that, because I am unusually clean about food, bathroom, and beds, and wash and things like that, but as far as somebody using the table to make something, carving, the chips might be there on the table until someone screams, "Take them off," so we never—— But I mean, generally speaking, we live. But she didn't miss a trick. She followed after me and hung up [my son's] clothes. [My son] never hangs up anything. His room looks like it's—well, a hurricane has struck. And she picked up after him and lectured him, and she felt very good. [My son] is a good kid. He took it. He said, "Gee, I wouldn't want you to be my sister. I wouldn't want you here all the time. I couldn't stand the strain." And she thought that was pretty good because he could joke with her.

B.M.: Did she actually ask for any advice? What do you do with Billy when——

MRS. E.: Yes, which was very good. And she also gave me advice freely as I've said, and one afternoon she said, "I'm going upstairs and take a nap. Watch the kids." Just like that. And I didn't resent it. I don't know why I didn't. If my daughter had said that I'd say, "Who do you think this is," you know, "old home week, or something?" But she said it, sort of, this is the way she is. And she did—she went upstairs and she took a nap. She said, "I don't like the mattress on that middle bed. I took one of those beds in the back room."

MRS. M.: She's a very honest person.

B.M.: Not many foster parents could put up with it, you know?

MRS. E.: Either that, or just plain stupid, but in a way she had a lot of nice things about her. I liked the way she treated Billy. I didn't like, perhaps, the way she worded some of the things. For instance, our family is moderately religious, I mean we go to church when the spirit moves. It doesn't move quite often enough, but we do go. It's a very mixed religion, but then father lived with us for years and he was a religious fanatic. So when he left our family, unconsciously I think, went the other way as far as saying grace. We never sat down without saying grace and now, nine times out of ten we sit down and no one says grace, which is kind of like a—almost like a reprieve after granpa left—because, you know, well, you couldn't take tea without saying grace and he'd forget he was saying grace and you'd have to stop and say, "Gramp, that's long enough," you know, and one of those deals. So all of a sudden we're a little bit on the lax side. I love dinner time, because everyone has so many good things to tell you. It's fun listening to the kiddos. But she soon realized we weren't saying grace and I'm sure she was trying to impress, so we sat down to the table and she snatches Billy and she says, "Cripes, don't eat that 'til you thank God for what you're eating!" I said, "Probably it's going to take more than thanks, because I am not a good cook. I am not a good cook. I like to cook certain things, but—— And [my husband], of course is very—— You don't joke with [my husband] easily. He's very quiet and I think sometimes he's very abrupt. But he looked up, but he didn't say anything and I was hoping he'd——

K.O.: He'd say grace.

MRS. E.: But he didn't. The very next day, I think a couple of days after she'd got back, I told you about the letter I received from her. She wrote Billy, wanted me to read it to him, and said, "In our family, we believe in God. And we are very happy to say grace for the little things we have. When you come home— God has taught me how to be good—and when you come home I'm going to teach you how to be good too."

B.M.: Or you'll go to hell, or something like that. Didn't she say something about hell?

MRS. E.: Yeah. So you won't go to hell when you die, Mommy's going to teach you how to be good. I think she felt if she had more time, she would teach me. And I suppose I could use it.

B.M.: It was interesting to see how the mother progressed, you know. She started out by being, you know, very dependent—"I don't know what to do, I don't think I can handle the kid, I'm sick, I can't take him, I'm scared." And then after this, she got really porky. Then she began to get really porky after that visit, you know. "It was too much of a strain for this kid to be subjected to different influences, the foster home and the home, and he needed to be home right away."

MRS. E.: I don't care what did it, but I'm glad it's done. Because I think it's given her enough that she can do it better than I, and I'm all for it.

B.M.: That's the way she turned, you know. She couldn't do anything at first, and then all of a sudden she could do everything much better than everybody else, and I hope she'll eventually find a stable middle ground, you know.

MRS. E.: Well, she's done a good job on the two children. And I don't think they got there by chance. I really don't.

B.M.: Well, this was a great help, too, because we were having great questions, trepidations, about sending the kid home. And Mrs. E. you know, told us that the other kids were great.

MRS. E.: They really are. They're nice youngsters.

B.M.: Which made us feel great, I mean better, about sending him home.

MRS. E.: She talks more than she acts. She's rough talking. They aren't frightened of her, and they are nice youngsters. They play well with each other, and they were nice when we had company. They weren't artificially nice. They weren't sugary nice. They were just nice, just wholesome youngsters. And they didn't talk the way the mother did. And I had a feeling that perhaps I was getting another side of her because she was—it was like a defense—you know this made her feel bold and strong and able to cope with us. She really was funny, 'cause I have—two of my boys are rather good looking, the two older boys, and she really was quite a flirt with them. They're both married, and their wives were there, and one wife is very, very fat, and she said, "You'd better watch it. You're so fat, you'll never hold on to your husband." And really, I mean, they wouldn't have taken this from anybody else, but they were wonderful to her.

B.M.: Also, when we were thinking of sending Fred home and what the parents would be like, you gave me a lot of help in understanding how the mother acted when she was on visits, and how passive she was when Fred cut his finger, and that kind of thing. It gives us a lot of help in understanding parents.

MRS. M.: Yes. The hardest thing I ever felt with Fred was when he came to visit, you know, the day before school started. I had to bribe the kid to get him home. I felt terrible. I think I called to say that, just in case it might make any difference. He just didn't want to go home. And I wanted to keep in touch with him, but after that day, I thought, well I won't, you know. Because I had to bribe him. He hid. He hid in the woods. He didn't want to go home. A dime meant a lot to him, you know, just a dime. If you gave him a dollar—oh, he went crazy. And I knew that's all I had to do. I said, "Here's some money for you and your sister to buy ice cream on the way home." So he went. But his mother didn't hear me doing that, because I didn't want to hurt her feelings to think he wanted to stay with us.

MRS. E.: Isn't that sad, though, when they're like that?

MRS. M.: Yeah. I felt sorry for her because I think she's really a nice, nice person.

MR. M.: He was a very unusual kid, you know. He could sulk and in two seconds it was all gone. He cried and screamed—two seconds——

MRS. E.: Aren't most children like that?

MR. M.: Well, comparing Fred to [his brother], which we've got now. Of course, [his brother] is much quieter. Fred was outgoing and wild and rugged and very lovable.

MRS. M.: Fred was fine until he had to come over here. He hated it.

MR. M.: He didn't like coming over here.

B.M.: That continued all the way through?

MRS. M.: I didn't know you people as well then or I would have said, well—

B.M.: I'll bet you wondered what I was doing to him, huh?

MRS. M.: I can understand, but sometimes I think maybe a change would be better, you know, cut it out once in a while or something. "Oh, you don't have to go this week, Fred," and make him feel good, you know? I don't know, but I many times thought it, but didn't have the nerve to say it at that time.

B.M.: Yeah.

K.O.: Why did he hate it so?

MRS. M.: I don't know why he hated it. I think because you talked about home, maybe, and his parents. And, plus, he missed playing with the kids, you know, after school. It was always after school, and he was playing with the kids.

MRS. B.: How old was he?

MRS. M.: He was 8.

MRS. B.: Same with my little 5-year-old. He can't stand anything that takes him from his friends. Even changing his clothes when he gets home from school takes too much time.

MRS. M.: [Fred's brother's] the same way. I can understand his feelings.

MRS. B.: Kid's like living in a rut. They don't want to be disturbed.

B.M.: Also, as you say, we talk about painful things. And the family was a painful subject.

MRS. E.: Is he home now?

B.M.: He's home now. We have his brother in the Village here, and Fred comes in sometimes.

MRS. M.: Do you see Fred?

B.M.: No, I haven't seen him. The parents come in for a parents' group.

APPENDIX B
FOSTER MOTHERS' ATTITUDES
TOWARD THE MORALITY OF
NATURAL MOTHERS

The following discussion is part of one meeting of the unstructured group, which took place about two months before the preceding discussion. At this time the author, Mrs. E., and a state social worker were coordinating efforts to return Billy to his mother. Mrs. E.'s anxieties about the child's return to his mother focus on the mother's morality. While living with a man to whom she is not married, the mother attempts to control Billy through instilling the fear of God in him. Mrs. E. is bothered by both aspects of the mother's morality. Mrs. G. is even more anxious about natural parents' "loose" sexual behavior than is Mrs. E. The psychiatrist questions the importance of these conventional moral judgments to a child's development.

One of the goals of the unstructured group was to encourage cooperative peer relationships between foster parents and professional staff. In this discussion, the psychiatrist challenges the foster parents' opinions, yet rejects the role of an "expert" whose judgment must be accepted because of his credentials. In the slippery realm of morality, he admits that there is no infallible word and that the question boils down to honesty and openness between people who are working together to do the best they can for children. Mrs. E. is comfortable with this kind of mutuality, but in the unstructured group discussion of 11-26-68 (Appendix F), Mr. B. indicates his need for a "strong doctor" who must remain emotionally detached in order to maintain a show of strength. This gets to the heart of the authority issues involved in professionalism, "expertise," and bureaucracy. An emotional detachment which professionals argue for to maintain objectivity has often operated to maintain arbitrary and irrational authority and to create antagonisms between people. Can one be an "expert" while maintaining full emotional contact with co-workers and clients?

The human service professions have precious little "absolute" truth to dispense. Much of what passes for truth is in reality a body of informed hunches— useful to guide one's actions, but always subject to revision in practice. F. Scott Fitzgerald once said that the mark of a mature person is the ability to hold two contradictory ideas in his mind at the same time. Many professionals cannot operate comfortably in this state of suspended judgment. They lay claim to a certainty which is not warranted by the state of the art in order to maintain their authority.

3-18-69: Unstructured Group Meeting

MRS. E.: I find it puzzling, that when children return to their own folks and I'm thinking specifically of Billy, who needs a lot of love, how can his mother allow that, who isn't married, and it bothers me terribly. She calls me up and I want to feel sorry for her, she calls me up 3 or 4 times a week. One day she called me three times, and she got me the third time and said, "Don't you ever stay home?" Yet all she wanted to do is call me up and tell me about [her paramour] and that Billy is going to come home and live. And I asked her if she was getting married, and she said maybe next week, she didn't know. To me——

PSYCHIATRIST: Is it bad for Billy?

MRS. E.: I don't want to say if it's bad for Billy or not. But I still say, I don't know.

PSYCHIATRIST: How much is morality and how much is good or bad for Billy?

MRS. E.: But I just have this feeling. It's not fair to repeat things that she said but, I just have to get this out. She said, "If I do get married, then my allotment from the State is out."

PSYCHIATRIST: Is it true?

MRS. E.: I don't know if it's true. But I feel like she's saying, "I get married and I'll stop living off your taxes." Really, I don't mean it. It is picky, but it's—I just have this feeling——. I wouldn't like to take Billy because I'm too old, I'd like to see him go with his mother but can she give youngsters—she has two lovely youngsters—can she give them a set of values which they can hold on to, something they can live by? But what is a good set of values?

PSYCHIATRIST: This is the very thing that Mr. B. was talking about before. How much is morality and how much is reality? We can get down to the real nitty-gritty right here of what's good for kids. Can a woman raise a child, sleeping with men, and still give them a set of values? I think so.

MRS. E.: Yes, but what happens to this child when it goes out into the world and it gets ribbed? A supersensitive child. I'm thinking of Billy right now. If someone says to Billy right now, like [another foster child in the home] said the other day, "I don't think you got any mother." And Billy said, "Yes I have, she's a bad mother." And I said, "Oh, come on Billy," and he said, "Yes, she is, she's bad because Mrs. S. [a former foster mother] said she's bad. Then I asked him what he thought bad was and he said, "I don't know, just bad."

PSYCHIATRIST: See, this is something that had been communicated to him by another person which has nothing to do with the morality of his mother.

MRS. E.: When he goes home, or goes to school, there will always be righteous people in the world and there will be poor little Billy. He has little defense now.

PSYCHIATRIST: Now, wait a minute [Mrs. E.] You're saying "poor Billy," and the reason I think you're saying that is because, I think we're getting into the question of values and children. It—how can you really say that Billy would have this kind of reaction if he never lived with his mother another day? He knows what other people think. Somewhere along the line, Billy has to start to develop a set of moral values. And really the decision of if his mother is good or bad is something that only he can say, irregardless of the people on the earth. And even if he doesn't see her again and someone says, "You mother is bad," and it won't really hurt him psychologically. It might hurt his feelings to hear this again and again and again. But it's something that he'll have to decide for himself.

MRS. E.: No, I get what you say, but I still have some reservations about it. I think this gal has a lot on the ball in many ways. But I'm not scandalous of her living with this [paramour]. We were talking about this, she's so innocent and gullible. [My husband] says she's not innocent, she's primitive. She really is. And I thought and thought about it, and she really is. She basically fights for her family in her own funny way. And hopefully it will work out all right, but I still worry.

MRS. G.: I was going to say that if this child was put back into this home, even if this is his natural mother and lives under the conditions of seeing her with not just one man, with more than one man, I think this mixes——. Even with one man, and with him living there, and as he grows older he realizes that his mother is not married. And don't forget that the children are cruel too. And—

PSYCHIATRIST: But the thing that we're talking about is now if Billy's going to get his feelings hurt, but this isn't anything we can stop. Kids can hurt his feelings about anything. They can hurt his feelings about being foster—it happens all the time. The thing that we really have to decide about is does it hurt him in his development, is it going to stifle his psychological growth? Ah, in all honesty, even though I'm supposed to be an expert, I don't think it will necessarily. I'm not saying that it can't, but that in itself really can't. But we get too close to the other thing. Do we want to stop from seeing his feelings hurt? And that's a different thing.

MRS. G.: Really though, but I know a boy and girl who live with their mother and she's not married and she's ashamed of their mother. And they know she's living with another man and they don't take any of their friends home, they try to hide their home. But if he goes back to this environment, if he goes back, and he has this set of morals and he goes and sees his own mother doing wrong, and they know it's wrong, and they become ashamed inside and they try to hide these things——.

MRS. E.: What I mean is that I don't feel that she's strong enough to make Billy feel part of the family and help him when the kids start poking fun at him. That's what bothers me. She calls me several times, and I talk to her because I feel sorry for her and she called me the other day and said, "I'm going to get married next week, but I called the doctor and he told me that my blood test wouldn't be ready by next week." Happy day in the morning. She isn't a bad person. She just comes out with whatever is on her mind. [When she visited us] we had a house full of company plopped down on the floor with one eye on the television and one playing cards with [another foster child] and had the radio blaring in her car. And one of the children was calling upstairs. And she turned around and yelled, "Shut up and get upstairs!" and turned around without ever batting an eyelash.

She isn't a bad person to talk to. She wrote a letter to us and told Billy that if he's bad he won't go to heaven. So that every time he's bad, she's going to see God and tell him that you're bad and he won't let you go to heaven. And we believe in God at our home and we have told him that we thank God before meals and we pray to God before going to bed at night, and I let her take care of Billy the couple of nights she was there, so I don't know how she knows how we feel, since we don't see her that much, but she has put so much fear in him. And he said to me, "When was I bad when my mommy was here?" And she said, "God said that He told [the state social worker and the agency social worker] that I am good now so I can have you back. Ah, I'm not that gullible. I don't believe that this was the girl that was in my home. She wasn't wicked or mean. She had affection. It was very natural feeling that she had for her children. It may not have been everything that you'd want, but they were lovely children. They were at ease, not too fresh or too quiet. And I really felt flattered when the little boy asked if he could call me granny. He said I looked older than his mother. And I really thought it was a nice little thing for a little boy to say. He said this spontaneously. I don't know if kids are easy to bring up or not. Billy certainly isn't. It's not a question if she's doing something wrong or not, but she has two other children who have had a different training from Billy, and Billy has had some training which would say some things aren't proper. I think he needs his mother desperately, but there are so many things going on in my mind about him.

PSYCHIATRIST: One of the toughest things, that's so very hard to tell. Ah——

MRS. E.: But he's made so much progress now. I think that we're looking for some reassurance—some peace of mind.

PSYCHIATRIST: You know [Mrs. E.], it feels so good to me to be able to talk to you, because I can't talk to some foster parents the way I talk to you. Ah, it gives me a sense of relief to be able to level with you and say, "I don't know and I don't know what's going to happen." I know that doesn't take the burden off your shoulders, but——

MRS. E.: It makes me feel better when an authority—well, it's like when I go to my doctor. He's the kind of person who levels with me and says, "Frankly, I don't know, but let's try this."

PSYCHIATRIST: I like that. What you just said. We don't have to know, but it's good to try. It's honesty, that between you and me and when we both sit down and neither of us know, and maybe we can't know, but it makes my life easier to know that, and makes me feel good to hear you say it too.

MRS. E.: Well, in the back of my mind I'm straightening things out. Maybe I shouldn't air all my doubts. But what would that gain? No one knows until she tries it. It may cure her in a sense. I think she has a very very——. She kept bringing up the subject that she never should have let him go in the first place. I must think that she's awful. I said I don't. At 17 or 18, my own daughters couldn't have coped with it.

SOCIAL WORKER: I think you're experiencing what many of us experience since you've been such a part of this decision, of whether he should go home or not. It's a problem that [the psychiatrist] and I face quite often, whether the kid should go home with his family or not.

MRS. E.: Each time that I thought of it, it made me ill. Billy's teacher, whom I had many reservations about her, she said, "Billy's not settling down now, is he moving?" I said, "That's not my decision to make," and I took the attitude that the kids have and said, "Those are the breaks," and walked out.

APPENDIX C
THE FOSTER CHILD GROWN UP

Two adults who were raised in foster homes tell foster parents what it was like. Mrs. A., who is now married with children of her own, cared for foster children until she had had her own. She has felt insecure all her life because of her many moves, and still vividly recalls feeling stigmatized as a "state child." As an adolescent she particularly resented the state taking some of her earnings—earnings she wanted to use to become independent. Mr. B. owns his own barber shop, is married, and has two sharp memories of social workers: one suppressed his grief over being moved from a home, and another was his friend. I wonder what happened to his grief and rage after the social worker slapped him for crying.

Foster Children, Now Grown, Talk to Foster Parents

1-7-69 Structured Group

Two former foster children, now adults, were invited to talk with the foster parents about their experiences. One, a woman, will be called Mrs. A.; the other, a man, will be called Mr. B. After the introduction, they proceed. Two different social workers co-chaired the structured group. They will be designated S.W.1 and S.W.2. Foster parents will be designated F.P.1, 2, 3, 4, 5, and 6.

MRS. A.: Well, my mother, when I was born, she put me in a home when I was 6 years old. Then I was taken home by my father. Then I was put into another home. The hardest thing that I found was being moved from one home to another. I felt secure in one home and I was moved. And all of a sudden I was someplace else. I think then and all through my life I feel the insecurity that I felt then, being transferred from foster home to foster home.

S.W.1: We hear this often from boys and girls who have been moved in foster homes from one to another. Do you remember the early years?

MR. B.: I left home right after I finished kindergarten. It was a very nice home with two other children. And I was the only foster child. I got along very well.

S.W.1: How many years?

MR. B.: Well, third grade, I'll have to go by grades. In the meantime, I went home for a year. I stayed there for a year, then went home with my parents for a year, my mother for a year, then went back to the same people.

S.W.1: Well, what about high school?

MR. B.: Well, I went home for another year and a half, then I went to a couple more. I went to the F.'s. I was always with a family.

S.W.1: What is your general impression of a foster home? The ones you were in? Were you treated well?

MR. B.: I always felt like it was my own. As long as I was there, the people were my parents and the other children in the home were my brother and sister.

S.W.1: Were you well treated?

MR. B.: Yes.

S.W.1: Was it from this agency?

MR. B.: Yes. Well, to start with, it was Catholic Diocesan Bureau until I was sixteen.

S.W.2: Well, here we expected to get a couple who have had a few lousy parents. Do you remember how you were treated by members of the community? Were you shunned or made fun of because you were a foster child? Or were you rejected in any way?

MR. B.: No, people understood what it was.

S.W.1: I remember, Mrs. A., that you mentioned on the telephone to me that one of the things that bothered you was this term, "state child." About how kids get tagged with this.

MRS. A.: My impression is that when you leave a home, most of the time the parents have had problems, divorce and things that weren't good. And the state child was rotten and no good.

* * *

S.W.1: Mr. B., do you remember anything that happened in relationships, being placed in foster care? Any unhappy experiences that you can recall?

MR. B.: No, I can't remember any unhappy experiences that I can recall. They were all happy. And for my own life, my happiest times were spent in foster homes. This was the best time of my life.

S.W.1: Well, can you remember any unhappy experience with the neighbors or schools in general?

MR. B.: Well, the only unpleasant experience I can remember, and this was in New York City, I was being taken from one foster home to another on the trolley, and I was crying because I was being moved, and the social worker wasn't too kind and she slapped me and told me to shut up kid, and stop crying. . . . But this is 25 years ago, and social workers are a lot different now than they were then.

S.W.2: Don't count on it. Do you remember any of these kinds of experiences, Mrs. A.?

MRS. A.: Well, my best life was in a foster home. Because I was in a foster home, I think that I'm a better person for it. I never got that attached so that I couldn't leave, or when children came and went. It didn't bother me. I just accepted it.

S.W.1: Everyone can't accept that though. Change is hard. In the first home you said you were the only foster child, in the last home you said there were other children.

MRS. A.: Well, there was quite a few—eight or nine.

F.P.1: Sounds like the Group Home.

S.W.1: Did you find that the natural children were treated better, or that foster children were treated better, or what?

MRS. A.: Well, the children were older, and I was the youngest so I got along quite well. I still feel that that's my home. And when I go home, I go home to my foster mother.

F.P.2: I was wondering if you kept up the contact.

MRS. A.: I feel that she's my own.

S.W.1: Do most foster children feel that their own parents are more important than foster parents? Do you still feel that the ties are so strong?

MRS. A.: Well, my foster mother is more important to me than my own mother.

S.W.1: Did you always look forward to seeing your own mother over your foster mother?

MRS. A.: Never. I always looked for my foster mother. I never knew my own mother, but I will say that my last foster home was with a fine mother. With five girls and me. And I wish I had kept up the contact when I was able to keep in contact. It did leave a good memory in my mind.

S.W.1: You said girls—were they foster children?

MRS. A.: No, they were natural children. I was the only foster child. And the other home had no children, only me.

F.P.2: Did you feel that you were picked on more because you were a foster child?

MRS. A.: No. What I liked about the home was that there were a lot of children, both girls and boys.

F.P.1: Well, having mostly boys I was just wondering how you got along, because it seems to me that in homes that are mixed, both boys and girls, that they seem better adjusted than if there is just boys or girls.

F.P.3: What, are they more polite?

F.P.1: No, not just that, but they seem more adjusted to life in general. I think I want to use the word "acclimated."

S.W.2: What I think Mr. T. wants [is] girls put in to make a more natural situation. [*Mr. T. is the foster father of an agency group home for boys.*]

F.P.1: Well it's not normal to have all children of the same age level in a home. They're in steps.

F.P.2: I have both boys and girls, but girls seem to adjust quicker, and they expect from the boys what they would expect from any boy. They seem to be more normal. They fight and compete against each other when I had only the girls, but now you should see the girls play with each other since I have the three girls and one boy. They compete but get along. They compete for the attention. It's because he is a boy, and it's a very normal type situation.

F.P.4: I think that it's because he's a small child. I think emotionally disturbed children should be put where there is a small child, because they can pour out their affection on him, because he is a small child, rather than on the adult.

S.W.1: Did you find that you could talk to the children in the foster home, or easier than talking with the foster parents?

MRS. A.: I could talk to the children easy, but also the parents, too.

S.W.1: But when you were angry at the foster parent, could you got off in a corner with another foster child and blow off steam?

MRS. A.: Go out and complain about it. But it's something children would do about their parents.

* * *

F.P.5: What about the business of each of the foster children having natural parents and each wanting to think that their parents were good people, but the fact that they're in a foster home would tell them that their parents aren't that great? Sometimes foster parents get their feelings hurt. Sometimes when they've spent years with kids and having it thrown in their face that they'd rather be home with their own parents.

F.P.6: A lot of the natural parents come visit the children and make a lot of promises of things that will never happen.

F.P.:2: How many kids don't believe their own parents?

F.P.1: Very few.

F.P.6: K. and R. lived with us for two years. They were brother and sister. And when they were moved, they were 10 and 12, and when they were moved we were just notified that they were to be moved. And they resented it terribly, and almost two years after that they came back and during all that time, K., in particular—R. is still withdrawn—but K., in particular, always figured if she always had her own parents. She's still very good, but she has this in the back of her mind. It wasn't until she was out of school and on her own did she realize that her own parents didn't mean a thing to her; and she considers us her parents. And, of course, when she did get on her own and went to her father, she went to him and told him that she feels no feeling there.

S.W.2: At what age were you when you realized that your mother would not accept you?

MRS. A.: I'm not sure. I think I always realized it. No one ever had to spell it out to me. I realized it when I was very young.

F.P.2: Did you make up your mind that you would build your own life? Is this what you prepared yourself for?

MRS. A.: Yes, ah, the foster parents that I had all along taught me their ways, the ways of their family. Basic things like manners and conduct, and sent me to school. I didn't want to go, but I knew it was important. And they pushed me through.

F.P.1: Did you have any brothers or sisters?

MRS. A.: Yes, both were put up for adoption.

F.P.1: Were you able to keep in touch with them?

MRS. A.: No, they were put right up for adoption.

S.W.1: Now, Mr. B. talked of the charming social worker who batted him. I was just wondering that you must have had a series of social workers; there's a turnover there, too! I was wondering if they kept in much contact with you?

MR. B.: I had a wonderful social worker from Catholic Diocesan Bureau. Her name was Mrs. D. She was my social worker from the time I was born to the time I was 16 and, ah, I always felt very close to her, like she was a relative. And we're still close. I call her once in a while. She's been to my home.

S.W.1: Were you able to get much help from her?

Mr. B.: Usually when she came I really had a good time. I was able to talk with her. I found that I could go to my foster mother if I had to. I'm close to her.

S.W.1: Do you still keep in touch with your foster mother?

MR. B.: Yes, that's my mother as far as I'm concerned. My foster father has passed on.

S.W.1: Mrs. A. has been a foster mother herself.

F.P.2: For larger children?

MRS. A.: Two small ones. A little girl, a year and a half, and her brother, 3. They just moved before my baby was born.

F.P.5: How do you feel being a former foster child and raising foster children? Do you feel that you favor them more?

MRS. A.: No, I treat them like they're my own, but no different. Not anything special, but not anything less.

F.P.5: The way you felt that you were treated.

MRS. A.: Yes. I try to.

S.W.1: Were there other boys or girls in the home that weren't happy?

MRS. A.: There was one girl who didn't like it. They were rotten to her, the same people. That girl went to a different place. She was never happy. You either find a home that you can make your own or you don't. I hang my hat where my home is.

F.P.1: Do you find that girls adjust to a foster home better than boys?

MRS. A.: I don't know.

S.W.2: Did you find the boys to be more complaining or less complaining, or couldn't you say? Which were the most troublesome?

MRS. A.: I think the girls. Teenage girls.

F.P.2: Do you find in the homes that you were in that there was much rebellion about doing chores? I mean was there a big conflict over this or did they accept the jobs as they came?

MRS. A.: Ahem, we weren't assigned anything, but I always felt that there are certain things that we should do. Like the dishes, doing the beds. If my mother was doing some kind of work, I joined in. I wasn't told what to do. If we were asked to do something, some of the children were insulted that they were asked to do something. I think that children have to do things in the home. As if it was their own.

F.P.5: Do many of them think that their foster parents were being paid a fortune to take care of them?

MRS. A.: Yes. I heard several times, you get paid for me, so I don't have to do this. I never felt this way but I know the feeling.

F.P.5: I don't think that part has changed. We still get that from many of our children.

S.W.: You get that from kids.

F.P.6: You know, from all the foster children that I've had, I've never had one to say that to me. Never.

F.P.5: It depends upon the parent, actually.

F.P.2: I never got it from the younger ones, but from my two older ones. Just recently. All of a sudden they were told that they shouldn't be told what to do. They should be allowed to do what they want to do. I mean this is the way they feel. And if you ask them to do anything, it's just like pulling teeth. Last week the answer I got to, "Wouldn't it be nice if you girls went upstairs to clean your rooms?—I'm sick of looking at the dust roll around under the beds." One of them said, "Why, you get paid to take care of us." And I have ten rooms.

F.P.5: Well, even if you have your own children they say things like this.

F.P.2: Well, I think with the older girls I get this kickback. With the younger ones—they're very willing to help. But this is something new; I was shocked because I never heard that before. But I did have it thrown at me, "You take care of me, what do you do?"

F.P.5: And the only time they give you a hand is when they want to go out.

F.P.6: When they want an extra favor or money.

F.P.1: We don't assign chores. The boys set it up themselves and they rotate. They have times when they swap. The boys have certain responsibilities all the time, or different things they do, clean their rooms. This is what we say, "This is your house too!" and we live in a clean house.

F.P.2: That's what I've been saying to the girls. I've stopped doing for the older girls, almost everything. I'm just there to see that they're in line. I just don't mean that I sit down and list rules, but that they get fed properly, go to bed on time. Do what they're supposed to do. I feel that at 17, 18 years they're old enough to take care of their clothing and such. I found out that since I have them do things for themselves that they're very resentful, that they feel that they're being imposed upon. Up to now, we haven't pushed it, but I've been having them take care of their own clothing, their own personal hygiene. I tell them if they're looking bad. But I've noticed that within the last six months they've become shoddy about themselves. And this is because I haven't been making them do things—with me telling them. They just don't care—they expect you to do it for them. And if you don't tell them, they keep going back further and further. We kind of let them go a little. One is an exceptionally neat [child].

F.P.6: Our own daughter is exceptionally neat and it certainly rubbed off on the others in keeping clean.

F.P.5: Were you made to keep your own things up?

MRS. A.: No, but I wish I was. Most of the things I took upon myself. My foster parents didn't make us do different things, but I think they should have. I think that children who are made to do things, made to have certain responsibilities, come out better. But he told me they started letting the older ones do things on their own and this is good. But if they start lagging off on things that they should [do], then it's time to blast.

F.P.2: You think that foster parents are justified in blasting off on children when they're not shaping up?

MRS. A.: Yes, definitely.

F.P.2: All three of our girls come back and thank us for making them do things that they didn't really want to do. And I think most kids eventually realize this. That they will look back and see why they had to do certain things.

S.W.1: To jump away, Mr. B. said he went to a school for a number of years, and certainly there were a great number of rules and regulations. Did you find that the other kids had many objections to chores and the like?

MR. B.: I don't think so. I think that, going back to what she said, you have to treat your own child the same way you do the foster child. You have to set up certain guide rules that they have to follow, and you have to have some method to ensure that you get this. But if you think that they will think evil of me when they get older, then you'll never accomplish anything. It's best to take a firm attitude.

F.P.2: I have one who turned 18 this week. And for the first time in her life she finally admitted that, and this is what shocked us—she said to the other 17-year-older, "Aren't you ashamed of your room? It looks like a pigsty. The other two girls at least try to keep things neat. Aren't you ashamed?" And she said, "That's the way I like it." And this one said, "Well, Mommy hasn't had you since you were 9 like she had me. Boy, if she had you since 9, you'd know how to be a lady, and keep your room clean. At least I have some good training and I'm ready for marriage." And this shocked me. She cooks, sews, keeps house, babysits. She just accepted a diamond for Christmas—which we're heartbroken about. She's in school. But they both agreed to wait. But she blasted the other girl and all these years we had her, and the things we had to do. We encouraged her to cook and things like that. We worked with her and taught her, and now she's able to relate to the other children. And you know what?—she keeps saying, "You got here when you were too old; if Mommy got you when you were younger, you'd know how to do these things now." And this is something we never expected to hear from her. Now she's able to say, "I was made to do it and I'm a better person for it." She's so well adjusted. I'm afraid we'll have to send her on her own soon. But, she did say, "You came too late."

F.P.3: Did you get engaged when you were there?

MRS. A.: Yes, twice. I got engaged, and my foster mother was happy about it—except I wanted to get married when I was still in school which was very upsetting. But she told me to wait 'til I got out of school, and my social worker stepped in and did something that hurt me awful. It was my last year of high school; I got a full time job, nights, to save money to get married, and the social worker decided that I'd pay my own way, but she was going to run my money— but I was always good at saving my money. We made an agreement of what I should pay to my foster mother—they still paid my doctor bills—and, the state worker went up to the bank with me and made me sign my money over to the state until I got married and they would hold it until then. And they said I could save $300, then start paying my board and bills. I did. I always saved my money. The state worker just stood in and took control of my money and it was very upsetting.

S.W.1: As if she didn't trust you to do it yourself.

MRS. A.: Yes, that's what hurt the most.

F.P.5: Do you feel that if the child has money that it should be in control of the foster mother?

MRS. A.: I would have went along with it.

F.P.5: Then that person had to cosign with you. You couldn't touch it without her okay.

F.P.6: There may have been a reason for that, where a foster child had taken advantage of a foster parent.

F.P.5: I think it should have been up to the decision of the foster mother.

S.W.2: Did either of you ever wonder why anyone would want to take care of you? You knew your own parents didn't want to take care of you, or couldn't, but did it ever enter your mind why these people would want to take care of you?

F.P.2: You mean why are people in the foster care business?

MRS. A.: They took care of children for the satisfaction that they got from children and the help that they could give them. It wasn't money. I guess there are some who do it for money.

F.P.5: Have you ever been in a foster home that you have felt [they] were in it for the money?

MRS. A.: No, but I've heard stories.

S.W.1: As a foster mother, have you found out how unprofitable it is?

F.P.5: Yes.

F.P.6: Is it better being with an agency or the state?—like clothing allowance and stuff like that.

MRS. A.: I don't remember.

F.P.3: I don't think most kids placed by the agency, between the ages of 6 to 16, have much control of their clothing allowance.

F.P.2: Well, with our agency, it drops the clothing allowance at 16—with the assumption that the [child] will get a part-time job to pay for some of the clothing.

S.W.1: We have a set amount for a kid from 6 on. It starts at around $8. Then it goes from $8 to $11 to $13. They get more, until they get to 17, then it drops drastically, to $11; and they're expected to pay for their clothes.

MRS. A.: My foster mother gave me my clothing money and knew I could handle it. Some of us did good. But others went out and spent it.

F.P.2: What did the foster parents do then, with kids like that?

MRS. A.: They went without. If they wanted it, they'd have to go out and work for it. I took babysitting jobs, shoveled snow, raked leaves in the fall. When I was 14 to 15, I worked in the tobacco fields for the summer. And that gave me enough money for spending during the year.

[*Discussion about working on tobacco fields. Girls bothered blacks, Puerto Ricans, and Jamaicans—not other way around. They didn't make much money, but had alot of fun.*]

F.P.2: Well, weren't you proud when you got your first paycheck?

MRS. A.: Yes. But I always felt a lot of shame being a foster child; only because my mother didn't pay my way, and I always wanted to pay my own way until, as soon as I could, I did.

F.P.2: I have found working with most foster children that they're ashamed at having to accept charity. My daughter related this to me. She said, "Mommy, how much longer am I going to have to accept charity?" I said, "What you're getting isn't charity but help." But she said, "It's so awful to have to say no if someone asks me if that's my real mother and I have to say no, it's my foster mother." And she said they say, "Oh, she gets paid for taking care of you." And she said this is what hurts. She'd like to say that she's on her own.

F.P.5: I think many children feel this way too. That they'd like to carry their own responsibility. I know my own kids like to say that board is their biggest bill, but it comes in regularly.

F.P.2: This is what I'm trying to say. E. hurts, really hurts over this. That many times she'd love to say, "No, nobody gets paid for taking care of me. I feel like I'm accepting charity. It's a sense of pride to be able to say I'm paying my own way, or that the state isn't paying my way."

F.P.3: We had the subject come up once, and I explained it to them this way. Ah, Dad pays for Carolyn's suit—these are our own children. Of course, your father can't pay right now, so the agency is taking his place and just paying what he would pay if he was here. And they seem to accept it.

F.P.4: I never worked a day in my life to pay my own way. And I never felt guilty.

F.P.2: But you weren't a foster child.

F.P.4: I just don't understand how money can play such an important part for teenagers or younger children.

F.P.6: Well, my daughter is clothes-crazy, and she knows that I certainly couldn't afford it. She buys her clothes.

F.P.1: Well, with foster kids we have to put a limit on it.

F.P.2: Not if they're earning it.

F.P.5: No, not if they're earning it. If we're paying for it. With a foster child you have to set rules and limits. You may have to say, "You're not allowed to have that." I have one who wants a tape recorder, typewriter, 4-speed bicycle, and we just keep putting her off, until we tell her we just can't afford it.

F.P.6: Well, if it was up to some of these foster children, if they had their way, they'd be continually asking for these ridiculous things.

F.P.1: If one of my foster children were fairly responsible and wanted something for $100 and he didn't have it and I did, I would loan it to him.

F.P.3: I think that's part of growing up—that if that's your responsibility. And I think that this has to be taught.

F.P.2: Well, I think that the foster children that I have are so emotionally upset at this time, that they need rules and limits.

* * *

F.P.1: Some of our boys were very self-conscious about living in the group home. They try to get all around the topic and avoid telling anyone where they live.

S.W.1: Yes, these were kids who moved from the Village to the Group Home and wanted no identification with the Village, the green bus.

F.P.1: But with the group we have now, this makes no difference to them.

F.P.2: Mrs. A., in the foster home that you were in, was it a mixed home, with white and black children?

MRS. A.: No. When I was there, there were all Catholics and whites.

S.W.2: What color Catholics?

F.P.2: Is this foster home still operating?

MRS. A.: Yes.

F.P.2: Do they still have this type of set-up?

MRS. A.: No, they take any race or religion. They don't choose.

F.P.2: Are there both races at the house now?

MRS. A.: Well, my mother takes them as they come.

F.P.2: Why I ask is that I just recently had the question come up if I would take blacks and how would I feel about it. The other day we were in church and my daughter turned around and said, "Mommy, there are colored people in church." And I asked her what was wrong with that. And she said she didn't know that any colored people were Catholic. And I said to her, "Okay. I have a question. If we were told that we have to bring a Negro child into this house——?" We waited for an answer. My husband looked around. And no one said anything. I asked again, then they all started to giggle and laugh, and I said I wanted an answer—not a giggle. And one of them said, "Would it make a difference if you have all colors? We have dark hair and light hair. Little ones and big ones. What difference if they're white skin or dark skin? I wouldn't care if you brought a Chinaman in here as long as it wouldn't change your attitude towards us." This is the way she felt. And I just wondered if this ever came across when you were a foster kid?

MRS. A.: Well, my mother has her own daughter, who is a foster mother who lives nearby, and has quite a few children who are half-and-half over to her house. And when she has new children come in, they realize that some of these kids are colored. And a it sort of shocks them, but then they don't give it a thought.

APPENDIX D
THE NATURAL PARENT

In the following discussion, a natural parent of foster children tells foster parents how she felt. The foster parents reveal their struggles between empathizing with the children's parents and resenting them. Foster parents have invested a greal deal of emotional and physical energy in their foster children, and one can easily understand their need to possess the children. I believe that this kind of direct discussion is useful in helping foster parents and parents to understand each other.

Foster Parents Talk with a Natural Parent

2-4-69 Structured Group

F.P.3: Sometimes I feel that natural parents should visit through the agency. I feel that some natural parents, not all, have a feeling of resentment towards foster parents.

F.P.4: This is what I have to face. I see these people and have to be nice to them, but you hate them. It's not right or logical, but you do.

S.W.1: I, at the beginning, prefer to meet the parents and if I have the feeling that they are upsetting the child or they are getting upset, then I think that they should meet at the office. I have one foster father who prefers visits through me. He thinks the child needs visits with the mother and so I don't fight it. Did you feel that when you went there, did you feel like you were being judged?

N.P.: Yes, I always felt low. Like I was kind of an outcast. I don't know why. This is just my nature.

S.W.2: Something wrong with somebody who doesn't take care of their own kids.

N.P.: Right. There got to be—I know people think I'm a drunkard. I was in a mental hospital for two weeks, and this had a bad effect on me. So I felt both insane and poor. I had no money. And you don't look nice, and you don't feel nice, you don't perform well.

* * *

F.P.2: . . . and anybody who has done what you did and let your children go is a big person.

N.P.: Well I'm glad you feel this way.

F.P.2: And you yourself said you felt this way.

N.P.: I don't think my [child] would have ever made it to college. At least she has the chance. I don't know if she'll make it, but at least she has a chance.

S.W.2: What bothers you is not being able to hear someone say that they're a failure.

N.P.: Right.

F.P.1: I don't really believe that the parents of these children are failures. I think that sometimes it can't be helped. Like I heard you say that you were sick and away for a couple of weeks and couldn't cope with the family and you voluntarily had to give them up.

N.P.: I begged and begged [the social worker] to help me find somebody to take care of them.

F.P.2: Well, just recently, the girl that works in the coffee shop—all these years I've had to get to know her, and just yesterday I found out that she had her children in foster homes for four or five years because she wasn't able to cope with them. She had a mental breakdown, she spent months in a mental hospital, and now she says, with her children home she feels resentful to the foster mothers who were taking care of the children because they [the foster mothers] had taken so much away from her, because they refer to their foster parents saying, "She did this that way, and she did that this way," and she feels that she failed her children. And I said, "How do you feel that you failed your children? You weren't able to take care of them." She said, "I wasn't. My husband was a drunkard, and I was sick and wasn't able to take care of them." I said, "Why do you feel that way? Now that you have your children back, don't you feel like you're a good mother?" She said, "Yes, I do, but I still feel that I should never had given my kids up."

N.P.: Right. You're never quite happy. I don't think that I'll ever be quite happy. Just the thought that I missed their childhood. I missed it. I can't bring it back. And although I was in such a state that I didn't remember my name or why I was at the hospital. And I needed someone desperately to take care of them. And two days later I was sitting there saying, "My God, what have I done?"

F.P.2: This is a natural reaction. According to this other lady, she was very unsettled. And she wondered how she could be so low, so mean. She considered herself the lowest of the low.

N.P.: Right. That's the way I felt.

F.P.2: But now that she's gotten back, she says she resents the fact that the foster mother had her children because the children keep reminding her of the foster mother. Even though she has them back, she has the feeling that she should give and give and give, that she shouldn't even take from them. And her husband has straightened out, and she's better. Or she shouldn't ever punish them; she feels so inadequate about it, so distressed, she keeps giving and giving, and they walk all over her.

N.P.: Someone asked me the other day what I was afraid of, if I put my foot down. Why was I afraid to? And I hadn't thought about it. But you are. You are afraid to say anything because you don't feel that you have a right.

S.W.2: What [did] you think of foster parents in general before you met these nice folks? . . . They're mean and ugly and they're only in it for the money. And they hated real parents and social workers and agencies. You never thought those things?

N.P.: No, before I had children, I never gave foster care much thought, but after I was having my own, I thought that anyone who would take care of someone else's children had to be good.

F.P.3: Or crazy.

F.P.4: I don't see where you can make that much money.

F.P.5: You speak about not being able to cope with children. I can say that I had a very normal life. And I can say many times I didn't know how to cope with my three girls. And would think that if anyone would come along and take them, that I would give them to them. I wouldn't even charge a nickel apiece. And I think this is something that is apt to come to any parent. Then when you have other problems, it can get——

N.P.: This is what I have to tell myself. I didn't have my physical health, I didn't have my husband, I didn't have any money, I didn't have anything. I didn't even have a decent place to live. So it was too many things. There was no way out. But here's a thought I had. How much should you tell your children about the hardship at home when they've been in foster care? If you don't tell them, they demand of you. If they do know they may go back to the foster parents, upset and worried about what's going on at home.

F.P.2: I had one girl who is 18, who is well on her way to being on her own. She's very well adjusted, well adjusted for a child who has been on foster care, and I've had her for ten years. And she can speak on the subject better than most girls. She said one day, "Mommy, if I had to go back there to my mother, I'd have to go back there with the guarantee that my mother would have to tell my why she gave me away. I said I know why, you told me, but I've been told, the social workers have told me, but I have to hear it from my mother's mouth for me to believe it, because I don't believe that any mother could give up her children that willingly unless there was an extra special reason." And I said, "There was an extra special reason," and she said, "Yes, I know, you told me, but I want to hear it from my mother," and I said, "Won't that make you dislike her, won't you feel more resentful to her?" And she said, "No, if I was facing her and she was telling me herself I could feel, I could see how she would feel about the subject." And this is a girl who is 18, she's a very perceptual child, not intelligent but grown up. We did something right. She's turned out to be a very compassionate child. She tries to understand everybody's problems. If one of the children doesn't get a letter from their mother or hear from their mother, she cries for them, because she's gone through this and she knows how they feel. And I think you'd be surprised— . . . but you'd be surprised at how compassionate they become. They really learn how to love their enemy. At the beginning they resent everything that is done for them. They resent being in foster care, but I'm sure that you would find in time they become very understanding about these problems and I wouldn't hesitate to tell them, because if they're any kind of children and if they have any kind of love at all, they'll understand, no matter what you tell them, they'll understand.

N.P.: There was one problem which I used to have and that was transportation. I don't have a car, and when my oldest boy went home for a weekend, it was up to me to get him home and get him back, and it had to be done by a certain time. Well, I had to ask a neighbor. I don't have any relatives in the state, I don't have anybody you can really depend on. So I would have to wait for somebody to decide to give him a ride home. And he was almost always in trouble, because I could never get him home in time. Sometimes he was supposed to be home at 3.

S.W.2: One of those uncooperative mothers.

N.P.: Yes, that's the way it seemed. [My boy] was always in the middle. It was nothing deliberate. I always tried to get him home on time. If I sent him home at 2 o'clock in the afternoon, this hurt him because he didn't have to be home until 7 and yet, but if I waited, everyone would be having their Sunday dinner between 3 and 6 and I couldn't get anyone to take him home.

F.P.5: Do you really know what happened, getting back to telling the child you know what happened. Could you really say you know this, this, and this happened?

S.W.2: Is it like that?

N.P.: No, that's not what I meant. While they're living in foster care.

F.P.4: But this is what the kids want. Like F. [a foster child] . F. came to us when he was 5 and saw nothing from his parents. Increasingly they showed up, and he was introduced to his mother. They didn't even recognize him. But he was introduced, and she said they were lovely children and they'd make a lovely life and she carried on how nice it was, how sorry it was. And little F. turned around and said, "If you're so nice"—and he's not a sassy kid—"and if daddy is so nice and our life is so nice, how come you got a divorce?" And she didn't have a good answer either. And he still wants to know. And myself, I'd like to know. When the real parents come into your home, when they do, and they tell you how nice they've kept things and how nice things went, and how everything was so nice, I find myself sorely tempted to say, "Well, if it's so nice, how come?"

S.W.2: Why don't you keep them home?

F.P.3: That's right.

F.P.1: You said that when you brought him home he was always in trouble. I think that if it's like this, then the social worker should have intervened and told.

N.P.: Well, this is what always saved the day. The social worker.

F.P.2: This is the wonderful thing. You can have the social worker act as the referee in the middle of these things.

N.P.: But that's bad. When [my son] was in high school, his foster parents moved to Delaware, and we had to decide whether he was going home, going to another foster home, or go with them. And that's a decision to make because that's a——

S.W.2: Who got to make it?

N.P.: As I remember it, the foster parents had already decided that they did want him to go, and so it was between the social worker, [my boy] and myself.

It included [my boy] because if I made the decision, it would seem like I was pushing him away, and I wouldn't do it. So I put it to [my boy], what do you think would be the best thing for you? And he indicated that he thought he'd like to go with them. And I think he made the right choice. They're very nice people, but I was never close to them, I never knew them. He misses them very much being in the service. He visits them, he divides up his leave so that he can spend time with them and time with me.

F.P.2: Do you resent them?

N.P.: Do I resent them? Well, at the time I resented the fact that they were so angry at this boy for not being home on time, while they have two cars sitting at home. They're sitting there in a comfortable house and I'm home with no milk in the house or no money, there's no buses. And I walked miles with him to get him back when the weather was decent. And frankly, I did resent it. I thought they could come over and get him.

F.P.2: The general feeling in the agency at that time was that we shouldn't get that friendly. Driving the child home would put us exactly in the spot of knowing where you lived and how you lived. And it would seem like a conspiracy going on about you and there shouldn't——

* * *

N.P.: I think that's bad.

S.W.2: Well, isn't there still a little bit of it?

F.P.3: I think that this agency is relaxed. I don't know which way it's going.

S.W.1: This agency has relaxed this rule.

F.P.4: Before it was almost a law that we didn't—— We weren't even supposed to keep in touch with the kids once they left. And that summer I was told that I was keeping too much contact with the children that were in my care and that I should drop it right then and there.

F.P.2: I think that in some cases, we're encouraged to associate with the parents of the children as much as possible, to find out just what our opinion is. Because lots of times the social worker don't get a true picture of what the parents are like. We come into the agency and we talk, and they come at their best. And if we possibly can be on a friendly basis with the natural parents we're encouraged to do it. They feel that the foster parents know more about what's going on in the child's mind. If he goes home for any length of time, like a weekend visit, they try to encourage the foster parents to go and see what kind of home the kids are going into. Lots of times the social workers don't even know what kind of home these kids are going into. They take these kids out of the home and they only have contact through the office.

F.P.5: I agree with you, that they shouldn't have too close contact with the natural parents. I find myself getting too closely involved with—— I would get involved if I had to bring the child home. I would begin to see the problem. I would then personally get in there and try to help when personally it is none of my business. Or, I would be very antagonistic and say, "This kid cannot go home any more."

F.P.5: This happened with one of our children. We were asked if we could drive this child home, since the father was unable to come after him—would we take him home on a Friday night. They would [pay] the transportation and take care of this. And would we take him back on Sunday evening. And I said fine, sure. We drove up to the house, it looked beautiful, it looked in good shape. We went to the door. We dropped the child off, we said, "Hello, Mr. and Mrs. So and So, here's your son, we'll be back for him Sunday night." All well and good. She looked like a nice lady, and her husband was all dressed with a shirt and tie; they were expecting us. So I don't know what the situation was. Oh yes, we had a death in the family. So I had to call up and tell her I'd have to pick him up a little earlier. Well, when I called, we got an answer. The small child answered and said, "I can't call my mother because she's sleeping, and my daddy isn't home." So I said, "All right, I'm coming to pick up So & So early and would you tell your mother when she gets up that I'll be there." And this is a good 50 mile drive from our home. We drove all the way there. The boy had the same clothes on that we left him off in Friday night. The mother, being intoxicated beyond the point where she could half stand, sleeping on the couch, half dressed. The father was in the kitchen, stark raving mad, throwing dishes and pots and pans. And the poor kid we had sent home was crying in a corner just afraid to move. And when he saw me, he ran just as fast as he could and he hung on to me like an octopus and just hung on. And when I told the social worker this, she said that they weren't under the impression that the mother was that much of a drinker. "We knew that the father had a terrific temper, but we didn't know the mother was a drinker. And he said—the little guy, I called him in and said, "Tell him why you're so upset." He was old enough, he was 9 years old. He said, "My mommy gets drunk all the time." And the social worker said, "Why didn't you tell me this earlier?" and he said "She told me not to, and nobody ever asked me before." So this is the kind of thing that we found. So in this case it was good that we brought this child home. Because we would have been sending this child home continuously weekend after weekend to the same situation. But this is only one particular case. Other times we've been to the homes and been invited in for coffee and high balls. And the first thing they can say is, "Oh, they take a high ball, they're drinking people, how can they take foster children." So we always have to be careful about things like that. But other than that, we've always been treated very cordially to the natural homes we've been to. With that one exception. I think it's a good thing to have contact with these people, because the foster parents are with these kids the most and it's important for them to know just what the situation is.

S.W.1: I'd like to ask, if in the future—four or five years—if they come, or came, and said, "Now we thought this home is ready to accept this child, how would you feel?"

F.P.5: I would feel very resentful because I would——

F.P.2: But the situation isn't there any more.

F.P.5: Perhaps the situation isn't there any more, but as a matter of fact I don't think it was there when the child left. The mother had joined AA. She was on the road to recovery, and the aunt had moved in to help supervise.

* * *

S.W.1: [*To parent.*] Would you feel resentful if the foster parents walked into your house and found this situation like this, knowing that they weren't coming earlier, but coming at 7 o'clock, and came earlier and found a situation like this. How would you feel? I don't know if this had ever happened to you, but let's say that it did, and you had the house all upset and you were in the process of cleaning it. Would you dislike the foster parents more for it?

N.P.: Oh no. I would if I was intoxicated, though. [My child's] foster mother and I are very close. She's a dear person. She has always visited back and forth. As a matter of fact, she had stopped over in the afternoon for [my child] to pick something up and we would talk. A lot of times she'd stop when our house was a mess.

F.P.2: Well, my house isn't always picked up.

N.P.: I think the worst she ever saw it was the time she came to the hospital to pick me up. I was in St. Francis Hospital and she was giving me a ride home. I had two children at home and my second youngest was returned from foster care home. I was rushed to the hospital from the supermarket, so I left my house in any order. And as I was shopping for groceries, I had to leave half my order and my money with my landlady. And after I go to the hospital, I called up my case worker and I said I need a homemaker or somebody to come in and take care of my house. So they came out there, and my landlady said that she would do it. Which I would never, I called them back and said, "No, don't let her do it, she's not responsible." She had seven children who were in her house all the time. Not her, she didn't come in to see if my children were supervised, or come in to get meals. She just allowed the whole neighborhood to play in my four-room apartment. My walls were banged up, lamps broken, ash trays broken, you can't imagine the shambles I came home to. Dirty dishes with maggots on them. My grocery money was spent on soda pop and they paid her for taking care of my children, not using my grocery money. And [the foster mother] brought me home and we walked into my kitchen and I said, "I couldn't believe it." And that's the most ashamed I ever was, and it's not my doing. Twice while I was at the hospital, I begged the state worker to please send someone over there; I don't want her taking care of my home, but they didn't. They said, "We checked and she said everything is fine." She's one who made money.

F.P.4: In a case like that, the social worker was negligent. The social worker should have gone and seen for herself and checked.

N.P.: You wouldn't believe this woman. She puts on the appearance of a real sweet motherly type. She just doesn't care. She fooled me for almost a year before I found out that she just doesn't care.

F.P.2: Maybe she cares and she just doesn't like housework.

S.W.2: What about the chronic suspicion of people who aren't able to take care of kids? Last year any more than this year?

N.P.: When [my son] came home from the Village—and I don't think that a good training program for any child to learn to get along in a home—he came here: go to your meals now, do this now and this now, and he didn't get along at all at home.

S.W.1: So you think foster care has its benefit. Coming from an institution like this, you feel that the child is less adjusted to society than a child in a foster home?

N.P.: Not adjusted to society, but not adjusted to live in a home where there is emotional problems. But as I look back on it, I pictured what would be best for them, and thought Children's Services could do it and, at the time, wanted military school for [my son]. I don't know why, but I thought that he would get along good in a school like this. And it's true, he did, he has made out well in the Marines. But he doesn't get along good in the home.

S.W.2: Are you saying that it's true, if you can't take care of a kid last year, then you can't take care of him this year?

N.P.: It's apt to be quite true, I think.

F.P.1: I don't think so, it depends on the circumstances.

F.P.2: I have one girl who has been with me for quite a while. And she went home for a visit, with the thought that we might be sending her home. Well, she did go home and her mother was very cordial about having her come home and very nice about the whole thing to the social worker. And it was fine until the child got home. She had her home for a ten-day vacation. Well, by the end of the tenth day the mother was so enraged she said if this is what I can expect from you when you get home, then I don't want you home. And she hasn't gone home and she's 18 years old. And I called the mother and asked the mother exactly what did this child do to upset you so bad for you to say this, and is there some way that we can talk to the child to make her understand? Well, I called her and she said, "I feel no remorse of here and now than I did five years ago, and if they're going to send that monster home to me, don't bother, because I don't need it." And, believe me, she hasn't made an effort to make even contact with the child for the past five years. And I don't feel that she's a monster.

F.P.3: I've had my girl for eleven years. She came to me when she was 11, and left when she was 21. She went to her father, and he thought of her as 11, and he wouldn't give her any idea of what kind of behavior he would expect of her being 21. He said, "When I get her, I'll give her the low-down." Well, it didn't work out. But [the girl] was very close to me and came back home to see me and my husband after she got married. She now has a little boy who is 4, and she's up the house quite often. And we talk about different things. And one of the things she said, and she said it quite a few years ago—she's 28 years old now—she said that when she left to go to her father's house, she left with a package full of resentment and that she was going to get even with him one way or the other for all he put her through. And I think that many of the children do this. Now we're going to screw things.

F.P.2: The mother that said this [called her daughter a monster] had six foster children who all went home in due time, and each one of them went home and proved her theory that they're no good, and after they went home, they all turned out no good. My daughter got a letter from her the other day, and she said, "Be a good girl, don't be like me. I'm three months pregnant, and the man is married." And this put my daughter in the state of shock where she couldn't believe it. She said, "That's what I have to look forward to if I go home to my mother and father. I'll stay here until I'm 50." That's the way she felt about it. Because each one of the girls did go wrong and the boys are all on probation, and she feels that the mother is to blame for this. That if they didn't send the kids home, then they wouldn't have turned out like this.

F.P.5: Well, I think that if you tell your kids that they're no good, then they'll turn out this way.

F.P.2: This is what the mother did. She said, "I sent you away because you're no good, and I couldn't take care of you, and you never were any good, you never will be any good. Even though these children went home after therapy, and went home well adjusted, it didn't take six months for her to turn each one of them. And it didn't take that long, and now my daughter is seeing this. You think she's going to be encouraged to go home to a home like this? This is the reason why we are making up plans for her future. She has made up her mind that no matter what they do, she's just not going home. . . .

* * *

F.P.2: [the foster girl] is 18. She doesn't care about leaving home. She's engaged and she's making wedding plans and she's going to give me a hard time about a big wedding and a big meal, but we're looking forward to it. Daddy [is] going to give her away. As a matter of fact, she doesn't even think she's going to invite her mother and father to the wedding. M. [another foster child] was talking about weddings one day. She's 12, and she comes from a background where life is pretty free and easy. In fact, one of her favorite remarks was that all married couples had boy friends and girl friends on the side whether they wanted to admit it or not. She said, "When I'm 18, I'm going to get married." So one of the youngsters asked her who she was going to marry. And she said, "I don't know, but when I'm 18, I'm going to get married." She said she'd pull the first guy off the street. It would be fun living with him. So she said, "If I didn't like it, I'd get divorced and get married again." So they kept this up, and finally C. [another foster child] said after a little while, "Mommy, are girls supposed to pay for the weddings?" I said, "Yes." And she turned around to M. and said, "I think that you better wait, because I don't think Mommy's going to pay for that many weddings."

We have this other one with us who has her mind made up that she's going to do just what she darn pleases and nobody's going to tell her what to do. First she says that she's going home, and wants to go home. Her mother writes and tells her how much she'd love to have her, but she'd like to have her grown up when she comes home because she doesn't want to be bothered with taking care of a child. So she said, "I want you to be a lady, I want you to grow up, I want you to be independent. I want you to be able to take care of yourself. I want you to come home but I want you to be able to take care of yourself. I don't have time to take care of a child." And she says, "Huh," she thinks, "I'm going to go home and take care of her, she's crazy." The next breath, she says, "Wouldn't it be wonderful to go home to [my] mother." But now that we're in the process of sending her home, she's beginning to back track; she doesn't want to go home.

F.P.5: She wants whatever she wants she won't be able to.

F.P.2: She wants the opposite to what we agree to. It's always the opposite. Oh yes, she wants a motorcycle.

Have you ever been able to relate what these kids are like towards their parents by what you felt towards your parents? Because I have. Well, when I was growing up I was often angry with my mother. We never had trouble, my family life was smooth. Especially in high school, she didn't agree with the kind of dresses, or the boy I went out with, and I resented it. But now that I look back on it, when I go visit her now, I realize that it wasn't what she was telling me, it was rather the way she was doing it which put me down. Because, she'll make me feel the same way now, but I'm adult enough to cope with it, and it doesn't bother you. But as a child it does bother you.

S.W.2: How would this carry over to how your child treats you?

F.P.3: I had no real trouble with my mother. But look at the trouble that these children have had with their parents, look at the resentment that can build up in a perfect relationship all the time you're growing up, and you still have these feelings.

F.P.1: [*Addressing parent.*] I know that it's kind of personal, but do you feel that your children have had trouble with you? Were you abusive to your children when you were so sick?

N.P.: No, I don't think I was abusive.

F.P.1: Well, if you weren't, they probably don't look at you as being abusive.

N.P.: No, none of us wanted to be broken up. Each of us, in a certain sense, knows that it was circumstances which caused the problems, all the things that happened. If they want to blame me for not getting along with my husband, they wanted to blame my husband for walking out, but, when you go back, you have to blame the union for calling the strike, you got to blame the twins because I had to have a hysterectomy, a fire—we were burned out. You've got to blame all these things. Every year there was a major thing. And we went a little further into debt each year. This is a thing that you can say, "Don't do this," but you can't plan a life and say, "Don't do this." You have to try.

F.P.2: I know what she's trying to say. She knows how she feels toward her mother. And have we ever thought of how the kids felt, have we ever looked at the kid's side?

F.P.3: No, did you ever think back about the problem you had with your parents, and have you ever thought of how much more intensive the problem would be with these children?

F.P.2: Yes, and I did have some of the problems that these kids had. I had a drinking father, and a mother who was a very hard worker. She had seven operations from the time I was 10 'til I was 17. I had the run of the house, I had four younger children at home. My father was a heavy drinker. And I know how I felt. I came home from a hard day at work, and I always had to rush right home from work to make sure that these kids had food in front of them, because I never knew if my father would be home to feed them. But, I will say one thing for my father, is that he wasn't abusive. . . . He was a heavy drinker, but he'd come home and plop himself down on a chair, and go to sleep.

S.W.2: But what she's saying is——

F.P.2: I know, what I'm saying is that I resented that I had to do all these things, I resented my mother.

S.W.2: Would you have preferred to be put in a foster home?

F.P.2: Would I like to have been in a foster home? It would have been a blessing, believe me. Then I would have been waited on and taken care of. As it was, I had to be the one to do all that. I can understand. My mother was very sick. And we were very poor, we wore hand-me-downs from other families. I'm not saying that we were the worst off. My father was working for the city. On pay day, he managed to spend half his pay on booze. And he would be half plastered before he come home. This wasn't all the time. This was pay night, or on weekends. And my mother was getting sicker and sicker and sicker. And with each child, she got sicker and sicker. And there's a difference of age for 17 years from the youngest to the oldest. So you see, it was always pushed on me to take care of the younger ones. And I resented it, because I felt that if I didn't have to take care of these kids, or if I didn't have to take care of my sick mother, I could just walk out the door and forget the whole thing. But how could I forget the whole thing when I knew they'd be abused. My father wouldn't abuse them physically, but——

S.W.2: Now if you had been in foster care, you wouldn't have gotten this responsibility.

F.P.2: If I had been forced into foster care, if my mother said I have to put you all into foster care, I think I would have been the worst foster child in the whole world. Because I would think that I could be sent home to help. This is why I can understand this child. I can see it step by step, and I can see what is coming next. And yet, in a lot of other ways it has made me a much stronger person. I am able to cope with a lot of problems.

F.P.4: Me, I never even knew about divorce. I never even knew about these problems. I grew up on a farm.

F.P.2: My husband is the only fella who had to take his future wife's family along with him on a date, because you never went any place without one or two kids coming along. This is the truth. When my husband and I planned on getting married, my mother was still very sick. And we still couldn't make up our mind, I was 23 and I still felt that I should stay at home. And finally my husband said, "Well, are you going to marry me or not?" By that time, I thought I was going to be an old maid so I grabbed the chance. We had been going out for some time and wherever we went, we had to drag a couple of the kids along, because my mother wasn't able to take care of them. But, when we were going out, he got so upset with me, are you going to marry me or not? And I thought to myself, "Boy, he's getting ready to walk out on me. I better grab him." And this is true. And this is why I think I can understand the kid's problems more. I feel for them because I had the same problems.

F.P.1: You can feel just so far.

F.P.2: Oh yes, that's why I turned hard. If my father had used the strap on me, I don't think I would be so resentful. I probably would have appreciated it more. As it is, I have a wonderful relationship with my parents. They're very good to us, and they're very good to my children. You'd be surprised at how good they are to the foster children. Exceptionally good. But I know what these kids are going through. When each one comes into the house I wonder, "Does he feel like I did?" I have one who comes from a large family. And he goes home to visit his mother and father, and he goes home to his father's house, and sometimes he comes back and says, "You should come home with me some day and live with my father." This is the way he talks, and I know how he feels. My husband has said that I'm a very fine mother. [*Laughter.*] He comes from his home, well he's only 5 and really doesn't know what he's saying, but he said, "You're coming home to live with my daddy, huh?" And I'll say, "Well, I already have a daddy," and he'll say, "That's O.K. He can stay here. Daddy knows how to take care of the house. My own Daddy doesn't know how to take care of anything."

F.P.4: I asked [my foster child] if he was going home to his folks, and he said, "No, I don't want to, but if I do, I'm going to be bad."

F.P.3: See, he gave you the answer.

F.P.4: And he's only 9 and if he goes home, he's going to be bad, because he doesn't want to go home.

F.P.2: Right now my girl has to make up her mind whether she's going home or going to stay with me, or—well, she has to decide which she thinks would be best for her. Because she's going to be given a certain amount to live on, and she has to earn everything she needs for college.

S.W.1: What do you feel about it?

F.P.2: I don't know, I don't know which would be best for her.

S.W.1: What would you like her to do?

F.P.2: I'd like her to have a home. But I don't want to see her get all messed up and unable to study and perform as [another foster child] did. I don't want to see—— She has a good relationship with her brothers and sisters when she goes home.

F.P.5: You don't think her mother would be mad if she stayed with you?

F.P.2: Well, she's used to what she needs. She is very used to having what she needs, when she needs it. And at her house she's not going to get what she needs. There'll be nights when there's no milk, and you have to do [*drink*] something else. And there'll be nights when . . . there isn't enough laundry detergent and not enough room, and there won't be enough closet space at all. She's not going to have a room to herself.

S.W.2: She should have poor foster parents.

S.W.1: Well, youngsters do reach the point where they can't go back to living the way they did before. I understand that you have rather a luxurious apartment?

N.P.: I do. I really do. I just painted it. And the landlord said he'd pay for the paint.

F.P.5: And watch next month, he'll raise the rent.

N.P.: It's the best I've had yet. And as far as the kids coming home to visit, there is room, but there is no privacy. One bedroom is so small.

F.P.2: Well suppose this girl would like to come to your care: "All right, I'd like to come live with you Mom, but I'd like to be independent enough so that I could have an apartment of my own, but you'd still be the boss, so to speak." If she can come home with this, would you be satisfied, if she was left on to have an apartment?

N.P.: I don't want her on her own in an apartment. And this is one of the reasons I'm wondering if I should tell her to come home and stay with me for the summer, because she said, and I quote, "The only thing looking forward to coming home to you is that I'll be able to go out more." She knows it, she can walk all over me. How many rules can you set up for her coming home a couple of weekends a month? How many rules can you have when you're going to be home for two weeks at Christmas? These are special occasions. You do let them stay up later. So she gets the idea that this is going to be the normal procedure. She has a boyfriend and, oh, she expects to go out with him every night. But when she's at [the foster home] there are limits. And I think they're good limits. They give her a fair and healthy way for living. And I'm not sure that I can set down these rules for her.

F.P.1: This is a problem that we run up against. We have boys, 15–16 years old, and we don't have any difficulty with them during the week. But they go home over the weekends. The parents feel exactly as you do. And so, when they go home and come back, home is so much nicer than here, but then after a while, the parents begin to complain because we're giving them all these things. Because there's no controls, they stay out late at night, they're out all day long. So our biggest problem is that the parents don't want to apply these controls because they want their children to love them—and not discipline them. So now we have to take the reverse action. Our boys can't go home for weekends, vacations, and holidays, until they can prove that they can carry over the discipline that they have in the group home. And it's hard to get the parents to go along with this because they don't want to set up these controls. So we say to the older boys, "It's your responsibility to set up the controls; you should not expect your parents to do it, because they don't know you that well." And this is very difficult, but at least there is a glimmer of hope that maybe it will work out, but it is a problem.

N.P.: Yes, now, once you've lost control of your children, once they've seen you this way, helpless and not knowing what day it was, how can you regain their respect? How can you get back your authority? Especially when they're all home. They're all bigger than I am. When they begin fooling around I say, "You have to stop or something is going to get broken." They all just look at me and laugh.

F.P.3: Our own children do this to us. I have two boys and they're 6'2". And they'll say, "What are you going to do about it, Mom?" But they don't mean it.

N.P.: Well, what if they want to stay up to 3 A.M. like he said, I don't feel equipped to make them go to bed.

F.P.1: I think that if a youngster is 18 years old and hasn't learned to put controls on himself, you and someone else has gone wrong some place. So they have to learn to put the controls on. I don't have to speak to my kids, and they're only 14. They know when they should go to bed.

N.P.: I have one like that, but the rest stay up all night long.

F.P.2: Well, I have a daughter to whom we have more or less given her her independence. We have said, "You're engaged, from now on what you want, we've taught you. And if you don't like what we've told you, then set up some rules for yourself, you're a big girl now and we want to know if we can trust you." And she has been given the right to date when she wants to, and go out to places that she wants to. I mean there's a limit to places we'll let her go. We don't want her to go to drinking places. And we do not want her home after 1 o'clock on any nights. And she uses good judgment. You'd be surprised how many nights she comes home at 11:30, 10:30, just depending on what she's done or where she's been. And if she is going to a place where she'll be home after midnight she will make an effort to call me. When she doesn't, I don't worry. I wait until 1 o'clock, and if she's not home by 1 o'clock, I get on the phone and call the boyfriend's house to see if he's home and then I start from there. I haven't had to do that—just once. But she does use good judgment.

N.P.: Like over Christmas. She planned to be home after midnight, she went to midnight Mass. And she went over to [the foster home] for hot cocoa. It was 1:30 when she got home, but she told me that she would be late. So, to me it seemed to me all right. But over this Christmas vacation she wasn't working— and any of her friends' skating parties, or if there was something she wanted to do, there was no reason why she couldn't. She could go out any night as long as she should be home when she should, and she was. But, is this going to be the rule?

F.P.1: What I do when I send the kids home—when I send the big ones home—I tell them, all right, you're going home for the weekend, you have the rules set here. I want you in bed by a certain time on school nights. When you're home, when you go home to your mother's and want to stay up to 1, 2, 3 o'clock watching television, don't expect to come back here and talk to me about it, because it's not going to make me very happy. So when they come back they talk to me about it, but they tell me how they told their mother that 11 o'clock is bedtime, and they took the mother along with this. And I have to agree. For some reason they have been very obedient about this part. But with one in particular [she] wants to be in bed by 10 o'clock when she's home because she can't keep her eyes open, and her mother kept saying, stay up a little longer, stay up a little longer. And she said to me, "You know what—my mother wouldn't let me go to bed until 1, and I was so tired by that time." And I said to her, "Next time tell your mother that you won't be able to go home if she doesn't let you go to bed when you want." And she did. And her mother never stopped her after that. But this is it. She just thought of this as part of her day. This is what I told her and she accepts it at that, because this is what I told her, and this is what she's used to. She came back from home Sunday night, and Monday morning she was so exhausted she couldn't keep her eyes open. This is what they did that weekend. But after that, I told her, "Do you want to go home? If you want to go home, you have to follow the rules, because if you don't go home and follow the rules, then you can't go home for good.

S.W.2: Have you ever had the feeling—because I've had the feeling when I've been working with kids in some situations when the kids have been in foster homes or here at the Village—life would sure be a lot simpler if these kids didn't have any natural parents. Because then the natural parents wouldn't be adding all these extra problems. All these questions of when are you going to take them back, and other people wouldn't have to be afraid to get attached to the kids.

N.P.: I feel very in the way many times. And very unnecessary. And the only thing that holds me back from committing suicide is that I'm afraid that one of the kids would feel guilty. They would blame themselves. And it's true. It's one thing that has stopped me because I get very very depressed.

S.W.2: (addressing F.P.4) Haven't you gotten into the situation with all the different kids that you've had, that it would be a lot easier to make it with him if the kid knew he had an age with you. That he wouldn't be upset by my mommy and daddy?

F.P.4: It would be like anything else. It would be quick and painful, but it would be over with and done with and the kids would be able to make a life. Where this way, they're tied.

F.P.2: Yes, but this way they wouldn't have a mother.

F.P.5: Yes, even when they get older, they still need a mother, even if they're married.

F.P.2: Someday you're going to be able to get all this with your grand-children, that you missed with your own children. Don't forget that. That's still coming your way.

N.P.: I hope so. I think about that sometimes.

F.P.5: Yes, but they need their mother even though you seem to think they don't.

F.P.2: Right at this moment they don't, but they do. Even in your own children. Sometimes they feel that way and don't feel that way, until they're grown up and married and have children of their own. You'd be surprised at how many times I've gone home and cried to my mother because of different things that has happened to me, that I never thought that I would be able to. I always felt that she was such a grind on me that when I grew up I was going to be an independent person, never going to go back and ask her for a thing because she was too sick to bother with me when I was younger. But you'd be surprised at now. Even though I resented her and my father—as much as he used to be offensive, and as much as I resented him—I still feel to this day that there was a lot of times that I can go back and say, "Pop, such and such a thing happened, what do you think I should do in a situation like this?" And my father is very helpful to me, even though I resented him for all those years. I have a different understanding now.

F.P.4: What would the situation be if you had the same parents? Like some of these kids have a couple of sets of parents. How would you feel about going home to [another] mother and dad?

F.P.2: Well, I have an aunt who was very close. When my mother was ever sick, or I needed help, or if there was a time when I ever needed anything, my aunt always got bombarded. I'd run to her with every little problem. Papa came home drunk last night, the man came and said the mortgage has to be paid before they foreclose on the house. And the light bill isn't paid. The man is at the back door and he wants to shut the lights off. These things came up. And my aunt acted like a second mother to me. And I depended on her a good deal, even after my mother was able to stand on her own feet, and my father.

F.P.: Some of these kids have a mother who has a boyfriend, or boy-friends. Father who is now married to some other woman, and has children also. Who [is] he really, his heritage?

N.P.: This is what bothers [my girl]. When she was staying at the [foster home] I was married twice, so she had a father she didn't know, a stepfather who walked out on her. And she had [the foster father]. So when she was making up papers at the high school and it said "father," the poor kid didn't know what to put down.

F.P.4: You know how my kids took care of that? They used my name and they put down "foster" in front of it. And for "nearest relative," they put down my brother's name. And these poor kids are so confused they don't know what to do.

F.P.5: The kids get around it after a while. But when they're first in the situation, they don't want to put down foster mother. But even after they've accepted the fact, they feel guilty about it, they feel like they should have their real mother's name on it somewhere. For [my foster child], this really bothered her.

F.P.5: We had an incident once with our 17-year-old boy. He started to look at it very realistically. His mother was never going to be strong enough to have him. And I'll never forget it. They were teasing me one day, as they sometimes do. I bet you wouldn't do that to your mother and he said, "Of course I wouldn't. She's my mother." And although she scorned him and caused him a lot of trouble, they never get over that, that that's their mother. And your children are going to be very much like that sooner or later. And there is no one else who could take that place. I'm sure of it. We have seen it so much. We had a boy who went home. He wouldn't go home to live, his mother has never been married, and she has three children and he resents this. But she is his mother and he respects her. But don't say anything against his mother. And there is this very strong tie which can not be severed.

F.P.2: This is the same with [my foster girl]. Although she's been told that she's going to live with us and then go out in the world and live on her own, she's going to be with us, and that her mother doesn't want her or have anything to do with her—and yet—say anything against her mother and she goes 20 feet in the air. You can't say two words against her mother. As much as she knows this.

F.P.3: Her mother may be very selfish. But she'll be sorry when she doesn't have anybody to call her grandchildren. She's going to have to think twice.

F.P.2: Well, we're kind of hoping that this kid would get on her feet and go see her mother and show her that she was making a pretty good life, working and all, good steady trade, going to hair-dressing school. We're kind of hoping that mother will come across and say, "All right, you can come home for visits." But we're not sure that this will work out. In lots of ways, we're not sure if the kid wouldn't be a lot better off without her own natural mother, but I wouldn't tell her this.

F.P.3: No, neither would I.

N.P.: Where does heredity come into this? I mean like with [my boy], I think there's a good reason why I don't get along with him. As long as he stays away, we get along fine. But he's like his father. He's like him. He never lived with him, but he walks like him, speaks like him, has a complete outlook like him.

APPENDIX E
THE FOSTER PARENTS'
OWN CHILDREN

Very little has been written or studied about the natural children of the foster parents. Clinicians know and studies show, however, that the foster parents' own children can help to make or break a placement. In this discussion, two adolescent children of a foster parent (Mrs. E. in the discussions of 11-26-68, App. F, 5-13-69, App. A, and 3-18-69, App. B) tell what it was like to have foster children coming and going in their home as they were growing up. The boy is more guarded than his sister, and quite certain that he would not want to take foster children when he grows up.

Foster Parents Own Children Talk With Foster Parents

3-18-69 Structured Group

* * *

S.W.1: [*Addressing the daughter*] Do you remember the first time a strange child moved into your home?

DAU.: . . . We were all the same age, that was another thing. K. [*foster boy*] was the same age as me. E. [*foster boy*] was a year younger. And S., too. We were all close in age, which I think made it a little more difficult.

S.W.1: I was wondering about this.

DAU.: There was a lot of competition with my brother. He was the smallest one, and all the others were big and strong. My brother's built like I am, small. So it made a lot of competition for him, three others. We got along. I never got in a fight with any of them, I was so small.

S.W.1: You couldn't compete.

DAU.: No, we all went to school together and worked in the summer. K. and I worked tobacco. We were all the same age so we did things together, we went to dances together, one weekend we went to N.Y. together, the boys and myself. Boy that was fun.

S.W.1: Did you ever ask your parents why they were doing this? How come these people are moving in?

DAU.: Well, no.

S.W.1: Or perhaps they explained it.

Dau.: Well, E. came first, because of his family. I knew that, and he wanted to stay. And I remember that he liked animals. And W. came, and my parents explained because he was having trouble with his mother. You know he was a big boy, and they told us that she couldn't handle him, his father was a cripple.

And they just said, "Why don't you ask W. if he'd like to stay for a few days." We weren't sure about him. They hadn't talked to anyone from Child & Family Service yet. And they just wanted to know for sure. And then they made sure and called and stuff.

S.W.1: [*Addressing the son.*] Do you remember this experience . . .

SON: . . . I was 7 or 8.

* * *

S.W.1: When your parents were having trouble with these boys do you feel that they were getting what they deserved, or did you resent these children for what they were doing?

SON: No, not at all.

S.W.1: Were you upset because they were upsetting your parents?

SON: Well, yes, that's natural.

S.W.1: What were your thoughts on that? Did you want to have it out right then and there?

SON: No. I sort of understood that they had problems so I didn't really mind.

S.W.1: [*Addressing the daughter.*] What about you? Were you wanting them to leave?

DAU.: No, I never wished that they throw them out, because we were all friends. But K. was hard. One night we were at a dance and he had a fight in the lavatory. And it's a reflection back on us. And he tore the whole place apart. And it was kind of a shock. But they were a lot of trouble, fighting and stuff like that. The thing I didn't like was the way that because—— Daddy never favored them—but being a girl I was never in competition. He was so fair. It was like S. was one of his boys. And it was hard. It was at a time when the boys were going out and stuff. He'd handle it great. I felt bad when W. left. He still lives in town. I still see him. We're good friends. And of course K. wanted to go home so badly that we were glad to see him go home. And he comes over too.

* * *

S.W.1: [*Addressing the son.*] Did you ever have any time that you had to discuss the other kids with your parents?

SON: I'm, well they'd ask, well, um, well, if something happened and I was familiar with it they'd ask me what happened. But I don't remember ever having to discuss a specific problem. With K. we might have. He was such a bully. K. and I got along, that was a good thing. So I played it right. I got him on my side.

* * *

S.W.1: [*Addressing the daughter.*] . . . you were the young one. But with the three you have now, you're the big sister.

DAU.: Um, L. came five years ago. He's 15. And of course he was the first little boy we had. And of course I was always my father's pet, being a girl. And all of a sudden I was really excited. Wow, having a little boy. Then all of a sudden he was a baby, and he got a lot of attention. At first I realized it, that I said to myself, I don't mean to feel like that. And Daddy would sort of tease me, saying I have to do this for the baby, and this for the baby. And this would get to me, but I'd get over it. Now he resents the foster kids. The first boy we had after him came awhile and he was older than him. And L. asked to leave, he told my parents he couldn't get along and asked to leave. This is the first time my parents had this happen. He was scared of him, the bigger boy. So when he left, L. was all set. But when T. and B. came, they became so close, it's terrific how they get along.

S.W.1: Yes, they're great big things, and he's such a small kid.

DAU.: But they're both in the same grade. And one is three years ahead. But they get along, and I think it's really great. It's working out better than when all the boys were the same age. Of course they were harder to handle. These boys aren't hard to handle. They really just fit right in.

* * *

S.W.1: Did you two find this, that you thought that your mother was giving the foster kids more attention? Did you feel neglected at any time at all?

DAU.: Well, yeah, I felt they were waited on a lot more than when I was that age. I'd say "You never let us do that when we were 5 years old."

* * *

SON: I did at first. My older brothers—I'm the youngest of my older brother and sisters, so I didn't think much of it because they were always home.

S.W.1: Did you think much of it. Did they say?

DAU.: Well, like I said, it bothered me at first. They did it a lot more about me. My brothers would come into the house and complain how I had something they never had, kind of making you feel good.

S.W.1: [Addressing the son.] . . . you didn't have just foster boys in your family, you had girls too. Previously before these three. As a matter of fact, one of the girls came back to visit with three of her own, didn't she?

SON: Yes. It didn't bother me too much. She was a lot older than me. But they did fight. And, ah, it really didn't bother me. She kept telling my brothers that she going to marry me. It was, well, sort of funny.

S.W.1: She had her eye on you.

* * *

S.W.1: [Addressing the daughter.] Did you ever wish . . . that your parents would have a girl?

DAU.: Well, at first that's what I wanted. I wanted them to adopt a baby. But then after L. came, I realized I was 15 and I wondered if I'd really like it. I always felt, I didn't know. Before I thought I might, but I've always been the only girl, so I don't know if I'd like it. If now someone said, it wouldn't bother me. But at 15 I'd say no. But at 12, I was all set for a girl, I wanted a girl. I think L. helped me get over this.

S.W.1: I was wondering about the contacts that the boys have had since they left. Do you keep in touch?

DAU.: Well, I see R., and I see B. all the time. When we were in college. my brother had a cottage in W. I was in my second year, he was in his first year. And they always came up, and I'd see him quite a bit. He still sees my parents. He really liked them, but he was glad to go home. He was glad to get out. He didn't have any restrictions, but he was older. and K., he'll drop in some times. And he stops me. And D., I wasn't home when he was there. But he was there last night. And when R. went away to school, but whenever he had time off, he'd always come back even though we had so much trouble and fights. Yeah, we see them all quite a bit.

S.W.1: [*Addressing the son.*] Do you see most of the kids?

SON: Well, yeah, once in awhile. E. comes back, just like she's part of the family. And M. comes back once in awhile.

S.W.2: Do you think that growing up in a home with several foster kids, and you becoming aware of some of their family stories, problems, and all that—did that make you any more or less tolerant of that, more able to handle some of your own problems than if you had a simple life?

SON: Well, I think you get to a point where you realize things. And it's good to look back on it.

* * *

S.W.1: . . . If you were to advise people about people entering foster care, would you say people should be very leary of it, that they should do it, that it's a good thing—from your point of view?

DAU.: I think it's good. I think that all the boys I've seen worked out good. The first boys came, and I think that when they first came, my parents had never had boys, so daddy would treat them different, and I kind of resented it, because—S. was good and never got in trouble, but when the others got in trouble, none of us could go to the dance, you know he didn't want to seem unfair. And this, I thought was kind of unfair. But, like the way they all turned out, I think it's great. I'd be very upset if my parents ever had to lose any of them. I would never want anyone to leave. I like the way they come back to see us.

S.W.1: I think the question [S.W.2] asked [the son] is a good one. What might it have given your life, compared to if you didn't have foster children? You and S. and the farm?

DAU.: Oh, well, for my parents, I think it's been great. They like children. And Daddy has really been happy. And the kids are very happy when they come back.

S.W.1: Is it the sort of thing that you'd ever want to do yourself? Can you look that far ahead?

DAU.: Yeah, I would like to have my own children and wait until they were a little older. I think that I'd like to be able to spend some time with my own children. But when they got older, and if I could, I would take care of foster children.

S.W.1: How would you advise a couple who came to you and asked you whys or what kind of answer, how would you advise people who would be thinking about this, you being the child of people who did this?

DAU.: Well, you have to be the type of people that can accept them. Not everyone can take a foster child. But if they're the type of people that can enjoy them and really interested and really want to and aren't afraid to punish them.

S.W.1: [*Addressing the son.*] What is your reaction to this question? Not, well, if you'd do it yourself, but do you think it's been a good thing for your family?

SON: Yeah, I do, but I definitely wouldn't want to do it. I would recommend it for somebody else if they wanted to do it. I would want to spend my time with my own kids. I think, well, it did do the family good, we all enjoyed it.

* * *

F.P.2: How do you feel with other people who ask the question, "Your mother keeps foster children." What kind of reaction do you have. Are you inclined to be proud of your parents? Do you feel that they're intruding to ask?

SON: Well, I did feel that. At a point, I don't think it's any of their business.

* * *

S.W.1: [*Addressing the daughter.*] What about you?

DAU.: Oh, well being right around town, a lot of people ask. I remember when M. was there and started school. She started her second year there. And the kids started teasing her, those aren't your real parents, she isn't your real sister. And I would get very upset. I'd say, "Listen, they don't know anything that is going on. Tell them what you feel, tell them that you are my sister, because sister, that's the way you feel. Just because you weren't born here, I still feel like your sister." And I was very upset. Most of my friends would ask, but I'd never get upset about it. I had one person who I knew well who thought it wasn't a good idea. And I really got upset. I told her, "You don't have to come over then." I got very upset she felt that way. I sort of feel the way [my brother] does, that I'd rather spend more time with my own children. I mean I don't——

* * *

DAU.: [*Addressing F.P. who had said she never had children of her own.*] I have a question. Why did you ever take foster children instead of adopting them?

F.P.2: Well, we thought about it for a good long time. My husband was in the service a good many years. And I was still at the time where I could still have children. We would go through this, I would be pregnant and have miscarriages, we'd go through this process. And we went to the priest, and I was very bitter, I had lost one of my babies very late in time. I was bitter against everything— church, the priest, God, everybody. And as far as I was concerned, there was no God. And we got to talking and the priest said, "Gee, why don't you try and take care of some children. Maybe if you have a child around you, maybe you wouldn't be so obsessed with this thing." So I said to him, well he said, "How about adopting one?" and I said, "well, not while I can still have my own, I don't want to adopt any." This was after a fourth miscarriage. So when we did take [a foster child] , we did it thinking that we needed a young person. We actually, well the money meant nothing, because we threw it away as fast as we got it, all on her. Consequently this is the reason for it, so when we did decide, before we knew it, we had the one, and then they asked us to take another one. And before you knew it, we had a third one. And by this time, we were so satisfied with what we were doing for the kids that we stopped thinking about having a child of our own. Then, when we did get to the point where we thought we might like to adopt one, but as far as adopting one, it never entered our minds until we knew we couldn't have any of our own.

DAU.: Well, I know I worried when L. first came. And, we got afraid in case he never got taken away. He saw his mother and that upset him. And that bothered me. He'd see his mother and get very upset. And that bothered me. He'd come home all mixed up. And that I didn't like. If we knew L. was going, we'd be upset as he was. Now, of course, he hasn't seen her for so long. We were afraid whenever he was taken away. And I was wondering if you ever had that fear, too, that the parents didn't want them back. What could you do to keep them?

F.P.2: Well, with [our foster child] , we knew that when we took her, the possibility of her going home was very slim. Her mother was very bitter towards her. As a matter of fact, there were six children in the family, and all of the children had homes with their own parents. But she was the one, right up to the very bitter end, even up to last week, her mother and father still refused to see her. And when she did go home, it was such an unhappy experience, that she was so happy to come back. We devoted all our time with this girl. This is why she feels like ours. She never had any love at home. From the time she was real tiny, she had been really abused. The mother resented her from the time she was born. We forced the issue of her going for a visit home—because she couldn't understand why they didn't want to see her. And it turned out to be a very unfortunate thing. It only set her back that much further. But once she was able to understand that they didn't want her any more, then she was able to settle in as our daughter. If she had her way, she'd use our name tomorrow. We knew that that would hurt her father, and he had a very bad heart, and I think that that's why [she] many years ago would have asked us to adopt her. But I think this is why she never asked us to adopt her. But as far as [she] is concerned, in her eyes she has no other mother and father.

S.W.1: L. puts your name on his lunch box.

DAU.: Yes. But, oh, when they first asked my parents to take L. . . . they didn't want to take someone little, because my mother knew that she would become attached, and was afraid of that. And that's why they had never taken a little one before that. And I mean it kind of scared us. If anyone had tried to take him now, they'd have a lot of trouble. Well, have you ever had one taken, or moved, whatever they do? Isn't that upsetting?

F.P.3: Well, with the last one it was.

DAU.: That's what I'd be afraid of.

F.P.3: Oh, I don't think upsetting the same way that you're referring. I think that when you take foster children, I wanted the condition that I wouldn't have the last say on these children. And I had three of my own. And I think when you have your own, it's easier to let go of someone else's children. So I always had it in the back of my mind that these kids were on loan more or less, so I was more prepared for them to go back. I think the reason for this, was that if you had a child who had a great deal of problems, and you spent a great deal of time, and then this child is taken, and to you it seems that he is placed back in a situation which is just as bad as he came out of, then you feel bad. We've had youngsters go up for adoption, which made us feel good, because someone who adopts a child accepts him with open arms and is ready to do whatever he can for this child. And this is good. But when you take a child from a bad situation and put him back into it, or a worse situation, or one that will develop into a worse situation, then it's bad.

F.P.3: I had a little girl who wasn't with us too long. But the day she walked in, she belonged. She walked in the yard and started playing with the toys, and one of the boys walked in the yard, and she said, "Do you live here?" and this was L., and she said, "Yes, I live here." And L. and this little girl look alike. Blond hair, blue eyes. And she said "Good, I live here too, fix this bicycle for me." Just like that. And the first night she was there we finished supper, and my husband went to sit in his chair, and my other daughter who was a year older, 6, went in and sat on her daddy's lap. And [the foster girl] went in and looked and said, "Move over, I'm coming up." And she belonged. And, well, they found adopted parents for her. And she said to me—she was a very smart little girl—and she said, "You know what I'm going to do," and I said, "No, what are you going to do?" and she said, "When they come to take me, I'm going to cry and I'm going to kick and I'm going to scream." And I looked at her and said, "You little nut." And she said, "I know." I said, "Oh, no you won't." And she said, "Why not?" And I said, "Little girls don't act like that." And the next day she behaved herself very well. And I said, "If we can get her out of here before I start to cry, we'll all be better off."

APPENDIX F
THE PAIN OF FOSTER CARE

There is a lot of pain in the foster care system: children's pain when they leave their families, and when they leave foster parents; parents' pain when they lose their children; foster parents' pain when they lose foster children; social workers' and psychiatrists' pain when they deal with all these other pains. The following discussion centers around pain that foster parents feel when they lose children, and the pain that social workers and psychiatrists feel. The psychiatrist James Black tries to focus the discussion on the grief that people feel when they lose children, on the grief that the children feel, and on how to deal with the grief. The foster parents, like most people, tend to veer away from the pain. They take flight from their anxiety in a variety of ways: keeping busy, talking about other things, making light of the pain, denying it altogether. The psychiatrist brings them back from time to time. Jim and social worker Kathleen Olmstead discuss how they and other professionals deal with pain. Professionals have protective devices not available to foster parents: work compartmentalized into time-limited spans (the classic 50-minute hour), professional detachment, "objectivity," "specialized training." The devices used by foster parents and professionals are examined in the following discussion. I have omitted some talk where it is not directly relevant to the issue.

Three of the foster parents are also involved in the discussion of 5-13-69 (App. A): Mr. and Mrs. B., and Mrs. E.

11-26-68 Unstructured Group

[Mrs. E. talks about the possibility of one of her foster children, Peter, going home to his mother, and the fact that Peter is not sure whether he wants to go home or stay with Mrs. E.]

MRS. E.: I'd like to see him sure. It would be better for Peter if he knew definitely what he wants. We want to make it clear that he's welcomed to come back. All my others have, and I think it makes him feel better. I wouldn't want him to think he has to come see me. Lots of times he'd say, "I'm coming to see [another boy], not you," and that makes him feel happy. . . .

J.B.: Peter's going home?

MRS. E.: What did you say?

J.B.: Does it look like he might be going home?

MRS. E.: I think perhaps. She [*the mother*] said she's going to petition for him after I get him through this year of school. But she should be aware of it. Peter has said, "I'm not going to work here and go home, so why should I work here?" He has a funny attitude. A little twisted. He fouled up at school. The teacher called up and said she thinks he copied from the boy next to him, and so they didn't even grade him. And this is the new boy, and we had this ever since he knew that his mother wants him back.

MRS. M.: Is he afraid of his mother?

MRS. E.: Oh, no. His mother, I think he loves his mother.

MRS. M.: Then why doesn't he want to go home?

MRS. E.: Oh, I don't know. Who knows what goes on in a little boy's mind? He's happy where he is—— What he wants to do to his own mother, I can't blame him. I think that if I was torn apart in so many ways that I would be worse than Peter at the same age.

MRS. B.: [My foster girl] is just the opposite. She can't wait to go home.

* * *

MRS. M.: How old is Peter?

MRS. E.: He's 11, but in many ways younger. But he's a pro in many, many others. He's very wise in the ways of the world. He plays better, gets along better with teenagers than he does with his own people his own age. He's sort of like a wise guy, but he has a pleasing personality. I have a firm belief that he could sell fur coats in the warm climates. And, all along he's said he'd go into being a salesman, but I hope he goes into religion or something like that—something worthwhile because he certainly can be the biggest con man. He could make me think that the world is beautiful right after he's taken everything out of my pocketbook and set fire to the chair. He doesn't do these things, but he could give me a big smile and tell me that life is worth living. Or he could walk by me and give me a pat on the back and say, "I really didn't do it," or, "I really didn't mean it." And sometimes I snap right back, "Look, that doesn't get you anywhere with me, but it will with a lot of other people."

J.B.: That's certainly going to tear you right up when he leaves, isn't it?

MRS. E.: It certainly is. I don't mind telling you that. Even though my husband said he's the hardest youngster that we've ever taken care of.

MRS. B.: Why do you think that you become most attached to the ones that are the hardest to handle?

MRS. E.: Because there's an awful lot of good in one. Because you let an awful lot of yourself come out. But there's an awful lot of good that Peter has let out. But he's afraid——

MRS. B.: Give him time.

MRS. E.: Oh yes, he has so many good points. You can see the way he is with animals and young children. He's absolutely wonderful with them.

J.B.: So when he's gone, part of you is gone.

MRS. E.: Worse than that even. I think that even all of me. Because he doesn't let me sleep in the morning. He doesn't let anyone sleep. And he wanders around and I think, "What is he going to do now?" But there's something——

[Conversation between Mrs. E. and Mrs. B. about their foster children's personality traits.]

MRS. E.: . . . One thing that bothers me about leaving, since we are talking about the situation like that, and the little Billy I was talking about, I have the feeling that he may be leaving shortly. Anyways, what bothers me is the way they react when they are told definitely that they are going. I think that scares Peter. I think it was a serious mistake to tell Pete, I don't know——

K.O.: Is he going?

MRS. E.: He might be going, but somebody has told him and deep down inside he's saying, "Just mark time since I am going." I'm not saying that the social workers did it, or I did it, but I think we all did it in our own subtle ways. Like Billy, who is going home, thought his mother was out of the picture, is going home tomorrow to see her. I have had the most miserable two weeks with Billy. For two cents I would give him back to the Indians. I don't think that would help Billy. I don't think anyone would have taken him, personally. Really, tantrum after tantrum. I'd say, "What do you mean, you're going into the agency?" And he'd say he's going into the agency to see MRS. B. [*his mother*] , "I think she said she was my mother." But, oh, he doesn't eat, he doesn't sleep. He does all the things that I said Billy would never do. Like flushing his shoe down the john, or taking everbody's toothbrush and flushing them down the john, and saying, "I didn't do it." And I heard somebody say, "I'm tired of walking into the bathroom into a puddle of water on the floor." There'll be Billy lurking in the hallway, wondering what'll be next.

MRS. M.: In anticipating of seeing his mother?

MRS. E.: If you were 7 years old and [had] seven different foster homes, and someone came and told him definitely that he was going to see his mother, and he doesn't know what your own mother means–he just thinks it's another foster mother. So he calls her Mrs. B. and he doesn't even associate his name with her name. He carries her name on a piece of paper and he'll say to me, "What does this say?" And I'll say, "Mrs. B." "And who's Mrs. B.? Another foster mommy?" Or else he'll want to hear me say that that's his own mommy. I've been trying to teach him this all last week. Since he wants to call her Mommy B., and doesn't want to call her just Mommy. "But she's not Mommy, you're Mommy."

J.B.: So if he calls her Mommy, then you're not Mommy.

MRS. E.: He can't conceive of having two mothers at the same time. It was all right when it was Mrs. B. When he was with Mrs. A., it was "Mommy." Then it was Mrs. H., which was Mrs. A.H. [*combining last names of two foster mothers*] .

J.B.: So in order to gain one, he has to lose one.

MRS. E.: Yeah. And-a- so he just says Mrs. B. So I said, "If you don't want to call her just 'Mommy,' call her 'Mommy B.' She'll understand that and it won't be so confusing." I thought he was mixed up. If he says 'Mommy," and calls me "Mommy," that that would straighten things out. But we're not getting very far. The school teacher just can't make things out. She said she was doing very well, except for these last two weeks. And then——

K.O.: How do you think about his seeing his mother?

MRS. E.: If it means something definite for Billy, I am very happy. [The mother] called me today from N., saying she didn't know if she should or shouldn't. It's the first time I had talked to her. And I thought it was a very interesting conversation. She didn't sound like she was apologizing or sound like she was guilty. She was just stating facts. And I said, "You don't have to explain to me because I'm doing the job, and hopefully I'm not getting too attached." And she said, "No, I just wanted to talk to you before I met you tomorrow. I thought that if I just talk to you before I met you, I won't seem so offensive, and maybe I won't be." That was the feeling I had. So I don't know. She sounds like she really wants him. I certainly don't want to judge. I have troubles enough figuring out who I am, and try to figure out Mrs. B. or who everybody else is. She could have been a victim of circumstances. And I like the A.A. motto, "There by the grace of God go I, because I live so——" I may not be an alcoholic, but that may be a cure. But I hope it's a good move for Billy, but I think she's a dreamer and I almost told her, but I better let Mrs. Mandell tell her. "Hopefully, I'll have him back by Xmas." I almost said, "Which Christmas?" but I didn't. If she could adjust that fast, good luck to her.

J.B.: Maybe he's upset because he's afraid that he may lose you.

MRS. E.: Last night, I don't think he'd mind. He doesn't like me to go out. We had six extra people for supper tonight. And I had the misfortune of saying I have to hurry, I have to go to Children's Village tonight. And right away Billy got upset and, boy, did he have a tantrum. So I didn't mean to say it, but our house is always full of people and you can't watch it every time you say a word for fear of what you might say. I don't live that way. If I'm going to do it, I'm going to do it, and they might as well know. So I imagine that he's in bed right now with my husband baby-sitting. One tantrum and off to bed.

J.B.: Maybe he links [another foster child] coming with his going?

MRS. E.: No, I don't think so. In our family there's too much commotion. I had my grandchildren there for two weeks visiting. He just assumes children are children and a part of this house. There's always someone there, and I don't think Billy knows anything different. He just knows that he's important, that he's the baby, and he likes being the baby. Well, he'll lapse into baby talk. And he'll never put his hands in his mouth, but recently I'll say, "Are you hungry, Billy?" Oh, no. He'll do this for awhile. And sometimes someone gets him something to eat or a glass of milk and he's all right. I think he's a very interesting little boy and I——
If she wants to love him and cope with him, then I'm quite happy, but oh-h-h——

K.O.: Hasn't he gone through this sort of thing so that children could be spared this turmoil between families?

MRS. M.: Terrible.

MRS. B.: I was just thinking it's too bad. But I don't see any way out of if either.

MRS. E.: You ought to face reality.

MRS. B.: I know our little boy is——

MRS. E.: How old is he?

MRS. B.: He's going on 3. He's very trying. He's very, very attached to me. And I can hardly leave the room without him being there. And if I get my coat to go out, well he's having a fit. He really has quite a tantrum. His folks come to visit him once very two weeks. And when they come, he runs and hides and won't have anything to do with them at all. So I figure the best thing is for them to take him out alone without me, when I'm not there. So they took him out for a short ride, which was kind of hard. It was hard to get him in the car. He was good for them, but I wasn't there. But when it comes down to choosing, then it's hard. He runs to me and I'm "Mommy" and he doesn't want to have any part of them. So they took him for Thanksgiving dinner Sunday and his mother really had an awful time. We had to place him in the car bodily. And he's screaming, scratched her, hit and bit, and did everything that he could possibly do. And she had two little ones with her, one a year younger, and they were both in the car and she was trying to drive and take care of the two of them, and it was really rough.

MRS. E.: Is he going home to her?

MRS. B.: Eventually, providing that everything works out for her.

MRS. M.: So really, if he's that unhappy, why does he go back?

MRS. B.: I don't know why. He really doesn't even know her, he's too young. He just doesn't want to go with her.

MRS. B.: He was put in the background and just left there. When I got him he was 2. He didn't know how to eat, stand up. He had no muscle development. He was suffering from malnutrition. He had a lot of problems. So maybe he remembers.

* * *

K.O.: What's he like now?

MR. B.: Like grab a tiger by the tail! He's in everything at every moment.

MRS. E.: Like a normal 3-year-old?

MR. B.: Yeah.

MRS. B.: All around rambunctious, like a disturbed 3-year-old. He has very, very bad temper tantrums. I've never seen a child with a temper tantrum as bad as his. Other than that he's fairly well. Except for the fact that he's not talking properly. In fact, I had kind of given up on him. Not given up, but wondering whether he has reached a plateau, a stand-still, where he isn't going to do anything, for a while.

MRS. E.: What do you do when he has a temper tantrum?

MRS. B.: Well——

MRS. E.: I'm serious. What do you do?

MRS. B.: Well, sometimes I take him and just put him in his bed and then leave, and he'll scream and yell for a minute, then he stops, I'll get him up. Just by leaving him by himself does it. He doesn't wreck the room. If he has anything within his reach, he'll take it and slam it around. Like today, he had a—— Many times he's grabbed me by the throat and I've had red marks.

MR. B.: The dog wasn't too happy the other day. He bit the dog.

ALL [*Laughter.*]

J.B.: Let's go back to something we were talking about a few minutes ago. When Mrs. E. was describing how Billy has been in the last few weeks and when Mrs. B. has been describing what it's like, when Carlos was being put in the car with his mother, how did you all feel?

MRS. B.: Very, very bad. I felt sorry for that little kid.

J.B.: No. I'm talking about how did you feel as it was being described? How did you all feel in the room here as it was being described? Pulling Carlos into the car, and Mrs. E. described what happened to Billy.

MRS. B.: You mean what was their reaction?

J.B.: What was everybody feeling?

MRS. M.: Well I feel that Carlos shouldn't be forced to go if he doesn't want to, if he feels that strongly about it. Obviously, it brings on or renewing a lot of unhappy memories, subconsciously. And I think that if this is the case, let him be secure where he is. Don't let the mother be involved. If this child has been taken away from her because of neglect, what good is it going to do to keep this relationship up? Who is saying let him go back? This disturbs me to no end.

MRS. B.: Well, it's a problem. They took him from her and put him here until they could get things squared away with her. He's the only thing she has. He should go back to her. You'll have this problem no matter when he goes back.

MRS. M.: But it would take many, many years if she did change, wouldn't it?

MRS. B.: I don't think he'd ever believe it unless it was proved to him. And the only way it can be proved to him is if he goes back to her and sees for himself. He isn't going to like going back. They probably think, they got it made, why should they?

K.O.: I think it might be compounded. Not only is it the fact that he has to go back, but he has to make new attachments that he has to leave.

J.B.: When this was going on, there was a hush in this room. I think that you could hear a pin drop while listening to you describe what was taking place when Carlos was being put in the car, and you describing what was happening to Billy in the past year. I felt like it was a curtain all over the room. There was just a hush, and I really felt that everybody was involved in an emotional kind of way with what was taking place.

ALL [*Jumble, indistinct talk.*]

MRS. M.: I don't think that a child should have to cope with this. Being forced to go with somebody, who they can only feel fear when they are with these people. I mean the child himself is upset. Don't you find a difference when the child gets back? Don't you find him all keyed up?

MRS. B.: I think he had an enjoyable day. They said he was good. The father did. And I have the feeling that the father is being truthful with us all the way. I think that he's trying to get things back to a normal situation. I really do. The mother, I can't say the same for, but if the father tells me something, I can believe it.

MRS. E.: Don't you think that children learn early in life when they can control a situation by screaming or yelling. . . . So he takes a tantrum. I have my own angel, and I use that term loosely. He wouldn't let me get out of the house without kissing him. And if I did it to the others, he'd come back, because if I didn't, [my boy] would have a tantrum and drive his father up a wall. And I'd have to go back.

K.O.: What if you spared him? You don't make him go. You keep him away from his mother because she's unfit, so to speak. What if three years from now she becomes fit?

MRS. E.: But who's to say though?

K.O.: What happens for that lapse of time? I don't know the time has been better, helped him forget some of these unhappy experiences.

MR. B.: I don't see how Carlos could remember too much at all.

MRS. B.: Yes, but he's had a chance to be more secure for a longer period, and maybe have a little more faith in others.

MRS. M.: Yeah, but all of a sudden you open the door and throw him out and he's back in the situation he was before. Even though it was a good situation for a while.

MR. B.: It's like saying you don't want the situation to happen. What it amounts to is saying, "You're an unfit person and we're going to take your kids away." If you don't want this situation to happen. But if you don't, the situation is going to happen. I don't think that you'll ever solve the problem.

K.O.: You said you cried, Mrs. B. Did you cry for Carlos, for the mother, or both?

MRS. B.: For both. I was crying, and my daughter's girl friend was there and she was in tears. She felt bad for Carlos. She thought it was a horrible thing to do. This was terrible. I have the feeling, that mainly because the mother has been through a lot and because I know a lot about the personal problems. And, all of a sudden, her and her husband had split up. But she came back, and she has gotten to the point where she can say that she has been bad, that she has made a lot of mistakes. As a matter of fact, I think she's beginning to know herself. In fact, in meeting her now she smiles, while before she was completely impassive. I couldn't get a smile off her at all. I can talk about Carlos. Before, she wouldn't say anything about Carlos, she wouldn't talk about him. But now, by just saying, "hello" I can get a smile from her. Maybe she's realizing, maybe she's trying. . . . It may be a slow start, it may only be a beginning. I think that she will realize that she can be somebody, that eventually she can be somebody.

MRS. M.: How old is she?

MRS. B.: She's only 20. She had a baby when she was 17. She was immature. And all young people have problems adjusting to one another. And the baby came right away. The father is Puerto Rican, where she's native, which I think makes a big difference.

MRS. M.: Oh I don't think so, not if they love each other. I married an Italian and it worked out all right.

[Talk goes on about the children's behavior. Mrs. B. tells of an incident when Carlos had a temper tantrum when she tried to take him home from a friend's house, indicating that he was not reacting only to his mother in the car incident.]

J.B.: I'd like to go back a few minutes again, because I think we're passing over something that's important to all of us. We touched on what was happening to each one of us when you two were describing the scenes that had occurred within the past two weeks. And since that time we have been talking about what this means to the youngsters and what it means to the parents. But we really haven't hit too much on what it really means to us. I think we really get involved too much with these youngsters and have a kind of sharing with them the kind of feeling they were having. And each one of us was feeling a sense of sadness, and maybe some anger, because maybe for a minute we were putting ourselves in their shoes. And the closer you are to them the more that happens. Perhaps it happens when you live with them. Perhaps you get so involved that maybe when something like this happens, you get sad and angry.

MRS. E.: It's a very different feeling in a household. Even the children sense it. Even the foster children, even [the boy] who has just come. Peter, who is debating whether he should go home this weekend, and [another boy] who is all of a sudden very jealous of Billy, about seeing his mother and all this, and I can understand why he is. And it's made a very tense atmosphere. And I'm glad I'm old and able to sit back and look at this realistically. Maybe if I was younger and in my twenties, like Billy's mother, she's 27, I would go all to pieces if this was something that was happening. And while I was crying, Billy would be tearing the house apart. So, I play games. I've played more games that I thought that I had forgotten.

J.B.: Maybe you weren't alone in your feelings, Mrs. E. I wonder how many here felt like crying. Maybe not that much sadness.

K.O.: I felt torn.

MRS. E.: I talked to Billy's mother on the phone. And I haven't talked to as nearly as many mothers as you people have. But I had this funny feeling—do you people usually have it? I'm very hard to hoodwink, but I had this feeling that she was sincere. She didn't say, "I love him, I love him, I love him." She didn't say, "I'm going to be a wonderful mother to him." She just said, "Gosh, I hope I can get to know him. I hope that I can make it so he can live with us. I just hope I can get my family back together. I have to try in some way and see if I can try to make something out of my life." And she talked about that—she's getting married again and she said hopefully it will be a good marriage. And I don't think she's the best educated, but what she said—and she didn't say much—sounded like she was sincere. Now she may be pulling a Peter on me, because as I said Peter could sell anybody anything, but she didn't sound it. . . .

[More talk in the same vein.]

K.O.: When this kind of situation comes up, when the child goes out to the car screaming and kicking, we feel sad for the parents who have to take this from the child. We feel a great deal of pain for this child. And don't we ourselves go through this? Don't we feel every bit of agony that this child is going through? And I think this is what we are kind of skirting around.

J.B.: We don't want to feel it. I think that each time we feel it we kind of move away from it, because look at how our trend of conversation has gone as we have felt——

MRS. B.: It's not that we don't know about it, it's that we don't want to talk about it.

MRS. M.: I know that I had a little girl—of course, I had her when she was 2½-months-old. I kept her for three years—my niece. And when my brother-in-law got married again, he never saw the child for three years. And when they took the child away, boy, you better believe me how, boy, I nearly ended up in Connecticut Valley [mental hospital].

MRS. B.: Were you mad because he had never come to see the baby?

MRS. M.: Yes I was. Because I—frankly, to tell you the truth, he had to take me to court to get her. Because he never contributed one nickel for her during the three years that I had her. In fact, I took care of her medical-wise and physical-wise. He married a young girl, 19 years old. Of course, he had four children. I kept all four of them for a year and a half, and then the older children, he took the three older children and—well, one brother took one, his mother took one, and his sister took one. And at the time, he said, "Keep the baby. I'll never come get her." I didn't have any children. We became very attached to this child and, as I said, when he did take the little girl back, I didn't want to fight with him, "She's yours and if you could do any more for her than I did, take her." Well, I know that at the time the child was very upset. For weeks the child was upset. And I wasn't very different. And just one toy in the house which belonged to her, and I would just break down and cry. For days my husband was the same way. And my husband is very stern. He doesn't get upset over things whatsoever. And this is just something I had to go get medical attention. I just couldn't get over the child.

MRS. E.: Was it a good home that she was going to, that she went to?

MRS. M.: Well, he married this young girl. And they stayed together approximately six months. Really, what he should have done [is] got married. At least he could have got adjusted to the new wife before taking the baby and asking a 19-year-old girl to take the responsibility of four children, just beginning a husband. Well, she was very abusive to the little child and ever to this day the child is retarded. I have pictures of her at home.

MR. B.: Well, This is a lousy situation anyways. Actually, when you had the child she was too young to——

201   THE PAIN OF FOSTER CARE

MRS. M.: This child never knew her father. He never came to visit with her. Christmas would go by, birthdays would go by. There was no reason why he didn't come visit with her. Even at one point the child had pneumonia and he was called two times during the night by the doctor, and he still didn't come, and he was 15 minutes away from the house. He didn't care about the child. But again, when he got married he wanted that child and he wanted it then. And as I've said, it was very upsetting to me and now when I see the little child, I still feel it, because there's no reason why this child is in the condition that she's in today. And if he left the child alone, she would not be in the retarded situation.

MRS. E.: Life is real, and life is—— And you have to face up to those things and there's nothing you can do about it. I feel good when they go if I had a good feeling about them.

MRS. M.: If she had gone to a home where she would have been loved and taken care of as she was. Not saying I have the best home in the world, but she did have a much better home and place where she could at least have the things that were necessary in life without abuse. The court never awarded him custody. The probate court said he's—as a matter of fact, Judge King—said to me, "Mrs. M., you can carry this further into higher court, but I think even in the end you'll find peace with the natural parent and you'll have to give her up. Again, but on the basis that he neglected and forgotten about the child, he said the court may stand behind you." And I just didn't want to fight over the child.

MRS. B.: I would have.

MRS. M.: Well, if I had to do it over, I would have gone farther with it. But at the time it was causing a lot of friction within the family. My husband is one of ten children. And I want the child, and this was very tearing. It took part of our life away from us.

K.O.: I suppose there's no way of avoiding that feeling.

MRS. M.: There is no way.

MRS. E.: I think there is. I had a large family, at first. I'm always happy. I love my children. They all come back to see me. We're having twenty-six for Thanksgiving dinner. They always come back every Sunday, and they want to build near us. I don't want to monopolize their life.

MR. B.: Most people wouldn't want fifteen or eighteen kids around them just to have that feeling.

MRS. E.: Well I enjoy that. Like tonight we had six extra people.

MR. B.: I bet you like the peace and quiet when they're gone, don't you?

MRS. E.: Yesterday, when they all went to school, I went over my son's who is building and I did all the taping of sheet rock. It was peaceful. And when I was done, I came home and did all my housework, and that was fine. But to get back to foster children—I was very happy when [a foster girl] went home today to her folks. But I knew Eva would never be happy with herself. And she's 17 years old. And I think she had the right to know her own folks. No one should have told her she shouldn't know her folks, they're not good for you. And when children are little, the same thing lies, if a parent has proven themselves up to a point, for who's to say?

K.O.: It sounds like you try to avoid feeling hurt.

MRS. E.: I feel hurt. Sometimes with my own children. Like yesterday I felt like, why did she have to come and get Billy?

K.O.: Then you do hurt.

MRS. E.: Certainly I feel hurt. I'm not that hard. I've built my defenses through the years. I hate seeing—— I have one daughter getting married, and she's moving to Ohio, and she's the most vulnerable in my family. And I have my qualms about it. But I still wouldn't say, "Look, I'm worried about you. I want you to stay here so I can watch you." I raised them so they can stand on their own two feet, and God willing, she'll be able to. I'll say, I mixed a lot of things. I know I've made many, many mistakes, even with the foster children. I shouldn't have, because I had seven of my own to practice on. But I didn't meet all these types to make these mistakes. But, to get back to Billy. I wouldn't care if Billy left tomorrow, but yet I like Billy. If I had to pick one child who was sweet and good and had given me the least problems, and gives all the love you want. Often children are very consoling for adults. Sometimes I'll say to Billy, "Come on and sit on my lap," and I'm not the kind of mushy person to get a bang out of Billy.

K.O.: You're pointing out lots of different ways that you've found for avoiding feeling hurt.

MRS. E.: You have to.

K.O.: No, I was just wondering what the others of you do to——

MRS. B.: What do social workers——

MRS. M.: To relieve yourself from this kind of thing. I'm sure they must become involved in a different degree than foster parents.

MR. B.: Well as professionals, aren't they taught not to show their feelings?

MRS. E.: They're not God. I'm sure they must have the same feelings, working with these children.

J.B.: Aren't we like the children sometimes? They've been through so many separations, comings and goings, that they form a shield around themselves that they don't hurt so much. When they're going through this kind of agony that you're all going through, what they do is have temper tantrums, get irritable, and get aggravated, because they don't want to face something that's more gentle to them and that makes them feel all torn up inside. Aren't we the same way? When I work for a long time, and he leaves the house for the last time, I really feel torn up inside and it's very hard to go on, and the way we hide it is go on with a new one. And we try to cover it over. Start with a new one.

MRS. E.: That's precisely what I feel.

J.B.: But is that good?

MRS. E.: Why isn't it? If you can let go of your feelings when you have to. I often go into my room when no one else is around and I'll cry, and my husband can tell you that I have been a real cry baby at times, but I get rid of it. I still get up at 4:45 and get my angels off and many times I'd like not to, but you have to. I can see, for example, this week Roger [*foster boy*] who is the saddest little boy I've ever seen in my life, like he didn't bring his report card home, and he was feeling this thing for Billy, and he wanted to show me that he was around. So he didn't bring his report card home. And I said, "Roger, where in the world is your report card?" And he said, "Oh, I'm just a mean old kid, and I threw it away." I said, "O.K. mean old kid, you better find it or I'll go to school tomorrow and get it." "Would you do that for me?" he said. I said, "I'd do it for me," but I just did it to prove that he was existing, and I didn't care about the report card.

J.B.: Now you have put your finger on one of the reasons why we do this. We don't want to have to experience what these children experience, and we want to hide from ourselves and other people how emotionally involved we are with those kids and how hung up we get.

MRS. E.: I don't hide it.

J.B.: Well, look what happened in this room tonight. We began talking about the youngsters and how we were involved with them, and we skirted away from—we talked about their parents and then—but we really didn't talk about the way we feel. And we were all torn up inside. I was, and I don't even know these kids very well. And I think when you know them, then you must really be torn up.

MRS. M.: I think that you see this. I've only had [my foster child] since March but believe me, I was in a situation like you—he gets me so mad. I said, "All right, I'll call [the social worker]." But I couldn't get anyone on the phone. So, while I was there, he came over and he says, "I'm not going to leave you. You still love me, don't you?" I got off the phone and I started to cry. And I was still so mad.

MRS. E.: Oh, they use that as a tool. To get back to my pride and joy Joe, he said to me last week something and I said, "We don't do that here and that's that." And he said, "At the Village——" and I've heard this 50,000 times, and I said, "But you're not at the Village, you're here." And he said, "The other day at the Village——" and I said, "Are you trying to convince me that you're unhappy here? You better forget it."

J.B.: Why do we hide ourselves from other people, about how we feel about these kids?

MRS. E.: Because maybe people don't like to listen to you.

K.O.: Does it, or do we teach the kids to hide how they feel, too?

MRS. E.: Could you go through life—I never never know what you're thinking.

J.B.: This is something that we all have in common.

MRS. E.: Don't you hate to be with the person who keep[s] saying, "I've had such an awful day." I wouldn't like to be with them. I've had scores of friends, and I'm reading the book *The Hobbitt*—you've all probably read it in college. It's a fairy tale, a fantasy. And I'd much rather talk about that than have somebody tell me, "Sit and listen how the youngsters did this and that." I feel for them, because I've been through many similar situations, but it's worse than to listen to someone talk about their golf.

J.B.: I think you started to ask Kathleen a minute ago——

MRS. E.: I did get my answer, because she looked at me very blindly and said——

ALL (*Laughter.*)

MRS. E.: I got my answer. You tell them what it was. She's showing on her face just what she wants to show. Same as I try, but I'm not as successful. Because I have so many things hammering at me. I'm sure she does, but they don't come in bunches like mine do.

K.O.: I don't know——

MRS. E.: Well come on and move out. We have room.

J.B.: Would you like to know what social workers feel?

MRS. E.: They probably feel the same way we do. Sometimes I feel they're very detached and then other times they seem just as emotionally involved as I am, as their defense mechanism is geared—

MR. B.: It doesn't depend on the social worker all the time. It can depend on the situation.

Which do you prefer? What kind of social worker, which kind of situation do you like to work with a social worker in?

MR. B.: I prefer a happy medium. Interested enough to really understand, but to be detached enough to be able to see it in a different light than I do.

MRS. E.: You have to keep on an even keel.

MR. B.: Everybody likes a strong doctor.

J.B.: So if the social worker gets too involved, then it's a bad sign.

MRS. E.: Who said it's a bad sign?

J.B.: I don't know, but that's what it seems.

MRS. E.: Well, it depends on how you look at it as far as I'm concerned. If a social worker has to stay in business the same way that I feel I have to. I tell you freely that I think I have to work for a living. It would be jolly if we didn't have to. And I'm sure the social worker has picked what she enjoys doing. If she got too involved, what would there be left of her? Her nervous system. She has to be like this or she wouldn't be doing her job well. If she was so involved with this one, she couldn't take care of Johnny the next day.

J.B.: Would she be weak?

MRS. E.: Would she be weak if she weren't involved? No. I don't think she should be a social worker if she couldn't carry out her job. Well, she has the parents to worry about, and definitely more children. You just can't worry about all these situations. They see them happening, and they have thoughts about it, there's no question about it. But they have to worry about the next child. They have to worry about the parent.

J.B.: You were saying before, Mr. B., that everybody wants a strong father. I don't want to say it against you—— Do you have the feeling that everyone wants a strong social worker?

MR. B.: What I meant by that is that everyone looks for a strong leader, and that's all.

K.O.: What do you mean by strong?

MR. B.: Well, your children come to you for information and safety and everything else. They learn to respect you for what they know you to be. They know this is the place to go for protection. Well, when I have a problem I have to have a place to go. Now, if this is a case with a social worker, I'm not going to bother her with petty things. I'm going to come to her with a problem. Now, if she can't handle it, she's going to look for someone stronger than her.

K.O.: Are you equating being strong with not letting your feelings out?

MR. B.: No, I have a hard time getting my idea across.

MRS. E.: I wouldn't want one without a heart, or one who could feel it but be able to control it and keep it in check, when I couldn't and she could. Because I have to live with them every day, and I don't think a social worker would be in that job if they didn't feel strongly for people; if they didn't you would be out of your work.

J.B.: Just like foster parents?

MRS. E.: Sure, I believe that. I've never said I don't have to work at this job. I like this job.

J.B.: Foster parents and social workers come from the same cloth.

MRS. E.: Oh I would say so. One is more trained. That's a broad statement.

MRS. B.: I believe that, because I always wanted to be a social worker. This is the way I feel. I know I can't go and spend eight years in college, because I have children at home and this way I can do part of it. I wish I could do more.

K.O.: I think social workers could become just as torn apart as foster parents. Take a child like Lola. I see the situation from the standpoint of her family, and I see it from the viewpoint of the foster family, and also Lola's. So I feel that I'm torn in three directions. It drives me nuts. You get so—— What one do you feel most for? You see a foster parent suffering because she might lose the child. You see the child suffering because she doesn't know where she wants to be or where to go. You get to the point where you feel terrible.

J.B.: What would you think if a social worker is working with a youngster for a long time, let's say five or six years, and was living in your home, and that child went home to his parents, and-a- both of you sat down and talked this over, and you both had a good cry together?

MRS. E.: I've done that. In fact, with a hard shell social worker, Miss L. Did you know her? I did that.

J.B.: But when it's happening, the social worker is just as much involved as you are and you just as much as the child is.

MRS. B. I think you have to be awfully stupid to think that the social worker isn't involved. It stems from the fact that they can't be in a job which they're unhappy in. I have a friend who thought she'd like to go into social work and was taking Child Development, but just couldn't take it. "Look, I just wouldn't be able to snap out of it and be able to work with another child. I would be a detriment to the profession because I wouldn't want to be involved with a new child for fear that it would happen again. So she went to be a program analyst and she's doing fine at that.

J.B.: You know what happens to us as social worker, psychiatrist, or foster parent. When we get involved, we close it off and we don't want to look at the way we feel, or that we're torn up. We're doing the same thing that we're saying is a problem for the youngster. Because they get involved and they close it off, and they fight it and they don't want to admit how they feel. So they have temper tantrums, wet their beds, have nightmares, all these kind of things.

K.O.: It's extremely hard to help the kids bring out how they feel. We've tried to do this with Lola, and the three adults sitting with Lola are more upset than Lola at times.

J.B.: You see if I close myself off from Billy, how can I say to Billy, "Billy, I got to know how you are feeling. You got to know how you are feeling inside. You have to know how much you're going to miss Mrs. E. You've got to realize how angry and enraged you are being taken away from her, and going to someone you don't even know because she's your mother." And if I'm going to say that to Billy, but shut myself off, I have to realize how much I feel and how involved I am, and it's hard to get Billy to realize this too.

MR. B.: So let's say he saw how shook up I was about this whole thing. Possibly he wouldn't come and talk to me about it.

J.B.: I think it might help Billy to know that I was torn up.

MRS. E.: What I said to Billy, and I don't know whether it was right. . . . And everybody in my family said, "Oh, just because you're going home——" And Billy and I was upstairs and he was having a real good tantrum, and I said, "Look, Billy, it bothers me too. I really love you. I feel unhappy. You're our baby. We have this nice little boy, and we're going to miss you. I'm going to get to know your Mommy, and we'll all visit." In fact, I like all my boys. In fact, all my kids come back. Joan [*former foster girl*] came for dinner. And I said, "Joan was my little girl. Joan's been my little girl for years." And he said, "She's a foster kid, too." And Joan's been brought up and has a family. And she comes back and I'm grammy to her children. And he said, "Can I come back, can I still call you Mommy?" I said, "I don't care what you call me, just call me." And we talked for a while, and he asked if I was going to cry or if daddy was going to cry, and I said, "Look, you have the whole family upset. Don't you realize it? Everybody talks about it. And I mean everyone feels bad." And he said, "Is everybody giving me presents?" I said, "No, we're not going to give you presents, we're going to pack you up and cry."

J.B.: That's good for him to know that you're going to cry.

MRS. E.: I said, "I'm not going to buy you anthing, Billy, but we'll probably all cry when you go." And Peter, as hard and tough as Peter is——

K.O.: So you did let him know how you felt.

MRS. E.: Why sure I let him know how I felt. I'm not hard with children. I get along much better with children than I do with adults. I really do. I like children.

J.B.: Do you know why it's good for him to know that?

MRS. E.: No, I just know he seems more relaxed.

J.B.: The reason is that if he knows that you are crying for him, and the reason he has to go is not because you don't love him, and that's the thing that he's afraid of, that he's always leaving somebody's house because they don't love him. Whether it's his parents, or foster parents, or an institution, that they don't care about him. And if you cry about him, then that means you love him. So he knows that there has to be another reason. And he has to look at the truth then.

MRS. E.: I'm thinking of A.R. who came to us at age 12, whose parents had been dead two or four years. And he had been in four homes and ours was the fifth, and he felt that he was rejected by everyone along the line, and in a sense he was, but he brought it on himself. He was obnoxious. He tested me. The first two weeks was a honeymoon period, everything was perfect. Then he began to test me, and we'd reprimand him. And he'd fly off the handle, and so this one particular time I told him that I just didn't know if I could take this any longer. And immediately he came out with, "Send me away," immediately on the defensive, "get rid of me if you don't want me." And I said, "I don't want to get rid of you, it's not you I don't like, it's the way you act and the things you do that I don't like." And he said, "How come you never show me that you love me," and this is a 12-year-old boy. And I said, "What do you want me to do to show you that I love you? I do things for you, I made things for you." "But you never put your arms around me." And I wouldn't expect a 12-year-old boy to say something like this. He had only been there a few weeks, and I really didn't expect it. So after that I made a point of physically touching him, patting him to let him know that there was a relationship there that he could depend on.

J.B.: Do you think, it's not fair to ask. Sometimes, I think leaving your houses is the best experience that these children ever had. Let me tell you why. It may be the first time that anyone has ever given them up, knowing that they love them, being aware that they are loved, but yet it is being done for their own good. What you think is their own good. If that happens, then at least they know there is somebody in the world that cares. There might be a real good reason for it, and it might be the only time it happens in their whole life.

K.O.: Look at how many times kids get moved for the opposite reasons, because he can't be tolerated any more.

J.B.: And usually they think, "Because I'm bad, they don't want me any more, because I'm not good."

K.O.: And usually that's why.

MRS. E.: When I had my very first [foster] child I had to get rid of him. He had tantrums which I just couldn't handle. He had seizures. And it got to the point where he had seizures and it got dangerous for my family and him. And I felt very badly. I felt I handled it very badly. But since then, I never let, well [the boy] know that I was happy to see him go, not because I think he knew we liked him, but he knew I was relieved, I couldn't help but show it. And, I'm not aware of what—— So after I had another one, in between there, there was really a problem, and I was, deep down inside, I was glad he was going to his folks, but I'm sure he never realized it. I think that when he left, he felt that he was the most loved little boy going. And-a- he came back for visits, and we made him welcome as all the rest, but I would never want [the second foster child] to know the load taken off my shoulders. But I made up my mind that I wasn't going to give in and say,

"Take him away," because he had done better at our house, better than anyone else's. And he had, well, because he was going back to his mother, and if I said, "Look, I can't take him," they might put him in two or three foster homes. But she still would have got him, because she had reached some kind of stability, which the state thought was a reasonable risk. So I knew he was going back, but there was times when I felt if I had to keep him another day, we'd all lose our sanity. But, I might add that now he's in . . . a school for boys. It was hectic, but he still calls me Mom, writes to me.

     K.O.: We need to stop.

     MRS. E.: And I like what I'm doing.

     J.B.: I do too.

     MRS. E.: But I'm looking forward to the day when I no longer have to work.

INDEX

Guardianship, 42

Hammel, Eugene, 52
Hawaii, 20–21, 41
Heymann, Irmgard, 115
Holman, Robert, 68
Homans, George, 112
Hooper, Anthony, 21–22
Horowitz, Meir, 12
Howard, Alan, 20–21, 27–28, 40, 41

Identity
    of foster children, 5, 66–67
    of adopted children, 113–114
Ideology, 97, 106
"Idlers," Russian, 105
Illegitimacy
    and family structure, 80–84
    and inheritance, 80–83
    in China, 15
    legal status, 80–84
    of adopted children, 6
    stigma of, 4, 7, 8, 77–78
Indenture, 34–35, 64
Immigrants, 34–35
Indian, American, 5, 60
Infertility
    of adoptive parents, 7, 37
Inheritance and adoption
    Ancient Greece, 4, 13
    Ancient Rome, 4, 13
    China, 4, 15
    Eastern Oceania, 20
    England, 16, 17, 78
    France, 3–4, 16–17
    Greece, 3–4
    Hawaii, 20–21
    India, 4, 14
    Islamic code, 12
    Japan, 4, 16
    Jews, 12
    Kapingamarangi, 24–25
    Latin America, 3–4, 16
    Mokil, 39–40
    Ponape, 25–27
    Prominence in laws, 12
    Nukuoro, 23–24
    Rangiroa Atoll, 22–23
    Rotuma, 27–28
    Russia, 5
    Scotland, 17
    Society Islands, 21–22
    United States, 16, 17, 38
Inheritance and illegitimacy, 80–83
Institutional care
    as a parent substitute, 63
    decline of, 35
    for the emotionally disturbed, 1, 35

for the neglected and dependent, 1, 35
for the poor, 2
parents' preference for, 64
segregation of, 35, 36
stratification of, 36–37

Jaffee, Benson, 7, 39, 44, 45–47, 55, 71–72, 86
Jenkins, Shirley, 5, 36, 59, 60, 66, 90, 95, 102
Jensen, Arthur, 2
Jeter, Helen, 72, 95
Johnson, Virginia, 63
Juvenile Court, 56

Kadushin, Alfred, 5, 34, 36, 37, 44, 48, 71, 110–111
Kapingamarangi, 24–25, 40
Kassof, Allen, 104–105
Katz, Sanford, 42, 56–58, 59, 64, 68, 83–84, 108
Kay, Herma Hill, 80, 82–83, 87, 92
Keesing, Roger, 52
Kibbutz, 98, 105–107
Kinderdorf, 106
King, Stanley, 39
Kinship
    and adoption, 28–29, 37–39, 64–66, 113–114
    and foster care, 35–36, 63–66, 69, 90
    and social class, 37–39, 90
    in American society, 29, 112–113
Kirk, H. David, 7, 38, 84, 85–86, 87, 94
Kline, Draza, 55, 71–72
Komsomol, 104
Kornitzer, Margaret, 12, 17, 18, 19, 33, 34, 43–44, 45, 78, 85, 86

Labeling, 35
Lambert, Bernd, 42
Larzerson, M., 2
Lasch, Christopher, 113
Lauffer, Armand, 33
Leslie, Gerald, 13, 14, 15
Levine, Abraham, 5
Levy, Robert, 41
Lieber, Michael D., 24–25, 40

Maas, Henry, 36, 37, 38, 39, 44, 47, 56, 58, 60–61, 64–65, 70, 72, 88–89, 108, 109–110, 119
Mace, David and Vera, 16
McAdams, Phyllis, 6
McKinley, Donald, 38
McWhinnie, A., 7
Malcolm X, 55, 63
Malinowski, Bronislaw, 61–62
Mandelbaum, David, 14
Mandell, Betty, 59, 73, 118

Marx, Karl, 97, 98, 99
Massachusetts Adoption Resource Exchange, 28
Masters, William, 63
Matrilineal societies, 4
Mayer, Morris, 63
Mead, Margaret, 68, 100–101, 107
Mech, Edmund, 67
Meier, Elizabeth, 89
Mexican-American, 5, 38, 60
Meyer, Carol, 101
Michel, Andree, 38
Miller, Henry, 57
Minority status
   in adoption, 2, 60–61, 65
   in foster care, 2, 5, 35–36, 60–61
   in institutional care, 2, 35–36, 60
   of adoptive families, 7
Mokil, 39–40
Mooney, B., 2
Moynihan, Daniel, 111
Murphy, H.B.M., 67, 87–88

Neglect
   legal aspects, 56–58
   parental, 114–115
   state, of foster children, 5, 56
Nemovicher, J., 44
Nibonicho, 104–105
Nixon, Richard, 2
Norman, Elaine, 5, 36, 59, 60
Nuclear family, 2, 3
Nukuoro, 23–24, 40

Olmstead, Kathleen, 123–152, 193ff
Orphanage, 35
Ottino, Paul, 22–23

Parental competence
   and social class, 42–48
Parents
   agency treatment of, 115–116
   contact with children, 7, 8, 28, 66–67
   health of, 5, 90
   housing of, 5
   poverty of, 5, 89–90
   rights of, 55–65, 70
   stigmatization, 7, 90
Parker, R.A., 48, 75, 95
Paton, Jean, 7, 71, 113–114
Patriarchal societies, 4, 5
Pearlin, Leonard, 47
Peterson, J.B., 68
Piven, Francis Fox, 58–59, 110
Ponape, 25–27, 41, 77
Portuguese-American, 60
Poverty
   and child neglect, 57–58
   and minority status, 1
   and state control, 58–59

and substitute care, 2, 58–59
   antipoverty program, 2
Primogeniture
   in Ponape, 26
   in Scotland, 17
Pringle, M.L. Kellmer, 7, 67, 88, 102, 108, 112
Problem families, 102
Professionals
   and agency culture, 109
   and class bias, 44, 57, 109–110
   hegemony of, 69–70
   in adoption, 43–44, 109–111
   in foster care, 43, 65, 90–92, 109, 111
   new breed of, 116
   social class of, 90–91
Property relations
   and adoption practices, 12
   and individual psychology, 12
   in feudal times, 33
Puerto Rican, 5, 59, 60
Purvine, Margaret, 44

Rabin, Albert, 105
Rangiroa Atoll, 22–23, 77
Redistribution of wealth, 1, 99
Reich, Wilhelm, 3, 30, 61–62
Reid, Joseph H., 2, 75, 108
Reiss, Ira, 100
Religion
   effects on adoption outcome, 44, 45–46
Researchers, 43
Ripon Society, 2
Ripple, Lillian, 44, 45
Ritz, Joseph, 58–59, 73
Rotuma, 27–28, 41
Russia
   family, 97–98
   October Revolution, 97–98
   school system, 104–105
   youth organizations, 104–105
Ryan, William, 44

Sants, H.J., 6
Sauber, Mignon, 66, 90, 95
Schaffer, Evelyn, 90
Schaffer, H.R., 90
Schneider, David, 112
Schwartz, William, 75
Separation, 67–68
Sex
   as related to placement outcome, 85–87
   of adopted children, 38, 85–86
Sexual anxieties
   of adoptive parents, 7
   of legislators, 61
Sexual permissiveness
   in America, 100
   in Ponape, 26, 77–78
   in Rangiroa Atoll, 77–78

in Trobriand Islands, 61–62
Sexual repression, 3, 61–63
Shinn, Eugene, 61, 74
Shireman, Joan, 28
Shockley, William, 2
Skeels, H., 2, 112
Smith, Raymond, 112
Society Islands (Tahiti), 21–22, 41
Spiro, Melford, 98, 106, 116
Stalinist regime, 15
State
  and stratification, 51
  control, 55, 65–66, 107–108
  denial of due process, 55–58
  economic exploitation, 58–59
  exclusion of parents, 55, 64
  neglect of foster children, 5, 56
Statistical Abstracts, 1, 37
Status
  and adoption, 37–38
  of adopted children, 6–8
  of foster children, 5–6, 42
Stephens, William, 102, 117
Sterilization, 2
Stevenson, Nicholas, 82
Stigmatization
  of adopted children, 6
  of foster children, 5–6
  of natural parents, 6
  of poor people, 8
Sturgies, C.H., 68

Taber, Merlin, 69–70
Tahiti, 21–22, 41, 97
Tal, Uriel, 118
Talmadge Amendment, 99
Task Force on Children Out of School, 76
Technocrats, 111–112

Thomas, Carolyn, 68
Thurstone, Henry, 35
Tillich, Paul, 97
Trasler, Gordon, 67, 102
Trotsky, Leon, 30, 97–98

United Community Services, 79
United Nations *Analysis*, 12, 16, 17, 18, 19
Unmarried mothers, 77–79

Watson, Kenneth, 28
Weckler, J.E., 39–40, 50
Weinstein, Eugene, 66, 75, 86
Whiting, Beatrice, 5
Whyte, William, 37
Witmer, Helen, 44
Witmer, T. Richard, 12, 16, 17, 18
Wittenborn, J.R., 44
Wolins, Martin, 2, 5, 55, 105–106, 112
Women
  adoptive mothers, 84–85
  as child bearers and rearers, 8, 84
  as fostered adults, 89
  devaluation of, 5, 7, 17
  foster mothers, 87–88
  in child welfare, 77
  natural mothers, 5, 77, 89–90
  social workers, 90–92
  unmarried mothers, 77–79
Women's liberation, 79, 85
  in kibbutzim, 98
  in Russia, 97–98
work homes 34–35

Yarrow, Leon, 113

Zalba, Serapio, 75
Zober, Edith, 69–70

ABOUT THE AUTHOR

Betty Reid Mandell is Assistant Professor of Social Work and Social Welfare in the Department of Sociology/Anthropology, Boston State College, Boston, Mass. Ms. Mandell has previously taught at Northeastern University, Boston, and University of Iowa, Iowa City. She is a member of the Editorial Board of *Social Work*. She received the MSW from Columbia University School of Social Work in 1952, and has been a social worker in child welfare and psychiatric agencies and settlement houses in five different states and Ontario, Canada. She has published numerous articles on social work and social welfare.